WOM
AND THE
NOOSE

WOMEN AND THE NOOSE

A HISTORY OF FEMALE EXECUTION

RICHARD CLARK

The History Press

Front cover from left to right: Charlotte Bryant, Kate Webster, Edith Thompson and Ruth Ellis (Courtesy of Topham Picturepoint).

Every effort has been made to trace all copyright holders. The publishers would be glad to put right any errors or omissions in future editions.

First published 2007
This paperback edition first published 2023

The History Press
97 St George's Place, Cheltenham,
Gloucestershire, GL50 3QB
www.thehistorypress.co.uk

British Library Cataloguing in Publication Data.
A catalogue record for this book is available from the British Library.

ISBN 978 1 80399 257 0

Typesetting and origination by The History Press
Printed and bound in Great Britain by TJ Books Limited, Padstow, Cornwall.

Trees for LYfe

CONTENTS

INTRODUCTION

The purpose of this book is to trace, through the cases of seventy women and girls, the history of British female executions from the early Georgian period to the final one in 1955, together with the development of the legal and execution processes and the changing attitudes of the media and the public towards capital punishment, particularly for female criminals.

There has always been a far greater interest in serious crimes committed by women than in those of most men, perhaps due to the comparative rarity of them. In the eighteenth century females accounted for less than 5 per cent of all executions. Large numbers of people, always including many women, would turn out to watch a woman die. Even after hangings ceased to be public spectacles there were often substantial numbers of women waiting outside the prison gates for the official notices of execution to be posted.

In the period 1735 to 1955 just over 600 women and girls were put to death in Britain (including Southern Ireland up to

1923). The majority of these women were hanged but approximately thirty-two were burned at the stake for High Treason or Petty Treason up to 1789. No woman was to be beheaded in this period and there is no record of a woman ever being executed by shooting.

It is not possible to be more precise on the numbers due to the paucity of the records for some counties in the earlier part of the eighteenth century and because one cannot always be certain whether a particular death sentence was carried out or commuted. In some cases broadsides were printed claiming to have details of an execution when the person was in fact reprieved.

The peak decades for female executions were 1740-1749 with sixty-two, 1750-1769 with seventy and 1780-1789 with seventy-five. However it should be noted that the courts tended to exercise greater leniency towards women, the reprieve rate in the period 1735-1799 being an average of 78 per cent steadily rising to 90 per cent in the twentieth century. The majority of women who were executed in the eighteenth and early nineteenth centuries had typically committed the more serious crimes, particularly murder, or High Treason in the form of coining, forgery or arson. When women were hanged for the less serious crimes it was often because they were repeat offenders who had already served lesser sentences or because the government of the day was keen to crack down on a particular type of crime.

The Murder Act of July 1752 required that murderers be hanged within two days of sentence, or the next 'working day' if the second day was a Sunday, which was a '*dies non*' or non-hanging day. After this date, murderers were often hanged alone to comply with requirements of the Act, which was not completely abolished until 1836.

Women convicted of crimes other than murder at the Old Bailey in London were usually executed several weeks after sentence when the Recorder had submitted his report to the Privy Council. Women were typically hanged along-side men. This was frequently the case at Tyburn and later at Newgate where quite large batches of prisoners would be executed together.

Those sentenced to die at County Assizes had a report on their case, forwarded by the trial judge to the Secretary of State for consideration for reprieve, containing his recommendation. Many Assize towns in the Shire counties carried out hangings on market day to ensure the biggest crowd, who were supposed to be deterred by the spectacle of the execution.

From 1868 the period between sentence and execution for murder was fourteen to twenty-seven days and from 1888 the Home Office directed that three clear Sundays should elapse.

Prior to 1836 there was no requirement for prisoners to be represented by counsel at their trials so most poor defendants had no legal representation at all. Circumstantial and hearsay evidence was deemed quite sufficient for a capital conviction. There was no appeal mechanism – the Court of Appeal did not come into being until 1907. After this date the period between sentence and execution could be up to six weeks where an appeal was lodged.

Age was no bar to execution and teenage girls under eighteen years old were regularly put to death up to 1849. The execution of persons under sixteen was not formally outlawed until the Children's Act was passed in 1908. The Children and Young Persons Act of 1933 prohibited the death sentence for persons under eighteen at the time of the crime.

A large prison-building programme was undertaken in the late eighteenth and early nineteenth centuries and executions were moved from their previous venues outside towns to in front of, or on top of, the gate houses of the new prisons. This did away with the lengthy and uncomfortable journey to the gallows by cart. At the same time the New Drop style of gallows was usually adopted which seemed to give a slightly quicker death.

Prior to May 1868 executions were carried out in public. Twenty-five-year-old Frances Kidder became the last woman to suffer this cruel and humiliating fate when she was hanged at Maidstone on 2 April 1868.

From 29 May 1868, the law required that all executions be carried out within the walls of prisons. Priscilla Biggadyke became the first woman to die away from the gaze of the masses at Lincoln in December 1868.

Ninety-five women received death sentences between May 1868 and December 1899 of whom twenty-two were to be hanged in the nineteenth century and a further one in January 1900.

One hundred and fifty-six women received death sentences in Britain during the twentieth century. Of these, seventeen were hanged including one in Scotland and two in Ireland. Ruth Ellis became the last woman to be executed in Britain on 13 July 1955.

Prior to 1874 criminals were given little or no drop when they were hanged and thus often struggled in the agonies of strangulation for some time after they were 'turned off'. As women were typically lighter in weight than men they tended to die harder still.

Francis Stewart became the first woman to be executed by William Marwood's newly introduced long-drop method in 1874, which was designed to break the prisoner's neck and cause instant unconsciousness, through the use of a measured drop calculated from the prisoner's weight and height. All subsequent female executions used this method.

From this time other changes were made to the execution process for both sexes in a continuing effort to reduce the prisoner's suffering. Executions became genuinely private affairs, with the press being increasingly excluded. The length of drop given was refined and codified in Home Office tables.

The design of the noose and pinioning methods were also improved. The distance the prisoner had to walk from her cell to the gallows was reduced to just a few paces with the introduction of purpose-built execution suites to replace execution sheds in prison yards. The last few female hangings took just fifteen seconds to carry out instead of minutes required in earlier private executions.

1

THE EARLY GEORGIAN PERIOD

The reign of King George II spanned the period from 1727 to 1760. In the period from 1735 to 1759, 151 women suffered the death penalty in Britain, fifteen being burned at the stake and 136 being hanged, giving an average of six female executions per annum.

Just over half of the women executed at this time suffered for murder, with highway robbery (what we would typically call mugging today), forgery and robbery in a dwelling house accounting for a significant proportion of the non-murder executions. In the cases of at least some of the others who died for the lesser offences, they had previous convictions and had already been reprieved once, receiving alternative sentences such as whipping, imprisonment or a period of transportation.

In this chapter we will look at four cases, of which three are of murder and one is of a repeat offender.

There was often a strange dichotomy between the severity of sentences and the actual treatment of the prisoner. Mary Blandy seems to have been remarkably well looked after even if she was made to wear leg irons. Sarah Malcolm even had her portrait painted whilst awaiting the gallows by no less an artist than William Hogarth who visited her in Newgate. Celebrity criminal Jenny Diver was in effect allowed to choreograph much of her execution, choosing the right clothes to wear and being allowed to hire a mourning coach to take her to Tyburn, to avoid having to mix too much with the common criminals.

Sarah Malcolm
Multiple Murder at
the Inns of Court

Sarah Malcolm is the first in this series of educated, middle-class young women who met her death at the hands of the 'common hangman'. She was just twenty-two when she suffered for the murders of three women during a robbery at the home of one of them.

Sarah originated from Durham and had been born in 1711 to a good family. However, her father had squandered the family's money and as a teenager, Sarah was forced to move to London and go into service. Initially, she performed her duties well but later got a job at the Black Horse, a pub in Boswell Court near Temple Bar, where she became involved with London's low life.

She left her job at the Black Horse and took a job as laundress to chambers above the Inns of Court, working for some of the tenants there. Among her customers was Mrs Lydia Duncomb, a wealthy but somewhat frail old lady, whose age is variously quoted as being between sixty and eighty, who occupied a set of chambers in Tanfield Court in the Temple. Lydia employed two live-in servants, Elizabeth Harrison aged sixty, who was effectively retired, and seventeen-year-old Ann Price, who had been employed to take over Elizabeth's duties. Elizabeth 'Betty' Harrison had been Mrs Duncomb's companion for many years.

The precise events of the night of Saturday, 3 February 1733 are unknown because Sarah never gave a credible account of them. She told her trial that she entered the old lady's apartment with Martha Tracey and the Alexander brothers, and they carried out the robbery while she kept watch on the stairs and thus took no part in the murders.

The first body discovered was that of Ann Prince with a knife wound to her throat. It was found in the passage leading to the apartment, her hands clutched to the wound. Elizabeth Harrison was found lying across her bed having been strangled with her apron string and Mrs Duncomb similarly lying across her bed. It seemed that she too had been strangled but that she might have died of shock and fright, and the weight of her assailant's body on top of her.

On the Sunday morning, one of Mrs Duncomb's friends, a Mrs Ann Love, arrived for a dinner invitation but could get no answer or see any sign of life. She went to fetch another of Mrs Duncomb's friends, a Mrs Frances Rhymer, and they could not raise any sign of life. Sarah also came up and Mrs Love, fearing that all was not well, sent Sarah to find a locksmith. Sarah returned later with Mrs Ann Oliphant, also a friend of Mrs Duncomb, who was quite a bit younger and managed to gain entry into the apartment. They were met with the horrific sights described above. They also realised that the apartment had been stripped of anything of value and Mrs Duncomb's strongbox had been forced open. Other neighbours came to see what was going on. A doctor was sent for by one of the Temple porters and Mr Thomas Bigg, a surgeon, made a preliminary examination of the three deceased women.

John Kerrel was also a tenant of the Chambers and he too employed Sarah. He had been out on the Sunday and returned home around 1 a.m. to find Sarah in his room. He was surprised to see her there at that time of night and being aware of the murders, asked her if anyone had been arrested. He also discovered that some of his waistcoats were missing and when he challenged Sarah about this, she confessed that she had pawned them. He told her to leave and was obviously not comfortable with her presence as he believed that who-ever had committed the murders knew their way around the apartments. Sarah left but now being thoroughly suspicious he made a search and in the Close-stool, he found some linen and underneath a silver tankard with blood on the handle. Under the bed, he found a bloodstained shift and apron. He immediately called the watchmen and they caught up with Sarah by the Inner-Temple Gate. They brought her back to John Kerrel's apartment who asked her if the tankard was hers and she told him it was and that it had been given to her by her mother. She was now taken to the constable and he took her before Alderman Brocas who sent her to the Compter (local lock-up jail) and on the Monday morning, committed her to Newgate prison. As part of the normal admissions pro-cedure, she was searched on arrival and was found to have a considerable amount of silver and gold coins about her, which she allegedly admitted were Mrs Duncomb's. They also found a purse containing twenty-one guineas in the bosom of her dress, which Sarah claimed she had found in the street. She offered these to Mr Roger Johnson the turnkey (warder) if he made no mention of them. He refused this and took the coins to his superiors and reported the attempt to bribe him. She also repeated to Mr Johnson that she had organised the robbery, but that she had stayed on the stairs leading up to the apartment while Martha Tracey and the Alexander brothers had carried it out.

An inquest was held into the murders and Sarah was indicted by the coroner's court.

Sarah came to trial at the Old Bailey at the February Sessions for the City of London and County of Middlesex which were held on Wednesday, 21 February to Saturday, 24 February. Sarah's trial was scheduled for Friday the 23rd and she was charged with the three murders and breaking and entering the dwelling-house of Lydia Duncomb. She pleaded not guilty to all of these charges.

As all of these indictments were capital offences, it was decided to proceed with the murder of Ann Price only, to save court time. The prosecution told the jury that if they were not convinced by the evidence and by the findings of the coroner's court, it was for them to say how Ann Price died. The basic chronology of the crime, discovery of the bodies and arrest of Sarah was now put before the jury.

John Kerrel was the first to give evidence and he told the court of the events leading to the arrest. His friend and neighbour, John Gehagan, also testified for the prosecution and confirmed the discoveries of the bloodstained clothes and the tankard. The two watchmen, John Mastreter and Richard Hughs, gave evidence of Sarah's arrest and told the court how she claimed that the blood on the tankard was her own from a cut finger. Frances Rhymer, who looked after Mrs Duncomb's financial affairs, identified the tankard and the purse that had been found on Sarah and told the court of the contents of the old lady's strong box.

Sarah cross examined each prosecution witness in minute detail and made much of any differences between the known facts and their recollections of events, in an effort to discredit their testimony.

Roger Johnson told the court how he had searched Sarah in Newgate and made his incriminating discoveries. He recounted that the purse contained a substantial number of high value coins and testified that Sarah had admitted to him that the money was Mrs Duncomb's, offering it to him to keep quiet about it. Johnson further suggested that Sarah had told him she had hired three witnesses to testify that the tankard was hers. Sarah claimed that she had given the money to Johnson for safekeeping and that he was to return it to her when she was acquitted. Johnson's superior, Mr Alstone, confirmed Johnson's account and also added that Sarah had told him that she had planned the robbery and had been assisted by Martha Tracey and the Alexander brothers.

The next piece of evidence was the statement, taken on oath, when Sarah appeared before Sir Richard Brocas on 6 February. In this, she affirmed that she had planned the robbery but that she had remained on the stairs outside the old lady's apartment whilst it was carried out.

Sarah was not represented by counsel but offered a spirited defence. She claimed that the blood on her shift and apron was from her period and was not that of the murdered maid. She claimed the blood on the handle of the tankard was from her finger cut. She admitted to planning the robbery and to being an accessory to the crime but implicated Tracey and the Alexanders in the murders. She told the court that she accepted that she would die for robbery in a dwelling house but that she could not confess to the killings, as she was innocent of them. She also asked the judge to order the return of the money found on her that was over and above that stolen from Mrs Duncomb. At the end of her speech, the jury retired for fifteen minutes to consider their verdict. Sarah was found guilty of the robbery and the one murder charge that was proceeded with and also guilty in accordance with the verdict of the Coroner's Inquisition, i.e. of the other two murders. The authorities had no evidence against Martha Tracey and the Alexander brothers and did not proceed against them.

Sarah was taken back to Newgate and the following day, returned to the court at the end of the Sessions to be sentenced to death, as were nine men. Her case was reported in the *London Magazine*, or *Gentleman's Monthly Intelligencer*, for March 1733.

In the condemned hold at Newgate, she continued to refuse to confess to the murders. Crimes like this were very rare, especially when committed by a young woman, and so she was seen as something of a celebrity. The well-known artist, William

Hogarth, visited her in prison two days before her execution and sketched her prior to painting her portrait.

At this time, as there was virtually no news media, in the case of particularly shocking murders it was arranged that the execution would take place as near to the crime scene as possible so that local people would be able to see that justice had been done. Sarah was reportedly distressed about the venue being Fleet Street as she would be executed among the people who knew her rather than at Tyburn where she would have been somewhat more anonymous. She confessed on the night before she was hanged and the details were printed in 'A Paper delivered by Sarah Malcolm on the Night before her Execution to the Rev. Mr. Piddington, and published by Him' (London, 1733). This was more of a self justification than a confession.

Sarah was to be hanged on Wednesday, 7 March. Newgate's portable gallows was set up in Fleet Street, in the square opposite Mitre Court, for the purpose. She was prepared in the normal way by the Yeoman of the Halter, her hands tied in front of her and the halter noose around her neck. She was placed in the cart with John Hooper, the hangman, to make the short journey to Fleet Street accompanied by a troop of javelin men and the under sheriff. Sarah is said to have fainted in the cart and also to have 'wrung her hands and wept most bitterly'. When she arrived at the gallows, she listened carefully to the Ordinary's prayers for her soul and again fainted. She was revived and just before the cart was driven from under her, she is reported to have turned towards the Temple and cried out, 'Oh, my mistress, my mistress! I wish I could see her!' and then casting her eyes towards heaven, called upon Christ to receive her soul. She was dragged off the cart by the rope and left kicking in the air, dying after a brief struggle. Her body was taken down and buried in the churchyard of St Sepulchre's church. Strangely, it seemed that John Hooper was the only person present to have any real sympathy for her. William Hogarth thought that 'she was capable of any wickedness' and the crowd surrounding the gallows were of the same view.

Sarah's bloodstained garments featured prominently in the trial. However blood typing had not been invented at the time and there was no means of knowing whose blood it was. She claimed it was her menstrual blood and it certainly could have been. Sarah did not deny being present on the stairs nor did she deny having the stolen property, both capital crimes in themselves.

It has been suggested as a motive for the crime that Sarah was having a relationship with one of the two Alexander brothers, whom she hoped would marry her and devised the plan to rob Mrs Duncomb so as to enable her to have enough money to get married on. She presumably saw her elderly client's apartments as a source of 'easy money'. Perhaps Ann Price disturbed her in the course of entering the apartment and was thus stabbed. Ann was presumably a fit teenage girl who would have put up a struggle, and no doubt this commotion would have alerted Mrs Duncomb and Elizabeth Harrison, so they too had to be silenced.

Sarah was fortunate in one way, in that had she been in the direct employ of Mrs Duncomb, she would have been guilty not only of murder but also of Petty Treason and would have been burned at the stake.

Jenny Diver
'Dressed to Die'

Unlike the majority of cases featured in these pages, our present subject was a street thief and pickpocket, rather than a murderer.

Jenny Diver's real name was Mary Young but she was rechristened by her gang as she was such an expert 'diver', as pickpockets were known. For simplicity, I have called her

Jenny Diver from here on in. She was a professional criminal who became something of a celebrity, ending her career dangling from London's Tyburn Tree. It is thought that she was about forty years old at the time of her death, although there is no precise record of her date of birth.

Jenny was born around 1700 in the north of Ireland, the illegitimate child of Harriet Jones, a lady's maid. Harriet was forced to leave her job and found lodgings in a brothel where she gave birth. She soon deserted Jenny who lived in several foster homes before, at about the age of ten, she was taken in by an elderly gentlewoman. She was even sent to school, where she learned to read and write and mastered needlework. Her quick-fingered dexterity fitted her well for her future life of crime. Her sewing was excellent and she was able to earn a reasonable living from it. So much so that she decided to go to London and become a professional seamstress.

There was a small problem however – how to raise the money for the ferry boat fare. She solved this by persuading one of her admirers that she would marry him if he found the money and went with her to England. He booked a passage on a ship bound for Liverpool. A short time before the vessel was to sail, the young man robbed his master of a gold watch and eighty guineas and then joined Jenny, who was already on board the ship. The crossing of the Irish Sea took two days and Jenny was very seasick. She and her young man took lodgings in Liverpool and lived together for a short while as man and wife. When Jenny had recovered sufficiently, they journeyed to London by road. The day before they were due to leave Liverpool her companion was arrested for the thefts in Ireland. Jenny sent him his clothes and some money before she departed, and he was returned to Ireland to stand trial. He was sentenced to death but this was commuted to transportation, as it was his first offence.

Once in London, Jenny met up with another Irish girl called Anne Murphy, who offered her lodging in Long Acre. Anne was in fact the leader of a bunch of pickpockets and introduced Jenny to the trade. As an apprentice pickpocket she was given ten guineas on which to live until she could start producing income herself. She was taken by members of the gang to suitable venues to observe their techniques and to practice lifting purses and jewellery. Jenny learned very quickly and was clearly going to be an asset to the gang. In fact she was so successful at crime that she was soon making a fortune and took over from Anne as head of the gang, who renamed her Jenny Diver. Anne and some of the other members often played the part of servants to her in her various scams.

Not only was Jenny nimble fingered but she was also extremely inventive. She was an educated, attractive and smartly dressed young woman who could mix easily in wealthy middle-class circles, without being suspected of being a thief. The story is told of how she went to a church service wearing two false arms which appeared to remain in her lap. Dressed in good clothes and sitting among the wealthier lady worshippers, she would wait her chance to seize their watches and jewellery, passing them to one of her assistants in the pew behind. Apparently to her victims, her hands had never moved throughout the prayers.

Another successful ruse was to fake sudden illness when in the midst of a crowd. This she did in St James' Park on a day when the King was going to the House of Lords. As she lay on the ground apparently in great pain, surrounded by people offering her assistance, she was systematically robbing them and passing the items back to other members of her gang who were masquerading as her footman and maid.

Jenny also went on expeditions with her boyfriend of the day, usually one of the gang members. In one of these adventures, she used the sudden illness ploy again but this time to gain access to a house in Wapping. While the owners went upstairs for smelling salts, etc., Jenny rifled through the drawers and helped herself to a considerable sum in cash. Her boyfriend was doing the same in the kitchen, stealing the best silver cutlery.

Jenny and her gang rapidly achieved notoriety and inevitably she was caught, for picking the pocket of a gentleman in early 1733. She was committed to Newgate and came to trial at the next Sessions of the Old Bailey, under the name of Mary Young, her real name, although she used many aliases. As this was her first recorded offence as Mary Young, she was reprieved to transportation to Virginia on America's east coast. She spent four months in Newgate, awaiting a prison ship. When the day finally came, she had a huge quantity of goods put aboard the ship with her, to enable her to fund a good lifestyle in Virginia. No doubt she used some of her wealth to bribe the captain to allow her to take all this and again the governor of the penal colony, when she arrived there to let her live well and not have to work in the plantations.

It would seem that she missed both the excitement of crime and the easy wealth she made from it because it was not long before she returned to Britain. Only 5 per cent of those sentenced to transportation for periods of less than life did return and to do so before completing one's sentence was a capital crime. However, Jenny was able to use her looks and money to persuade a returning captain to take her back to London.

She returned to her various forms of thieving, but she was getting older now and her fingers were stiffening with arthritis. At the age of thirty-eight, on 4 April 1738, Jenny was caught red-handed with two male accomplices trying to take the purse of a woman named Mrs Rowley in Canon Alley, near London's Paternoster Row. This time she gave the name of Jane Webb and under this name, was once more sentenced to transportation after her trial eight days later.

Remember there were no photographic or fingerprint records at this time so the authorities had to accept the name she gave and seemed unable to unearth her previous conviction and sentence. It would seem that journalists of the day had no such problem making the connection between Jane Webb and Jenny Diver and her true identity was reported in the *London Evening Post*. Members of her gang made every effort to save her from transportation, but on 7 June 1738 she was once more put aboard a prison ship, the *Forward*, again bound for America. Jenny did not learn from this and within a year, using her usual method of bribery, she landed back at Liverpool.

She made her way to London but her old gang had dispersed, retired, transported or hanged. Jenny was finding it much harder now to make the good living she had been used to in her younger days.

Nemesis finally overtook Jenny on Saturday, 10 January 1741, when she was caught trying to rob a purse containing 13s ½d (a fraction over 65p), from a younger woman, Judith Gardner, in Sherbourne Lane. Jenny had set up a scam with Elizabeth Davies and an unidentified male member of her gang, whereby he would offer to help ladies cross some wooden boards laid over a patch of wet ground. As he held Judith's arm, Jenny put her hand into the woman's pocket. Judith realised this and grabbed Jenny's wrist still within her pocket. Jenny hit her round the head but she maintained a firm grip on Jenny's cloak until passers-by managed to arrest her and Elizabeth. A constable was summoned and they were taken to the compter (a local lock-up jail). Their male accomplice managed to escape.

She was examined the next day by the magistrates, who committed her to Newgate to await trial. This time she was identified by the authorities and appeared before the next Sessions for the City of London and County of Middlesex at the Old Bailey, a week later on Saturday, 17 January 1741.

She was charged, together with Elizabeth Davies, with highway robbery in the form of 'privately stealing' (picking pockets to the value of more than 1s) and also with returning from transportation. She had been caught red-handed so had no real defence to the first charge and equally little to the second.

The principal prosecution witness was the victim, Mrs Gardner, who described the attack on her to the court and was cross-examined on her testimony by Jenny herself. Mrs Gardner told the court how she had been put in fear by the attack and how she had struggled with Jenny. Several other witnesses gave evidence of the crime and subsequent arrest of the two women. There was no counsel for the defence in those days but Jenny did her best to defend herself and brought forward character witnesses for both herself and Elizabeth Davies, not that these convinced the jury who brought them both in guilty, to use the parlance of the time. At the end of the Session, the Recorder sentenced them to be hanged at Tyburn. In all, thirteen prisoners were sentenced to death from this Sessions, seven men and six women. Both Jenny and Elizabeth immediately 'pleaded their belly' (claimed that they were pregnant), but the panel of matrons charged with examining them found this not to be the case. At the end of the Sessions, the Recorder prepared his report to the King and Privy Council recommending who should be reprieved and who should hang. Predictably, Jenny's name was not on the reprieve list. Elizabeth had her sentence commuted to transportation.

It seems that the enormity of her situation finally hit Jenny and she turned to religion. Religion and repentance were seen as very important and even criminals like Jenny would have become very concerned about the afterlife and the fate of her soul. She would have been repeatedly told that if she confessed and repented her sins, then she could avoid going to 'eternal damnation in the fires of Hell', or some similarly emotive phrase. As will be seen, she clearly took this message to heart. On her last Sunday, she and her fellow condemned prisoners were taken to the chapel and seated in the Condemned Pews where they were made to endure a church service with a coffin centrally placed on the table in their midst.

Wednesday, 18 March was to see one of the largest multiple hangings at Tyburn for many years. The prisoners had been convicted at the December 1740, January 1741 and February 1 741 Sessions. In all, sixteen men and four women were to suffer that day. The women being Jenny, Elizabeth Fox and Priscilla Mahon who had been convicted of robbery in a brothel and Dorothy Middleton, convicted of burglary.

On the morning of her execution, Jenny, being wealthy, dressed in a long black dress with a black bonnet and veil. Many of the women hanged at this time would wear a cheap shift as it was all they could afford and in any case, their clothes would become the property of the hangman afterwards.

Jenny was led from her cell to the Press Yard in Newgate, accompanied by the tolling of the bell of St Sepulchre's church just across the road. The Yeoman of the Halter tied her wrists in front of her and put a cord around her body and elbows. He put the noose around her neck and wound the free rope around her body. At this point, her nerve failed her for a few moments but she soon recovered her composure. The other nineteen were similarly treated and then led to the three carts and seated on their coffins. Jenny was allowed to go to Tyburn in a mourning coach, attended by the Ordinary of Newgate, Reverend Boughton, to whom it was reported that she confessed her sins and declared her religious beliefs.

Like anybody else about to suffer an imminent and painful death, Jenny was no doubt inwardly terrified of what was about to happen to her, but she had to maintain her image and put on a 'good show' for the crowd. Then, as now, 'celebrities' captured the public's imagination and she would have been expected to justify her celebrity status.

The journey to Tyburn, some 2 miles, could often take three hours or more to complete so it was usually around noon or later by the time the prisoners arrived. The procession comprised marshalmen, javelin men and constables armed with staves, all led by the City Marshal and under sheriff on their horses. The route led west out of the City of London, along Holborn, St Giles, and the Tyburn Road (now called Oxford Street) to the gallows at what is now Marble Arch at the north-eastern corner of Hyde Park. Extraordinarily as it may seem now, the procession would make at least two refreshment stops where the prisoners were allowed to have food and alcohol, before reaching Tyburn. The first was at the Bowl Inn in St Giles, the second at the Mason's Arms in Seymour Place.

Once at Tyburn, Jenny was helped down from the coach by Reverend Boughton and took her place in one of the carts. It is probable that the four women would have been placed in the same cart and the sixteen men divided up between the other two carts. The hangman, John Thrift, uncoiled the free rope from around her and threw the end up to one of his young assistants lying on top of one of the three cross beams, who secured it leaving very little slack. This process had to be repeated for each prisoner, so took some while to complete. Jenny may well have slipped John Thrift a small bribe to ensure he did his job well and positioned the knot under her left ear instead of at the back of her neck. When all the 'sufferers', as they were known, were secured to the beams and had finished their prayers, night-caps were drawn over the faces of those who could afford them. Jenny did not require a night cap, instead preferring her veil. The signal was given by the under sheriff for the carts to be whipped away by their drivers. As the cart moved from under her, Jenny was dragged from it, dropping just a few inches to be brought up with a jerk, causing the noose to tighten around her neck. Swinging back and forth under the beam, amid the writhing mass of her fellow prisoners, she made choking and gurgling sounds, her feet paddling in thin air. Jenny was fortunate, only struggling for a few moments before going limp and passing into unconsciousness, according to contemporary reports. It is not known whether her friends pulled on her legs to shorten her suffering, although this was a common practice. It is reported that some of the spectators offered up prayers for her soul as she dangled there.

She had arranged for her friends to claim her body when she was cut down to prevent it falling into the hands of the dissectionists and was buried at her specific request in St Pancras churchyard.

One hundred and eighty-two women were hanged at Tyburn in the eighteenth century, so female executions were comparatively rare. Jenny's would have been reported in the press as there were several titles by 1740 and there were execution broadsides published detailing her crimes, confession and execution. This mass execution drew a huge crowd of people of all classes. Wealthy people paid substantial sums for seats in the grandstands around the gallows. These were known as Mother Proctor's Pews, after their owner, who no doubt made a fortune from them. In the crowd there were quite possibly pickpockets operating, irrespective of the fact that it was one of their number who was the star attraction that day.

Was it simple greed or the love of London and the thrill of crime together with the easy living she made from it that led Jenny to continue down the path that she knew would inevitably lead to the gallows? She was an intelligent woman who would have been fully aware of the likely punishment for her crimes and yet, it seems, she could not resist the excitement and glamour of being London's most successful pickpocket.

Mary Blandy
'For the sake of decency, gentlemen, don't hang me high.'

Mary Blandy was thirty-one years old when she was hanged in 1752 for the murder of her father by poisoning. Her father, Francis Blandy, was a prosperous lawyer and the town clerk of Henley on Thames in Oxfordshire at the time of his murder.

So Mary lived a comfortable lifestyle at the family home in Hart Street and had been given a good education.

Francis had unwisely advertised a dowry of £10,000 – a huge sum for those days, for the man who married Mary. This attracted plenty of suitors, all of whom being promptly rejected except one, the Honourable Captain William Henry Cranstoun, who was initially acceptable. Cranstoun was the son of a Scottish nobleman and therefore seen as a suitable match. By all accounts he was not a physically attractive person but seems to have been able to take Mary in completely. All went well to begin with but then problems arose when it was discovered that Cranstoun was in fact still married, having wed one Anne Murray in 1744 in Scotland, although he had been living in the Blandy household for a year. Mary's father became very unhappy about Cranstoun and began to see him for what he was. To get over Francis' hostility, Cranstoun persuaded Mary to give her father powders which he described as an ancient 'love philtre' and which he assured her would make Francis like him.

He knew what the powders contained but presumably didn't mind letting his girlfriend murder her father to get the £10,000 dowry. Ironically Francis Blandy's estate came only to around £4,000. Under the law at the time, this would have automatically passed to him if they married.

Mary seemed to be totally taken in by Cranstoun and administered these powders, which were in fact arsenic, in her father's tea and gruel, causing him to become progressively more ill. The servants had also become ill from eating some of the leftover food although they all recovered. None of this seemed to register with Mary – that the powders might be the cause of the problem.

When her father was obviously near death, Mary sent for the local doctor who advised her that she could be held responsible for poisoning him so she quickly burned Cranstoun's love letters and disposed of the remaining powders. Susan(nah)

Gunnell, the housemaid, had the presence of mind to rescue some of the powder from the fire when Mary tried to destroy the evidence and took it to a chemist for analysis who found that it was arsenic.

Francis realised he was dying and asked to see Mary, telling her that he suspected he was being poisoned by her. She begged for his forgiveness, which he indeed gave her, despite the fact that she did not admit her crime to him. He finally succumbed on Wednesday, 14 August 1751. After her father's death, Mary was kept for some time under house arrest in her room, under the care of Edward Herne, the parish clerk of Henley. However, she was able to get out on one occasion and went for a walk around the town. The local people of Henley were hostile to her and chased her across the bridge over the Thames, into Berkshire, where she took refuge with a friend, Mrs Davis, the landlady of the Little Angel Inn at Remenham.

In spite of this popular suspicion, it was some time before Mary was arrested. As soon as he got wind of Mary's likely arrest, Cranstoun deserted her and is thought to have escaped abroad and died penniless in France in late 1752. An inquest was held which found that Francis Blandy was poisoned and accused Mary of administering it. On Friday, 16 August, the coroner issued a warrant for the arrest of Mary and for her committal to the Oxford County Gaol. Mary was made to wear leg irons whilst awaiting trial as there was some concern that she would try to escape.

She came to trial at Oxford Assizes on 3 March 1752 before the Honourable Heneage Legge, Esq., and Sir Sydney Stafford Smythe in the hall of the Divinity School. The normal venue, the Town Hall, was being refurbished at the time. The trial was of particular interest because it was the first time detailed medical evidence had been presented in court on a charge of murder by poisoning. Although Dr Anthony Addington had not been able to chemically analyse Francis Blandy's organs for traces of arsenic as the technology didn't exist at the time, he was able to convince the court on the basis of observed comparison that the powder Mary had given her father was indeed arsenic.

She defended herself with the help of three members of counsel, with what has been described as 'intelligence and zeal' although her case was hopeless. She made an impassioned speech for her own defence in which she totally denied administering poison but did admit that she had put a powder into her father's food. The servants gave evidence against her, telling the court that they had seen her administering the powders to her father's food and drink and trying to destroy the evidence.

At the end of the thirteen-hour trial, the jury swiftly convicted her of murder and she received the death sentence. She was then returned to Oxford Castle where it is reported that the keeper's family were all very upset by her conviction. Mary allegedly told them 'Don't mind it', 'What does it signify? I am very hungry; pray, let me have something for supper as speedily as possible.' They gave her mutton chops and apple pie. She apparently got on well with her jailers and was well treated by them.

She was allowed nearly six weeks between sentence and execution and appeared completely unmoved by her situation. The trial judge would have sent his recommendation to the Secretary of State, and this would have been considered by the King and Privy Council at a 'Hanging Cabinet.'

In July 1752, the Murder Act was passed which stipulated that all persons convicted of murder were to be fed only on bread and water and hanged within two days of sentence and that their body be dissected afterwards. Fortunately for Mary, she missed the advent of this new law.

Mary's case was the main news story in the early part of 1752 and there were endless articles about her in the press. She also wrote a great deal in the condemned cell including 'Miss

Mary Blandy's Own Account of the Affair between her and Mr. Cranstoun', which was described by Hoarce Bleakley as the 'most famous apologia in criminal literature.' She corresponded with various people, including another woman under sentence of death, Elizabeth Jeffries, whose case is looked at next. A middle-class lady who visited Mary in prison was shocked to find that Mary was sympathetic to Elizabeth who she regarded as a common criminal who deserved her fate. Mary was recorded as saying of her 'I can't bear these over virtuous women. I believe that if ever the devil picks a bone it is one of theirs.'

There seems to be some difference of opinion as to the place of execution. According to some accounts, she was executed in the Castle Yard at Oxford, a large open space, and in other accounts the gallows was set up on a raised mound at the Westgate. Both are quite possible.

Mary was hanged on Monday, 6 April 1752 from a gallows consisting of a wooden beam placed between two trees. She chose 'a black crape sack dress, with her arms and hands ty'd with black paduasoy ribbons.' She was attended by Rev. Swinton and behaved with bravery and penitence to the end although still protesting her innocence. A relatively small crowd had gathered to watch her die.

Her last request to the officials was 'for the sake of decency, gentlemen, don't hang me high.' She was naturally modest and concerned that the young men in the crowd would look up her skirts if she was too high. She was then made to climb a ladder draped in black cloth, whilst the hangman climbed a ladder beside her. Mary was noosed and her hands were tied in front to allow her to hold her prayer book. She covered her face with a large handkerchief.

It had been agreed that when she had finished her prayers, she would drop the book as signal to the hangman to 'turn her off' the ladder as the saying went. She passed into unconsciousness very quickly, reportedly, dying without a struggle, probably due to carotid reflex. She was taken down after half an hour but there was no coffin for her so she had to be carried back to the castle by six men. It is said that a blackbird perched on the beam during the hanging, and that no blackbird has ever sung there since.

Mary was buried in the early hours of the Tuesday morning in the chancel of Henley Parish church, between the graves of her father and mother. Her ghost is said to haunt the Westgate and the Little Angel Inn.

Mary was notably brave in the way she faced her death. She would have expected that death by hanging would be slow and painful even though in the event it seemed not to be. Her last words 'for the sake of decency, gentlemen, don't hang me high' became instantly famous although they hardly seem those of someone who is terrified, rather more those of someone concerned with preserving her modesty than with her imminent death.

Mary must have been totally devastated at the knowledge that the man who she thought loved her had duped her into murdering her own father and then immediately abandoned her to save his skin while sending her to the gallows. But how could an educated and mature woman be so taken in? Sadly she was by no means the first, nor will she be the last to murder for love. She must surely have had her suspicions when everyone who ate the food to which she had added the powders became violently ill and yet she brushed these aside in the hope that Cranstoun would marry her.

By the standards of justice prevailing in 1752, Mary had a fair trial and a fair sentence. Ironically, modern forensic science would have simply made it easier to convict her. The only doubt as to her guilt is that of her intention. She loved her father and I feel sure she neither meant nor wanted to kill him but rather wanted to believe what Cranstoun had told her even though she had clear evidence that it was a lie. At one time, arsenic was used as a tonic, and this may account for why her father seemed actually better the first time she gave it to him.

Elizabeth Jeffries
The Murderous Niece

The British public and therefore the British media have always enjoyed a 'good murder'. The early months of 1752 brought not one, but two such events. Their cases filled the newspapers for weeks. In the previous pages we have looked at the case of Mary Blandy and, as mentioned, the other case was that of Elizabeth Jeffries who had aided and abetted the murder of her uncle.

Mr Joseph Jeffries was a wealthy but childless man who lived in Walthamstow, Essex, and who had adopted his niece, Elizabeth. He made his will in her favour but threatened to change it because of her rebellious teenage ways, her good behaviour being made a condition of inheritance. Elizabeth had been thinking of murdering her uncle for some two years but did not see a way of doing it unaided. Finally fearing that he would carry out his threat to disinherit her, the by now twenty-one-year-old Elizabeth enlisted the help of Mr Jeffries' gardener, John Swan, with whom she was believed to have been 'intimate', to use the contemporary term. They had tried to persuade a former servant, one Matthews, to kill Mr Jeffries by offering him a substantial share of the proceeds, but in the end he declined, although he was probably present at the killing.

The plan to kill Mr Jeffries involved Matthews obtaining a brace of pistols for which Elizabeth had given him half a guinea. He spent this on drink but still joined the others in Mr Jeffries' house at around 10 p.m. on the night of Tuesday, 3 July 1751. Matthews hid himself in the pantry and was joined there by John and Elizabeth around midnight. They asked him if he was ready and where the pistols were but he told them, 'I cannot find it in my heart to do it.' To which the furious Elizabeth replied: 'You may be damned for a villain, for not performing your promise!' Whether John feared that Matthews would prove unreliable, we don't know, but he had brought a brace of pistols. He also produced a book and insisted that Matthews should swear not to disclose what had passed between them, 'unless it was to save his own life.' Matthews then left Mr Jeffries' house but remained long enough to hear a pistol shot. Elizabeth and John had devised a plan whereby they would both pretend to have been in their respective rooms at the time of the shooting, having first staged what was to appear to be a botched robbery by hiding some plate and silver in a sack downstairs. Later that evening, they would raise the alarm and claim that Mr Jeffries had been robbed and murdered by an intruder.

Initially the authorities arrested Elizabeth as there was no sign of forced entry, and began a search for Matthews whom she had implicated. However, they could produce no evidence against her and she was released. She now took control of her uncle's assets and began spending them. In the meantime Matthews was located and gave a full statement of events, if only to save his own neck. On receipt of this information Elizabeth and John were re-arrested and committed to Chelmsford prison for trial at the next assizes.

They were tried together some eight months later at the Essex Assizes before Mr Justice Wright on Tuesday, 10 March 1752. They had missed the previous year's assize which had opened on 31 July 1751. Matthews was the principal witness for the prosecution and both were found guilty. The Crown counsel summed up Elizabeth's motive for killing her uncle thus 'to alter his will, if she did not alter her conduct.' John Swan, as he was a servant of Mr Jeffries, was convicted of Petty Treason 'for the cruel and wicked murder of his late master', and Elizabeth 'of aiding, helping, assisting, comforting and maintaining the said John Swan to commit the murder'. Note that she was not charged with murder, as she would have been under the doctrine of common purpose that applied in the twentieth century (see Edith Thompson), but rather with the crime she had actually committed. She reportedly confessed her part in the crime on the Thursday and they were brought back before the court on the Saturday to be sentenced. She fainted as her death sentence was pronounced. Nine men also received death sentences of whom five were reprieved and the other three hanged at Chelmsford on 26 March. The Court ordered that Elizabeth and John be executed near the scene of their crime.

The execution procession led by the under sheriff of Essex left Chelmsford Gaol at 4 a.m. on Saturday, 28 March, with Elizabeth riding in a cart, sitting on her own coffin and accompanied by the hangman. Because John had been convicted of Petty Treason, he was drawn along behind tied to a sledge, which was a mandatory part of the punishment for that crime. On arrival at the gallows, which was near the sixth milestone in Epping Forest near Walthamstow, some 23 miles and perhaps eight or nine hours away from Chelmsford, he was made to get up into the cart with Elizabeth and stand beside her.

A huge crowd had assembled to witness the proceedings; such was the public interest in the case. The prisoners did not communicate with one another at all, not even by glance, in the cart. Elizabeth was made to stand on a chair as she was of small stature and fainted several times as she was being prepared. It was reported that both confessed their guilt and justice of their sentences to a member of the jury who questioned them before they were turned off. After they had hung for the requisite time both bodies were taken down. Elizabeth's corpse was taken away in a hearse to be delivered to her friends for burial, but John's was hung in chains in another part of the Forest, said to be near the Bald Faced Stag Inn in Hainault Road, Chigwell, Essex, as a warning to others.

A broadside of the trial and execution of Elizabeth and John was printed. With the typical inaccuracy of these publications, the date of the murder is a year out.

Clearly Elizabeth's desire for money was the prime mover in the crime and it seems that she sucked John Swan into the plan by the offer of sexual favours. It is not clear more than 250 years later whether she was really interested in John as a person or rather just saw him as an available assistant. No doubt she would have been happier to have paid Matthews to commit the crime and so put a slightly greater distance between it and her.

Mary Blandy had become aware of Elizabeth being in a similar predicament to her own and was allowed to write to her while both were in prison. The ensuing correspondence, between 7 January and 19 March 1752, was published under the title of 'Genuine Letters between Miss Blandy and Miss Jeffries.' Initially both women protested their innocence to each other, but later Elizabeth acknowledged her guilt to Mary. In her last letter to Elizabeth on 16 March, Mary reportedly wrote: 'Your deceiving of me was a small crime; it was deceiving yourself: for no retreat, tho' ever so pleasant, no diversions, no company, no, not Heaven itself, could have made you happy with those crimes un-repented of in your breast.' So, with the promise to be 'a suitor for her at the Throne of Mercy' Mary finished the correspondence.

2

LATER GEORGIAN PERIOD AND THE 'BLOODY CODE'

In the period 1760-1799, 205 women were executed, seventeen at the stake and 188 on the gallows. This was an average of just over five a year. One hundred and eight of these women had been convicted of murder.

The effects of the 'Bloody Code' as it was known became apparent during this time with a general increase in executions of both sexes, particularly in the period from 1775-1790.

The English Penal Code in the period from 1723 to 1820 became increasingly severe, mandating the death penalty for ever more offences. The year 1723 saw the introduction of the first of the (Waltham) Black Acts and these continually increased the scope of capital punishment over the next ninety years. In 1688 there were fifty crimes for which a person could be put to death. By 1765 this had risen to about 160 and to 222 by 1810.

It should be noted that only twenty or so crimes typically resulted in the execution of women and that in the vast majority of cases (69-70 per cent) the death sentence was commuted.

The huge number of capital crimes was inflated not only by endless acts of Parliament mentioned earlier but also by the minute subdivision of capital offences into individual categories. For instance there were seven individual capital offences of arson.

The country was run by the property-owning middle classes who were understandably keen to protect their property from the large underclass who were seen as feckless and whose lives were considered to be of little real value. In the period from 1735 to 1800, an amazing 1,596 females were condemned to death with 1,243 being reprieved and 356 executed, 32 by burning and the remainder by hanging. A total of 169 women and girls were executed for crimes against property whilst 187 were to suffer for murder: most of them were convicted on circumstantial evidence or on the strength of their confessions after very short hearings, often without any real defence in trials that would be considered wholly inadequate by today's standards.

The non-murder cases break down as follows:

CRIME	NO. EXECUTED
Highway robbery	42
Robbery in dwelling house	35
Burglary	25
Arson	16
Housebreaking	9
High Treason Coining	8
Forgery/Uttering/Personating	7
Riot/destroying property	7
Stealing in a shop	6
Horse/sheep theft	5
Privately stealing from a person (Pickpocketing)	5
Returning from transportation	3
Sacrilege	1
TOTAL	169

With over 1,000 men and women a year being sentenced
to death, although only a small proportion were actually
executed, there was growing activism in the early part of
the nineteenth century to reduce the number of crimes for
which people could suffer the ultimate punishment.

Sir Samuel Romilly (1757-1818), attempted to get Parliament
to de-capitalise many minor crimes. On 17 January 1813, he
introduced a Bill in the House of Commons 'to repeal so
much of the Act of King William as punishes with death the
offence of stealing privately in a shop, warehouse or stable,
goods of the value of 5s'. This Bill was thrown out by the
House of Lords.

After Romilly's death in 1818, Sir James Mackintosh, who
had supported Romilly's proposals, took up the abolitionist's
cause. On 2 March 1819, he carried a motion against the government for a committee to consider capital punishment, by a
majority of nineteen. In 1820 he introduced six Bills embody-
ing the recommendations of the committee, only three of
which became law. Lord Eldon, the Lord Chancellor, secured
an amendment to keep the death penalty for stealing to the
value of more than £10. On 21 May 1823, Mackintosh put
forward a further nine proposals to Parliament for abolish-
ing capital punishment for less serious offences. He wanted
to include forgery but this was opposed by Sir Robert Peel.
Shoplifting ceased to carry the death penalty in 1823.

Between 1832 and 1837, Sir Robert Peel's government
introduced various Bills to reduce the number of capital
crimes. Sheep, cattle and horse stealing were removed from
the list in 1832, followed by sacrilege, letter stealing, returning
from transportation in 1834/5, forgery and coining in 1836,
arson, burglary and theft from a dwelling house in 1837.

In the period 1800 to 1833 a further thirty-three women
were to hang for crimes other than murder. The last of these
was Charlotte Long who was hanged for arson in August 1833
at Gloucester.

This period in penal history became known as 'the Bloody Code' and the following pages look at the crimes that sent eleven women to the gallows and one to the stake.

Mary Jones
Hanged for Shoplifting

Mary was thought to be about eighteen or nineteen years old but was already married with two children when her husband, William, was press-ganged into the Navy to go to the Falkland Islands, leaving her virtually destitute. She lived with her friend Ann Styles in Angel Alley in the Strand and was at times reduced to begging to feed herself and the infants. It is said that she had her baby with her in the cart as she was taken to Tyburn to be hanged.

There had been a spate of shoplifting incidents in the Ludgate Street area of London during 1771 and the shopkeepers were on high alert and keeping watch for suspects. On Wednesday, 7 August, with one of her children in tow, Mary and Ann Styles went on a shoplifting expedition in Ludgate Street. They may have had other accomplices with them although no one else was arrested. Mary and Ann were observed going in and out of a large number shops. Thomas Ham, a shopkeeper himself and a witness at the trial, was suspicious of their activities and kept a close eye on them. He estimated that he had seen them go into as many as fifteen shops in the street, between 3 and 6 p.m. that afternoon. Finally the pair went to the drapery shop owned by a Mr William Foot and expressed interest in buying a child's frock. Nothing that they were shown appeared to be what they wanted and Mary made to leave the shop but Mr Foot's assistant, Christopher Preston, noticed that she had something concealed under her cloak. He went after her and brought her back into the shop where he discovered she had concealed four pieces of worked

muslin which she had taken from the counter. Christopher
Preston told the other assistant, Andrew Hawkins, to fetch a
constable while he kept the women in the shop. The constable
arrested them both and they were taken to the Compter (a
local lock-up jail).

Both women were charged under the Shoplifting Act with
the theft of the muslin which was valued at £5 10s. The actual
offence at this time was called 'privately stealing in a shop'.
The value of the goods stolen, being more than 5s, made it a
capital crime. The pair were tried at the Sessions of the Old
Bailey held on Wednesday, 11 September 1771. Thomas Ham,
Christopher Preston and Andrew Hawkins each gave evidence
for the prosecution.

Mary and Ann were permitted to speak in their own
defence. Mary told the court of her struggle to support two
children without her husband and that she had always been an
honest woman. Ann told the court that she had merely gone
with Mary to buy the child's clothes and that she had nothing
to do with the theft.

The trial lasted no more than two hours and Mary was
convicted as she was actually in possession of the stolen
items but Ann was acquitted. Mary received the mandatory
death sentence and was transferred to Newgate to await her
trip to Tyburn. When the Recorder of London prepared
his report for the King and Privy Council there was no
recommendation to mercy for Mary, despite her age and
circumstances. As was normal for non-murder cases she was
to spend some time in the Condemned Hold until the next
'hanging day'. She would have been regularly attended by
Rev. John Wood, the Ordinary (Newgate's prison chaplain)
and would have been expected to attend Sunday religious
services. She and the other condemned criminals had a special area in the centre of the chapel, surrounded by a high
partition so that they could not be seen by or communicate
with the other prisoners.

On the morning of Wednesday, 16 October she was brought to the Press Yard of Newgate where the halter noose was put round her neck, and her arms tied to her body with a cord above the elbows. She was made to get into the cart and sit on her own coffin.

With her for her last journey were four men: James Allen who had been convicted of stealing in a dwelling house, William Penn, Richard Thompson and John Hughes who had all been convicted of highway robbery.

The procession consisting of a court officer responsible for prisoners, the Ordinary, the hangman and his assistants and a troop of javelin men started out for Tyburn, about 2 miles away. The procession made its slow and bumpy passage along Holborn, St Giles, and the Tyburn Road, to Tyburn itself near what is now Marble Arch. A stop was made at St Sepulchre's church where the bell would be tolled, and the minister would chant, 'You that are condemned to die, repent with lamentable tears; ask mercy of the Lord for the salvation of your souls.' As the procession passed on, the minister would tell the audience, 'All good people, pray heartily unto God for these poor sinners who are now going to their death, for whom the great bell tolls.' Here friends might present the criminals with small nosegays (bunches of flowers).

On arrival at Tyburn around noon, some two to three hours after they had left Newgate, the prisoners were greeted by a large crowd.

Mary's cart was backed under one of the three beams of the gallows and Edward Dennis, the hangman, uncoiled the free end of the rope from her body and threw it up to one of his assistants balanced precariously on the beam above. They tied the rope to the beam leaving very little slack. The Ordinary prayed with her and when he had finished the hangman would have pulled a night cap over her face if she had been able to afford one. As you can imagine the preparations took quite some time where a batch of five prisoners was being hanged.

When everything was ready, the City Marshall gave the signal and the horses were whipped away, pulling the prisoners off the carts and leaving them suspended. They would only have a few inches of drop at most and thus many of them would writhe in convulsive agony for some moments, their legs paddling the air, 'dancing the Tyburn jig' as it was known, until unconsciousness overtook them. The hangman, his assistants and sometimes the prisoners' relatives might pull on the prisoners' legs to hasten their end. It is not recorded whether or not Mary struggled or was one of the fortunate few who quickly became still. The five bodies were left to hang for an hour before being cut down and claimed by relatives or friends and taken for burial.

One can well understand why the law in this period in history is now referred to as the Bloody Code. Of the 294 people executed at Tyburn in the decade from 1765 to 1774 only twenty-five were to die for murder and three for rape. The rest mostly suffered for various types of property related crime, such as highway robbery, burglary, housebreaking and forgery.

It seems amazing today that a young mother should be hanged for what would now considered to be a minor crime, yet in 1771 nobody would have thought anything of it – it was a regular and perfectly normal event. If it was Mary's first offence, as she claimed, she would probably get a community service order now, especially as she had dependent children. However Georgian justice was being applied increasingly severely at this time. Sixty-two men and six women received the death sentence during this year, of which thirty-four of the men and another of the women, Frances Allen, were to share Mary's fate. Frances Allen was hanged on Wednesday, 7 August for housebreaking.

A few years later Mary's case was raised in Parliament by Sir William Meredith, the Whig Member for Liverpool, when he was opposing a motion to make yet another offence capital. He told the House that he did not believe 'a fouler murder was ever committed against law, than the murder of this woman by law'. His eloquence was to no avail however and the Bill was carried.

Elizabeth Taylor
Burglary in a Dwelling House

Elizabeth became only the third woman to be hanged on the New Drop gallows outside Newgate, the previous two being Frances Warren and Mary Moody.

Elizabeth and her brother Martin were convicted of burgling the house and shop of Samuel Hooker at Highgate in London on the night of Sunday, 7 May 1785. They got quite a haul, nearly £200 worth of goods comprising 60yds of Irish linen cloth, ten linen handkerchiefs, 250yds of thread lace, 2,000yds of silk ribbon, 30yds of muslin, two silk handkerchiefs and some silver spoons and tableware. Elizabeth had been a servant in the Hooker household and had left his employment about sixteen months earlier.

That evening Mr Hooker locked up as usual before going to bed and was satisfied that everything was secure. Sometime after midnight Elizabeth, Martin and possibly a second man arrived at the house where they carefully removed four courses of brickwork from under the kitchen window without disturbing the sleeping occupants. Martin was able to get through this hole and then went into the shop, taking anything of value and passing it out to Elizabeth.

The crime was discovered the following morning when Mr Hooker came down and was surprised by the amount of light in his kitchen from the sun shining through the hole. He checked round and went into the shop where he noticed various items missing. In a state of agitation he went next door and fetched his neighbour to look at the situation. He then fetched the local constable, Mr Thomas Seasons and reported the burglary and the considerable loss of stock to him.

On 18 May, Mr Hooker and Mr Seasons went to Martin Taylor's home and searched it. They discovered a cap which had some lace on it and a few yards of ribbon which Mr Hooker was able to identify, but none of the other property. Martin was arrested at the house. Mr Hooker and Mr Seasons then went to the home of a friend of the Taylor's, Mrs Halloway, who was a part-time dressmaker with whom Martin had lodged. She claimed in court that Martin had asked her to make two shifts for his sister from the material that he had brought to her. Mrs Halloway knew Elizabeth from her visits to the house. Here Mr Hooker and Mr Seasons discovered pieces of the Irish linen cut up into panels for shirts and shifts. They also discovered one of the handkerchiefs that had been stolen. Further searching of the house revealed some more of the items in the upstairs room of another lodger, Mrs Powell. Mr Hooker and the constable's next visit was to Bow fair where they apprehended Elizabeth who tried to make a run for it with the help of some of the bystanders. When she was searched a small quantity of ribbon was found in her pocket book. She was taken back to Mr Season's house and then before a magistrate where she made a confession to the burglary.

Elizabeth and Martin were committed for trial by the magistrates and appeared at the June Sessions of the Old Bailey which opened on Wednesday the 29th, before Mr Justice Buller. Mr Silvester led the prosecution and the defence was handled by Mr Garrow.

Various witnesses were called including Mr Hooker, Mr Seasons, Mrs Halloway and Mrs Powell, each giving their account of the events and each being cross-examined for the defence. Mr Garrow questioned the constable as to the circumstances in which Elizabeth had made her confession and whether or not he had placed her under duress to extract it. He suggested to the constable that he had threatened her with being hanged if she did not confess, something which Mr Seasons denied, telling the court that he tried to dissuade her from making a confession to him and that she continued because she thought, in his opinion, that it might save her from the gallows.

Martin Taylor was allowed to make a personal statement in his defence in which he told the court that he had bought 14yds of the linen for 22d a yard from an acquaintance in the borough with the intention of having it made up by Mrs Halloway into clothes for his wife and sister. Elizabeth simply told the court that she knew nothing about the crime at all. Not a statement that was likely to impress the jury in view of the evidence against her.

Both Elizabeth and Martin were convicted and sent back to Newgate to await sentencing at the end of the Sessions. No less than twenty-two men and three women were condemned to hang on that Friday. However fifteen men and the other two women were reprieved and had their sentences commuted to transportation.

The execution of the eight remaining prisoners was to take place on Wednesday, 17 August 1785. With Elizabeth and Martin on the gallows were James Lockhart who had been convicted of stealing in a dwelling house, John Rebouit, John Morris and James Guthrie convicted of highway robbery and Richard Jacobs and Thomas Bailey who had also been condemned for burglary.

At around 7.30 a.m. the condemned were led from their cells into the Press Yard where the under sheriff and John Villette, the Ordinary, met them. Their leg irons were removed by the prison blacksmith and the Yeoman of the Halter supervised the proceedings as the hangman and his assistant bound their wrists in front of them with cord and also placed a cord round their body and arms at the elbows. White nightcaps were placed on their heads. The prisoners were led across the

Yard to the Lodge and then out through the Debtor's Door where they climbed the steps up to the gallows. There were shouts of 'hats off' from the crowd. This was not out of respect for those about to die, but rather because the people further back demanded those at the front remove their hats so as not to obscure their view of the execution. Once assembled on the drop, the hangman, probably Edward Dennis, put the nooses round their necks while they prayed with the Ordinary. Elizabeth might have had her dress bound around her legs for the sake of decency but the men's legs were left free. When the prayers had finished at about 8.15 p.m., the under sheriff gave the signal and the hangman moved the lever, which was connected to a drawbar under the trap, causing it to fall with a loud crash, the prisoners plunging down 12in or so and usually writhing and struggling for some seconds before relaxing and becoming still. If their bodies continued to struggle, the hangman, unseen by the crowd and within the box below the drop, would grasp their legs and swing on them so adding his weight to theirs and thus ending their sufferings sooner. The dangling bodies were left hanging for an hour before being returned to their relatives. It was not recorded whether Elizabeth struggled or whether she died easily.

Although still by no means an instant death at least being hanged outside Newgate and being given some drop was a considerable improvement over executions at Tyburn with the long and uncomfortable ride to the gallows where prisoners typically died a much slower death.

Phoebe Harris
Burnt at the Stake for Coining

We have a perception of what the modern crime of High Treason is, but up to 1790 it also encompassed several other offences, notably coining. The crime of coining was subdivided into individual offences relating only to gold and silver coins, e.g. clipping coins to provide coin metal for forgeries, colouring coins to make them appear of higher value, making counterfeit coins and having the equipment to do any of the above. Coining was considered treasonable because it directly affected the State and confidence in the currency.

Under the name of Mrs Brown, Phoebe Harris had rented a room from one Joel Sparkes at No.19 Swan Yard, a house in Drury Lane, London, before Christmas 1785. A friend of hers, Francis Hardy, had recommended her to Sparkes, describing her as a captain's widow with a private income. In reality, it seems that Phoebe had been separated from her husband for two or three years. Whilst Phoebe lived at this address she was regularly engaged in filing and clipping coins and then using the metal to make new counterfeit coins in sand moulds. Francis Hardy was the person who was later to inform the police of the criminal goings on at No.19. There was a suggestion, flatly denied by him in court, that he had had a relationship with Phoebe. He did, however, take her teenage daughter in as a servant on the day of her mother's arrest.

At about 5 p.m. on Saturday, 11 February 1786, John Clarke (a constable) went to No.19 in consequence of the information he had received and found Phoebe Harris and Elizabeth Yelland in the first floor room. He and his assistants, George Meecham, Patrick Macmanus, and William Andrews, broke down the locked door and arrested the two women. They then searched the room in which they found some counterfeit coins and the necessary equipment for coining in an adjoining closet.

When John Clarke compared the counterfeit shillings to genuine ones, it was clear that they had been cast from a mould made from a genuine shilling. In all, some twelve counterfeit coins were discovered, both shillings and sixpences. One of the genuine sixpences had a hole in it and this was evident in the counterfeits.

A little later, after the rooms had been searched, Elizabeth's brother, Joseph Yelland, returned home and was also arrested. All three were taken to Bow Street to appear before a magistrate. They were remanded in custody to Newgate to stand trial at the next Sessions of the Old Bailey.

Capital trials at this period took up very little time with a number being conducted during a single day. The April Sessions of the Old Bailey in 1786 opened on Wednesday the 26th of that month, before Mr Baron Eyre. Among those indicted were Joseph Yelland, otherwise known as Holman, Phebe Harris (spelling of Phoebe as given in the original indictment) and Elizabeth Yelland, who were jointly charged with two specimen counts, as follows:

> for that they, on the 11th of February last, one piece of false, feigned, and counterfeit money and coin, to the likeness and similitude of the good, legal, and silver coin of this realm, called a shilling, falsely, deceitfully, feloniously, and traiterously did counterfeit and coin, against the duty of their allegiance, and against the statute.

There was also a second count of coining a sixpence. The shilling is the equivalent of the current 5p coin, whilst a sixpence is the equivalent of 2½p. Although, in 1786 these two coins had much greater purchasing power they were still coins of small denomination.

The prosecution was opened by Mr Silvester, assisted by Mr Wilson and Mr Garrow led the defence. The case was heard before the second Middlesex jury, consisting of twelve men. Both sides were able to call witnesses and cross-examine those for the other side. In this case, the Crown called the constables involved in the raid, together with the landlord and his son. They also called Francis Hardy, who gave direct eyewitness evidence of the manufacture and colouring of the counterfeit coins. The coining equipment found in the rooms was produced in court as evidence. Hardy suggested that the group had bought forged coins from other criminals to pass off as good, also a capital crime then, known as uttering. He stated in his testimony that Phoebe continued with the coining business even though she knew that Hardy was fully aware of what she was doing. It appears that there had been some disagreement between Hardy and Phoebe and this may have led to him informing on her.

The defence was principally based upon the testimony of character witnesses for each of the defendants who averred them to be people of good character. Phoebe addressed the court as follows:

> My Lord and Gentlemen of the Jury, I am an unhappy woman; I was desired by a young man of the name of John Brown, to take the room which I did and he brought the things found in the room; and desired me to secrete them, and I not knowing the nature of them, or for what purpose they were intended, did do so, and so I told the gentleman when they came and took me: as to my sister in law, I being very ill, she came to clean the room for me, and the gentleman found her cleaning it on her knees: and my brother-in-law came some time after the gentlemen had been in the room.

She also called two character witnesses.

The jury took some time in their deliberations before finding Phoebe guilty and, despite Francis Hardy's evidence against them, acquitting Elizabeth and Joseph Yelland. Sentencing of all those convicted, took place at the end of the Sessions. Nine prisoners were condemned to death, these being Hannah Mullins, William Smith, Edward Griffiths, James May, George Woodward, Daniel Keefe, Jonathan Harwood and William Watts, who were to be hanged while Phoebe was sentenced to be burned at the stake. Many other prisoners were sentenced to transportation or imprisonment. Hannah Mullins and James May were subsequently reprieved to transportation.

Phoebe Harris was to be the first woman burnt at Newgate, as distinct from Tyburn or Smithfield, and her execution was carried out just after 8 a.m. on the morning of Wednesday, 21 June 1786. A huge crowd, estimated at some 20,000 people, had turned out to watch this gruesome spectacle.

At 7.30 a.m. six men, Edward Griffiths, George Woodward, William Watts, Daniel Keefe, Jonathan Harwood and William Smith were brought out through Newgate's Debtor's Door and led up onto the gallows. They were prepared in the usual way and the drop reportedly fell around 8 a.m. After they were suspended, Phoebe was led from the Debtor's Door by two sheriff's officers, past the gallows to a stake that had been erected halfway between the gallows and Newgate Street. The stake was some 11ft high and had a metal bracket at the top from which a noose dangled. Phoebe was described as, 'a well made little woman of something more than thirty years of age, with a pale complexion and not disagreeable features.' She was reported to be terrified and trembling as she was led out. She mounted a stool, the noose was placed around her neck and she was allowed a few moments to pray with John Villette, the Ordinary, before her support was removed and she was left suspended. According to V.A.C. Gatrell's book *The Hanging Tree* she died hard – he reported that she choked noisily to death over several minutes. After hanging for half an hour, the executioner put an iron chain around her upper body and fastened it to the stake with nails. Two cart loads of faggots were now piled around the stake and then lit. It is reasonable to assume that she would have been quite dead by this time. After a while, the fire burnt through the rope and Phoebe's body dropped, remaining attached to the stake by the chain. It took over two hours to be completely consumed by the fire, which continued to burn until midday.

Only two more women were to suffer Phoebe's fate. These were Margaret Sullivan on 25 June 1788 and Christian Murphy on 18 March 1789, both for coining. At the April Sessions of 1790 Sophia Girton was also convicted of this offence but her execution was delayed until after Parliament had passed an Act (Act 30 Geo. III, c.48) substituting ordinary hanging for coining offences on 5 June 1790. In fact, Sophia was ultimately reprieved, on condition of transportation for life to New South Wales, on 12 June 1790.

Executions by burning at Newgate were distinctly unpopular with the local residents of what was a respectable business area of the City. They had sent a petition to the Lord Mayor requesting that Phoebe's execution be carried out elsewhere. This was an early version of 'not in my back yard' rather than a protest against the severity of her punishment. It was later reported that some locals became ill from the smoke from her body. There were similar protests over the Sullivan and Murphy executions and a great feeling of relief when Sophia Girton was reprieved, and the whole ghastly business passed into history. The sheriffs were becoming increasingly unhappy about attending burnings, and it was they who brought forward the Bill to end this practice. Even though the condemned woman was dead before the faggots were lit, it must have still been a gruesome and revolting spectacle and one which conveyed a feeling of injustice. Men convicted of coining offences were hanged in the same way as other condemned males. *The Times* newspaper took up this theme after Phoebe's burning and printed the following article:

> The execution of a woman for coining on Wednesday morning, reflects a scandal upon the law and was not only inhuman, but shamefully indelicate and shocking. Why should the law in this species of offence inflict a severer punishment upon a woman, than a man. It is not an offence which she can perpetrate alone – in every such case the

insistence of a man has been found the operating motive upon the woman; yet the man is but hanged, and the woman burned.

One can only agree with the 'Thunderer's' sentiments as *The Times* came to be known. Other London newspapers carried similar articles. Again similar outrage was expressed two years later at the burning of Margaret Sullivan, although strangely there was little media interest in Christian Murphy.

Elizabeth Sedgwick
A Pyromaniac?

Arson was an offence for which reprieves were quite rare. Sixteen women were to die for this crime between 1735 and 1799 with a further five between 1800 and 1833, when Charlotte Long became the last, being hanged at Gloucester on 31 August of that year. Many buildings of the period were still of largely wooden construction and burnt easily, there was no real fire brigade and no insurance so the building's owner was normally left facing a huge financial loss as a result.

John Taylor, a farmer of Feltham Hill in Middlesex, suffered two major fires on two consecutive Sundays. This led to the arrest of one of his servants, nineteen-year-old Elizabeth Sedgwick, who subsequently confessed to the arson attacks and who was hanged at Newgate on 24 April 1787.

Elizabeth had worked for John Taylor and his wife Ann for about three months, mainly helping to look after the house. She did not have a boyfriend and was said to be close to her parents. It is probable that she was illiterate, as many were at this time, and that she had received little or no formal education.

On the evening of Sunday, 10 December 1786 a major fire broke out which destroyed Mr Taylor's straw barn that adjoined the farm house. At around 5 p.m., her main duties being over for the day, Elizabeth sat down to have tea with the family and having finished hers, asked Ann Taylor if she could go to her room and change her petticoat. Her room overlooked the barn and a short while later Elizabeth came rushing back and told John Taylor that she had seen a man with a lantern and candle in the yard. John went to the window to be confronted with the site of the barn well ablaze. He immediately evacuated the house in view of the risk of the fire spreading to it. The Taylor's and their staff endeavoured to rescue as much as they could from the flames but the buildings themselves were completely razed. At this time no suspicion was attached to Elizabeth.

One week later at teatime on Sunday the 17th, disaster was to strike again. As before, the family and Elizabeth were sat down to tea when Elizabeth noticed a bright light in the farmyard and shouted out to the family. John looked out the widow to find both his barley and wheat barns on fire and also the hayricks and the stables containing his six horses and various farming implements. This fire destroyed all the buildings mentioned and was greatly more serious than the previous one, representing a massive financial loss to the family. John was later to testify to the court that he was so frightened by what he had seen from the window that he had difficulty finding his way out of the house.

As was John's normal practice he had checked round the farm before going in to tea on this Sunday and had particularly noted that his large pig was securely tethered in its sty. The pig was seen in the farmyard immediately after the alarm was raised and this aspect struck John as more than a little odd.

One fire may be seen as unfortunate but two in seven days seemed too much of a coincidence. John's neighbours put up a £20 reward for information leading to the perpetrators and as a result a man by the name of Hanking was arrested, but it soon became clear he had nothing to do with the fires.

On 12 January one of the Taylor's staff found a handkerchief in the remains of the barns which Elizabeth identified
as hers and told them it had been taken from her by force by
two men at the bottom of the stairs. This seemed implau-
sible at best and so John Taylor took her to the local
magistrate, Richard Taylor. Richard was laid up with the
gout so Elizabeth's statement was taken in his bedroom by
the doctor who was attending him. She accused two men,
Winden and Goring, of being the persons who had taken
the handkerchief from her. Taylor was not satisfied with this
story and decided to remand Elizabeth for three days pending
a further examination, when he was well enough. It should be
noted the Elizabeth would have received no formal caution
and was not represented at this interview.

At the second interview Elizabeth made a confession and
this time she was cautioned by the local judge, Justice Bond,
not to say anything that was untrue and assured that she would
be allowed to correct and amend the statement when it was
read back to her. John Taylor, who was present at this examination, was later to tell the trial jury that Elizabeth had not
been threatened or brow beaten and that Richard Taylor, the
magistrate who took the confession, stopped after reading each
section of it back to her and asked if it was correct. She seemed
satisfied with it and put her mark, probably her thumb print, at
the bottom of it. It was signed by Richard Taylor and witnessed
by John Taylor.

Elizabeth claimed that the first fire was a pure accident. She
had gone into the barn with a candle to check the hens for
eggs and had fallen over in the poor light and dropped the
candle stick. She assumed that as the candle light had disappeared the candle had gone out and she could not find it in
the dark. So she left it and returned to the house but did not
tell Mrs Taylor of what had happened. She swore that there
was no intent to cause a fire and this seems credible. The following Sunday however, Elizabeth stated that she was seized

with the desire to start a fire in the barn and deliberately took a candle for the purpose of doing so. She placed the lighted candle under some straw in the barn and it soon caught fire. On her way back to the house she released the pig from its sty where John Taylor had seen it tied up securely a little earlier. She also stated that she had not been induced by any third party to set the fire and that it was entirely of her own volition. As a result of the confession she was arrested and committed for trial. Richard Taylor made an order that only her parents should be allowed to visit her and that she not be allowed a candle or any food or drink that could upset her nerves. He was satisfied that she did not appear to be suffering from obvious mental problems at the time she gave her confession, although from the conditions of his order he obviously suspected that she might have some.

Elizabeth's trial opened at the Old Bailey on 1 February 1787 before Mr Baron Thompson and the second Middlesex jury. She was prosecuted by Mr Garrow, presumably the same Mr Garrow from the earlier cases. She was charged with the 17 December fire and there was a second count against her for the 10 December. She pleaded not guilty to both counts. Evidence was given against her by John and Ann Taylor and also by the magistrate, Richard Taylor, and Henry Wilkinson the constable into whose charge she had been committed. Wilkinson told the court that he had followed Taylor's orders and had not allowed her candle, fire or visitors, other than her parents. It was to him apparently, that she confided her wish to make a confession and to withdraw the allegations against Winden and Goring. He also told the court that she seemed not to be under duress or intimidated when she made her confession to Mr Bond and Richard Taylor. The written confession was produced in court.

John Taylor told the court that on Sunday, 17 December, the date of the second fire, Elizabeth had several times said to him and his wife that she hoped there would not be any accident on that day as there had been the previous Sunday. This struck him as a very odd remark to make and raised his suspicions over Elizabeth's involvement in the incidents.

The court enquired both of John Taylor and Richard Taylor (the magistrate) as to what they thought of Elizabeth's state of mind and indeed her sanity. Even in 1787 there was concern about executing someone who was obviously insane. There were, however, no real signs of mental abnormality that could be found. Nowadays she would be examined by psychiatrists to establish whether she had a personality disorder such as pyromania. It seems quite possible that she did. If one accepts that the first fire was an accident, it is possible that she found it very exciting and this was what made her decide to start the second which was definitely a deliberate act. Other than pyromania what motive was there for it? She seemed to be well treated in the Taylor household by the standards of the day and bore no known grudge against the family. John Taylor was not critical of her personality in court. This was confirmed by Constable Wilkinson who told the court that Elizabeth spoke well and in respectful terms of the Taylor's. The only defence witness, Mary Sedgwick, her brothers wife who had known Elizabeth for five years, described her being of even temperament and not insane.

Inevitably Elizabeth was convicted by the jury and condemned to hang. In view of the magnitude of the damage caused there was to be no recommendation made for a commutation to transportation. During her time in the condemned cell she was visited frequently by John Villette, the Ordinary, who would have made every effort to get her to accept responsibility for her crime and accept her death with true penitence.

In accordance with her sentence, Elizabeth joined the other prisoners in the Press Yard of Newgate to be prepared on the morning of Thursday, 26 April 1787. No less than fifteen people were to hang on this occasion from the two beams of Newgate's black-draped gallows. Of these, seven, including another woman, Elizabeth Connolly and her co-defendant Michael Daily, were to die for burglary; four men were to hang for highway robbery; and one each for coining, personating and housebreaking. Notably not one person was being hanged for murder.

Preparing fifteen prisoners would have taken William Brunskill, the hangman, quite some time to complete, so it was not until around 8.20 a.m. before the drop fell. In most other respects this hanging would have been very similar to that of Elizabeth Taylor's. The behaviour on the gallows of this Elizabeth was not recorded, nor were details of her death. It is therefore likely that she expired quite quickly with minimal struggling as was not unusual with New Drop hangings. The execution would have been reported in the newspapers of the day but would have been seen as wholly unremarkable. The fact that one prisoner was an illiterate nineteen-year-old girl with probable personality defects would have raised little or no comment at all. A broadside was printed by D.W. Murcutt of Long Acre, London which stated, rather typically, that all the prisoners were very penitent on the gallows.

It is worth noting that arson still carries a maximum sentence of life in prison even today. No less than sixteen women were serving discretionary life sentences for this crime in 2002, according to a ministerial answer to a question in Parliament.

Sarah Lloyd
Hanged for Burglary

Sarah Lloyd was a young maid servant in the household of Mrs Sarah Syer in Benton Street, Hadleigh in Suffolk. Her precise age is unclear, being given as both nineteen and twenty-two years old. She was described as being small with dark hair, large eyes and a somewhat child-like demeanour.

She had a boyfriend, Joseph Clark, who it was thought by some to have put her up to the crime of robbing her mistress' home.

On the night of 3 October 1799 she let Joseph into the house and they took various items of jewellery from Mrs Syers' home, including a watch. Before they left the house they started a small fire at the bottom of the stairs leading to Mrs Syers' first floor bedroom. Fortunately this was quickly spotted and extinguished with the help of neighbours before it could cause injury or do any serious damage to the property.

Sarah was the chief and only real suspect, particularly as she had gone missing. She and Joseph were quickly arrested and taken before a magistrate, both being committed for trial and sent to Bury St Edmunds Gaol. There were two assizes a year in Suffolk at this time (Lent and Summer) and Sarah spent over five months on remand.

Sarah eventually came to trial at the Suffolk Lent Assizes which opened at Bury St Edmunds on Thursday, 20 March 1800 before Sir Nash Grose. The details of the crime were presented by the prosecution and Sarah's previous good character by the defence. However, this was not enough to save her from a guilty verdict from a jury of twelve men on the charge of stealing in a dwelling house goods to a value of more than 40s. They acquitted her on the charge of burglary and Joseph Clark was acquitted on both counts. The potential charges of attempted murder and arson were not proceeded with. It was not unusual then, as now, for the prosecution to proceed on the charge that is easiest to prove.

At the end of the assize all the convicted prisoners were sentenced together and six men and two women, including Sarah, were condemned to death. The other woman and five of the men were subsequently reprieved. Sarah was returned to Bury Gaol where she was visited on several occasions by a radical local magistrate called Capel Lofft, who had watched her trial, and by a small number of other local people of high standing in the community. He got up a petition for a reprieve which was signed by many locally who sympathised with her plight and sent it to the Home Secretary, the Duke of Portland. Lofft pleaded on her behalf that the extenuating circumstances of her age and immaturity should have been taken into account at her trial. Her age was given as twenty-two to the court but was not quite nineteen according to Lofft. He thus contended that her death sentence was excessive. Whilst over 200 years later it is easy to agree with him, it should be remembered that it was the mandatory sentence for the crime, although there was the possibility of commutation to transportation. It is probable that the judge also took into account the aggravating circumstances of the arson, which could easily have killed Mrs Syer had it not been quickly spotted, in his decision not to recommend a reprieve.

Although we may see the theft alone as relatively minor, Sarah's crimes were viewed very differently at the time as is shown by this extract from *The Times* of 11 April 1800:

> The circumstances attending the case of Sarah Lloyd are perhaps unequalled for the atrocious intentions of the perpetrator, who was a servant to a very respectable lady, residing at Hadleigh, named Syer. On the 3rd of October last she set her mistress's house on fire in four different places, and robbed her of some considerable property. Her intention was the destruction of her protectress, for, to prevent the escape of her mistress, the principal combustibles were placed under a staircase which led to her mistress's bedroom, and, but for the timely assistance of the neighbourhood, she would have perished in the fire.

Capel Lofft wrote on Sarah's behalf to various publications rebutting what he saw as obvious hostility towards her in the press, including a letter to *The Monthly Magazine* in which he set out the details of her crimes and the fact that she was acquitted or not tried on all but the least serious count. However all this was to no avail and Sarah's execution date was set for Wednesday, 9 April. On the 8th John Orridge, the keeper of Bury Gaol, received a reprieve for one 'S. Hop'. He had no prisoner by this name and thus decided to postpone Sarah's execution until he received clarification from the Duke of Portland. This duly arrived by messenger, the letter also saying that 'the great object of punishment is example'. A new execution date was therefore fixed for Wednesday, 23 April.

Capel Lofft went to Bury St Edmunds Gaol on the morning of execution and Sarah told him that she had managed to eventually get off to sleep the night before and that then she had woken and got dressed. John Orridge had allowed her to say her goodbyes to the other prisoners before she was prepared for execution. The morning of the 23rd was a typical April day, both windy and rainy. Lofft had brought an umbrella which Sarah managed to hold over herself, as the cart conveyed her to the gallows set up on Tay Fen, about a mile's journey from the Gaol on the other side of town. Lofft accompanied her on the journey. The procession was led by the under sheriff of Suffolk on horseback and a small number of javelin men to prevent any rescue attempt. It is probable that the hangman sat in the cart with Sarah.

According to Lofft the hangman was also affected by Sarah's brave demeanour and appeared nervous as he went about the preparations for her death. It is reported that Sarah pulled back her hair for him as he put the noose around her neck, although it is unclear whether she did this at the gallows or at the gaol before he pinioned her.

When the procession reached Tay Fen, Lofft got up into the cart and stood beside Sarah, launching a tirade at the large number of spectators against her punishment and the intransigence of the Duke of Portland that lasted a full five minutes.

Sarah stood calmly beside him until he had finished and then as was common at the time she was allowed to give the signal to the hangman to proceed. She was now 'turned off' and after she had been hanging for a minute, both hands were twice raised slowly and evenly toward her throat. These movements were interpreted by Lofft as signifying 'content and resignation'. No convulsive struggles accompanied her death and she died quite easily for the time. After she was taken down Lofft paid the hangman for her body so that he could give her a proper burial that evening at St Mary's church. A thousand people attended her funeral and Lofft told them that Sarah's mother had tried to hang herself when she had been told that there would be no reprieve. Two months later a tombstone was erected over Sarah's grave and this can still be seen today. It is engraved as with the following words 'She suffered a just but ignominious death for admitting her abandoned seducer into the dwelling house of her mistress and becoming the instrument in his hands of the crime of robbery and house burning.'

Lofft was summarily dismissed as a magistrate for his activism in trying to save Sarah and for his impassioned attack on the Home Secretary at the execution.

Sarah clearly impressed Capel Lofft, John Orridge the jailer and perhaps even the hangman with her femininity and bravery and found it easy to sympathise with her. However the outcome of her actions could have been very different if the Mrs Syer had died in the fire, which is why *The Times* and other newspapers took the view that they did.

Sarah Lloyd was one of seven women hanged in 1800, six in England and one in Ireland and the only one for this offence. Only three more women were to be hanged for stealing in a dwelling house, although it continued to attract the death penalty until August 1834 when John Young became the last to be executed for it at Winchester.

Ann Hurle
A Major Forgery

Ann Hurle was one of twelve people to be hanged for forgery in 1804. The law took a very severe view of this offence at the time and few forgers were reprieved.

Ann was an educated young woman of twenty-two, living in London, who had devised quite an elaborate plan to defraud the Bank of England of £500, which was a very large sum in those days and would now be the equivalent of over a quarter of a million pounds. The crime was perpetrated on Saturday, 10 December 1803 when she met stockbroker George Francillon at the Bank Coffee House and persuaded him to obtain a power of attorney for her to enable her to sell some Bank of England 3 per cent stock belonging to one Benjamin Allin, an elderly gentleman from Greenwich. Mr Francillon had known Ann for some six months and therefore was not overly suspicious. She told him that she had lived in Mr Allin's house as a child, where her aunt was the housekeeper, and that he had given her this stock in return for the aunt's service to the household and the kindnesses she had shown him. Mr Francillon obtained the power of attorney for Ann on the Saturday, and she told him that she was then going to take it Greenwich to get it signed by Mr Allin.

Ann returned on Monday morning with the document purportedly signed and witnessed by Thomas Noulden and Peter Verney, who both ran small businesses in Greenwich. Ann met Mr Francillon at the Bank of England where he took the document to the Reduced Office for verification. Ann meanwhile went off to sell the stocks. Mr Thomas Bateman, the clerk in charge of powers of attorney, asked to see George Francillon with Ann and informed them that Benjamin Allin's signature on the power differed from that on the specimen held by the bank. Ann told Mr Bateman that she knew Mr Allin and that as he was nearly ninety years old, in poor health and nowadays wrote very little, it was not surprising that his signature differed. She also offered to take out another power of attorney and obtain a new signature on it. Mr Bateman did not feel that this was necessary but wrote a letter to one of the witnesses to the document.

During the conversation in Mr Bateman's office, Ann mentioned that she had recently married and when asked by Mr Bateman why she had not taken out the power in her married name, she told him that she feared her marriage to one James Innes was not a good one. She suggested that he had stolen her money and then boarded a ship at Bristol and that he was already married to another.

Ann left the bank and returned on the following Tuesday. In the meantime, Mr Francillon had become suspicious when he checked the document. He put their main meeting off to the following day while he did some further research, including going to see Benjamin Allin. As arranged, Mr Francillon met Ann on the Wednesday morning at the Bank of England. He had previously had a meeting with Mr Newcomb the principal clerk in the Reduced Office and explained his suspicions. He and Mr Newcomb had a meeting with the governors. Ann came to the Bank with a young man but must have realised from the delays in seeing her that all was not well and left. She was arrested the following day in Bermondsey and taken to the Mansion House for questioning. The young man turned out to be James Innes, who was also questioned. She was charged with the forgery and he with being an accessory to the crime, although it seems that his case was dropped as there is no record of a trial for him. The case was obviously unusual and of some public interest as it was reported in *The Times* of Wednesday, 21 December 1803. Ann was committed for trial at the next Sessions of the Old Bailey in London.

These Sessions opened on 11 January 1804, before the Lord Chief Baron of the Exchequer, Sir Archibald Knight. Ann was charged with four offences. The first was:

> feloniously, falsely, making, forging, and counterfeiting, on the 12th of December, a certain instrument, or letter of attorney, with the name Benjamin Allin thereunto subscribed, purporting to have been signed, sealed, and delivered, by one Benjamin Allin, of Greenwich, in the county of Kent, gentleman, a proprietor of certain annuities and stock transferable at the Bank of England, called Three per Cent. Reduced Annuities, to sell, assign, transfer, and convey, the sum of five hundred pounds of the said transferable annuities, the property of the said Benjamin Allin, to her, the said Ann Hurle , with intent to defraud the Governor and Company of the Bank of England.

The second count was, 'For uttering and publishing as true a like forged deed, knowing it to be forged, with the like intention.' There were two further counts on the indictment against her, being the same offences against Benjamin Allin. Mr Garrow led for the prosecution and Mr Knapp for the defence.

George Francillon and Benjamin Allin were the principal prosecution witnesses. Mr Francillon related the above story to the court and Mr Allin examined the power of attorney document and declared that the signature was not his and that he had never signed such a document. Thomas Bateman, Peter Verney and Thomas Noulden also testified against her. Ann's aunt, Jane, told the court that Ann had not visited Mr Allin's house recently and neither had Messrs Verney and Noulden, the two purported witnesses to his signature on the document.

The witness' testimonies were cross-examined at this time but Ann offered no actual defence leaving this to her counsel. She was thus convicted and remanded to Tuesday, 17 January 1804 for sentence. Four men and three women were bought before the court to receive their death sentences that Tuesday, with the Recorder of London making particular reference to the gravity of Ann's crime and the fact that she preyed upon 'an infirm and imbecile old man'. He opined that only death was sufficient punishment for such a crime. He then proceeded to pass sentence on each prisoner. When Ann's turn came, she was asked in the normal way if there was any reason why sentence of death should not be pronounced against her and replied that she thought she was 'with child' (pregnant). She did not make this claim with any apparent confidence so no further enquiry into its validity was made. Sarah Fisher, another of the condemned women, also claimed to be pregnant but did so much more forcibly, thus requiring the court to empanel a Jury of Matrons, who examined her and declared that she was not. It is feasible that both women could have been in the early stages of pregnancy, although neither was 'quick with child'. Only if the prisoner was obviously pregnant was her execution postponed until after she had given birth. In most cases she was reprieved altogether and her punishment commuted to transportation. 'Pleading the belly', as it was called, was a frequently used tactic at this time by women desperate to avoid the noose.

The Recorder of London reviewed the cases of those condemned to death and made a recommendation in each one. He then presented his recommendations in person to the Privy Council, which was chaired by King George III. In Ann's case, there could be no recommendation for a reprieve. She was therefore scheduled for execution, along with Methuselah Spalding who had been convicted of sodomy at the previous Sessions held on 30 November 1803. It is interesting to note that Spalding was the only one of five condemned men at that Sessions not to be reprieved and that Ann was the only one out of the six men and three women at the January 1804 Sessions not to get a reprieve. Non-murderers normally had a period of two to three weeks before execution at this time and Ann's execution was set for Wednesday, 8 February.

For reasons that are unclear, the normal New Drop style gallows at Newgate was not to be used for these two hangings. A simple gallows was erected at the top of the Old Bailey, near to St Sepulchre's church.

On the morning of execution, Ann and Spalding were brought from their cells and pinioned in the Press Room. They were then taken out into the yard and loaded into a horse drawn cart covered in a black cloth which emerged from the prison at about 8.10 a.m. for the short ride to the gallows. The cart was backed under the beam and the two prisoners were allowed to pray with the Ordinary and make their last statements. Ann was dressed in a mourning gown and wore a white cap. She made no address to the multitude that had come to see her die but prayed fervently with the Ordinary for five minutes or so. William Brunskill, the hangman for London and Middlesex, placed the rope around her neck and when she had finished praying, pulled the white cap down over her face. The cart was now drawn away leaving them both suspended. It was recorded that Ann let out a scream as the cart moved and that she struggled hard for two to three minutes before becoming still, her hands were observed to move repeatedly towards her throat and her unpinioned legs kicked and padded the air. No doubt the eyes of the crowd were riveted on her poor writhing form. After hanging for the customary hour, they were taken down and returned inside Newgate from where they could be claimed by relatives for burial.

An angry letter appeared in *The Times* newspaper the following week castigating the authorities for the execution on the grounds of cruelty compared with the New Drop and the difficulty in seeing the prisoners and thus taking a moral lesson from their demise. It was alleged in the letter that the reason for the change of gallows was that the Newgate staff were too lazy to assemble the New Drop gallows. Whether this was true or whether the drop mechanism had become defective we will never know, but it was returned to service for the next execution, that of Providence Hansard for the same crime on 5 July 1805.

It seems surprising looking back two centuries that Ann, acting alone, would have devised such an ambitious plan to obtain this large sum of money. However, no evidence was offered at her trial to show that anyone else was involved, other than perhaps James Innes on the periphery of the crime. It must have taken quite some time to think through and make the necessary contacts, such as George Francillon, who would be able to obtain the power of attorney for her. It is hard to believe she was not aware of the risk of failure and the deadly consequences that would follow it. In the period 1800-1829, an amazing 218 people were to die for forgery in England and Wales. Another two women were to follow Ann to the gallows outside Newgate over the next two years: Providence Hansard mentioned earlier and Mary Parnell on 13 November 1805. Forgery ceased to be a capital crime in 1832 and the last execution for it took place on 31 December 1829, when Thomas Maynard was hanged at Newgate. Over two centuries attitudes have altered, had a modern day Ann committed the crime in the twenty-first century, she would have been given somewhere between four and five years in prison and have been released on licence half-way through this sentence.

Melinda Mapson
The 40 shilling question

The savagery of the law in dealing with crimes against property in the eighteenth and early nineteenth centuries is well demonstrated by our next case.

Melinda Mapson was a thirty-year-old married servant woman who took up a job in the household of Mr William Dignam in New Street in London's Covent Garden, on the evening of Friday, 10 February 1809, to replace Margaret Garey who had left his service earlier that day. It was to be a very short-lived job. Mrs Dignam gave Melinda instructions as to what she wanted doing and showed her where to sleep and then went on to bed. Mr Dignam came home a little later in the evening and spoke to Melinda, telling her that after she had put out the kitchen fire she could retire for the night and then he went upstairs to join his wife.

When Mr Dignam got up the following morning he noticed that a watch, a basket of clothes and a quantity of silver cutlery together with the sheets from the servant's bed were missing and that the front door chain and bolts were undone. Melinda was gone too. Only three people had been in the house that night – Mr and Mrs Dignam and Melinda – and Mr Dignam distinctly remembered locking and bolting the front door and putting the chain on, so suspicion immediately fell on Melinda. A closer inspection revealed that their former maid's trunk had also had the lock forced and some of the contents stolen. Margaret Garey had left her trunk at the Dignam's to await collection on the Saturday.

The thefts were reported to the local constable, Joseph Snow, who began a search for Melinda, which finally led to her arrest ten months later, on 21 December 1809, in the Wagon and Horses public house in Newington. He searched her and found that she was carrying a pocket book containing some pawn brokers' receipts (duplicates as they were called at the time). She denied any knowledge of the Dignams and so Snow kept her overnight and summoned Mr Dignam the next morning to identify her. Further investigation by Constable Snow's father showed that the pawn brokers' receipts matched some of the items that had been stolen and all were in different names: Mary Green, Mary Mapson and Mary Fuller.

The property recovered was identified by Mrs Dignam and Margaret Garey and Melinda by at least one of the pawn brokers with whom she had placed it.

Melinda was taken before the local magistrate and committed for trial at the April Sessions of the Old Bailey which were held on the 11th of that month before Mr Baron Thompson.

The indictment against her was as follows:

That on the 10th of February 1809, about the hour of twelve, in the night of the same day, being in the dwelling house of William Dignam, two shifts, value 5 s. the property of Margaret Garey; - a tablecloth, value 5 s. a silk handkerchief, value 3 s. a gown, value 10 s. a silver punch ladle, value 12 s. a shift, value 3 s. a counterpane, value 5 s. a silver tablespoon, value 10 s. and a pelisse, value 20 s. the property of the said William Dignam, feloniously did steal, and that she did afterwards burglariously break to get out of the same.

The Dignams, Constable Snow, Margaret Garey and the pawn brokers gave evidence for the Crown and there was considerable discussion of the security of the house to see whether it was possible that someone else had broken in and stolen the items. Mrs Dignam was asked to put a value on the goods stolen from the house and claimed that they were worth £30.

In her defence Melinda claimed that she heard a knock on the door after Mrs Dignam had gone up to bed and that she opened it to find her seaman husband standing there. He threatened her with violence if she refused to allow him in or made a fuss and she was so frightened that she left and went to her lodgings near Temple Bar. He too returned to Temple Bar later with the stolen property. Melinda had left London for a few days before returning and finally being apprehended by Constable Snow, who she claimed told her that Mrs Dignam would forgive her if she handed back the property.

The jury were not convinced by this defence. However they had a very important question to answer which was were the goods stolen worth more or less than 40s. If they decided the value was more that this sum Melinda would hang. It was not by any means unknown for a jury to decide on a lower value for stolen property despite its apparent worth, if only to save a prisoner's life. When they did so, it was known as a Partial Verdict. Melinda was not to be so fortunate and the jury 'brought her back guilty' of stealing in a dwelling house to the value of 40s. She was remanded to Newgate for sentence at the end of the Sessions and was duly condemned by Mr Baron Thompson. She had now just a month left to live. She would have been expected to take part in Sunday religious services and would have listened to Brownlow Forde, the Ordinary, preach in the special area reserved for condemned prisoners. In the centre of this enclosure was a table on which rested a coffin to remind the condemned, if they needed such a reminder, of their imminent fate. Meanwhile her case would have been considered by the Recorder of London and a recommendation made to the Privy Council. This was not favourable to her and there was to be no reprieve, even though there was no record of her having committed any previous offences.

Her execution took place outside the Debtor's Door of Newgate prison on Wednesday, 13 June 1810, alongside thirty-four-year-old Richard Jones who had been convicted of personating. William Brunskill led them up the steps of the gallows that had been brought out from the prison the night before. Melinda's arms were secured round her body with her hands in front. Her legs would probably have been pinioned at this time. After the usual prayers with the Ordinary, white nightcaps would have been pulled down over their faces and soon after 8 a.m. the pair were 'launched into eternity' together. The onlookers were only able to observe their upper bodies struggle for a few seconds before becoming still. They were left hanging for the customary hour before being taken down for burial.

Melinda was one of six people hanged at Newgate that year and the only woman.

Eliza Fenning
Hanged for the Attempted Murder
of her Employers

Elizabeth Fenning (always known as Eliza) was an attractive and petite 21-year-old girl who worked as the cook in the household of Robert and Charlotte Turner in London's Chancery Lane. Robert Turner was a law stationer and also employed a housemaid, Sarah Peer, and two male apprentices, Roger Gadsden and Thomas King, all of whom 'lived in'. Eliza had worked for the Turners for some seven weeks before the incident occurred.

On 21 March 1815, Eliza prepared rump steak, potatoes and dumplings for the family's lunch to be served at 3 p.m. She had made a beefsteak pie for the servants' lunch, the crust of which had been made from the same flour as the dumplings and was eaten by them without any ill effects. Robert Turner's father, Haldebart, had come to dine with his son and daughter-in-law that day, and soon after eating the dumplings, the whole family were suffering severe stomach pains and vomiting. Eliza and Roger Gadsden were in similar condition in the kitchen, having also eaten some of the dumplings. Roger had started to eat a dumpling but Eliza persuaded him to stop, on the basis that they had not risen. He was well enough to go to Lambeth and fetch Mr Turner senior's wife, Margaret, to come to the family's aid. The victims were all attended that evening by the family doctor, John Marshall, and all made full recoveries.

Mr Turner suspected that they had been poisoned, as a packet of arsenic kept in an office drawer had recently gone missing. Arsenic and other poisons were freely available in those days and were often bought for killing vermin. The following day, he asked the doctor to examine the contents of the pan in which Eliza had cooked the dumplings, as he thought there was a strong possibility that it contained arsenic. Eliza was arrested on 23 March and charged with attempted murder. She was taken before a magistrate and committed for trial at the Old Bailey at the April Sessions, being remanded in custody to Newgate prison next door in the meantime.

She was tried before Sir John Silvester, the Recorder of London, at the Old Bailey April Sessions, which opened on 5 April 1815, on four counts of administering poison with intent to murder.

Mrs Charlotte Turner told the court that she suspected that Eliza had been seeking vengeance on the family after Charlotte had discovered her in the room of two of the apprentices one night in a partly dressed state and threatened to dismiss her. Charlotte told the court that Eliza had remained sullen and disrespectful towards her after this. She also said that Eliza had asked to be allowed to make some yeast dumplings for the family on several occasions. On Monday, 20 March, she came into the dining room and said the brewer had brought some yeast, which Charlotte had not ordered, so on the Tuesday morning Charlotte agreed to the dumplings being made and directed that they were to be mixed with milk and water. Charlotte testified that Eliza was alone in the kitchen while the dumplings were being prepared. About three o'clock, the family sat down to lunch and the dumplings were brought to the table. Charlotte remarked to Sarah Peer that 'they were black and heavy, instead of white and light'. She told the court that after only eating less than a quarter of the dumpling 'she felt an extreme burning pain in her stomach, which increased every minute'. It became so bad she was obliged to leave the table and go upstairs. Other members of the family recounted similar stories in their evidence.

The Turners kept a packet of arsenic in an unlocked drawer in the office, to control the mice that infested that room, which the court was told was clearly labelled as poison. It was determined by the judge that Eliza could read and write and would, therefore, have been able to know what was in the packet. Also kept in the same drawer was scrap paper used for fire lighting. Eliza regularly went to the drawer to get paper for this purpose, according to Sarah Peer.

Roger Gadsden told the court that on 'Tuesday, 21 March. I went into the kitchen between three and four in the afternoon; I had dined at two (on the beef steak pie) I observed there a plate on the table with a dumpling and a half; I took a knife and fork up, and was going to cut it to eat it; the prisoner exclaimed, Gadsdell, do not eat that, it is cold and heavy, it will do you no good; I eat a piece about as big as a walnut; there was a small quantity of sauce in the boat; I put a bit of bread in it, and sepped it up, and eat it; this might be twenty minutes after three'.

William Thisselton, who had arrested Eliza, told the court that he had asked her whether she suspected there was anything in the flour. She said she had made a beefsteak pie that day with the same flour that she had made the dumplings, and she said she thought it was in the yeast – she saw a red sediment at the bottom of the yeast after she had used it – or alternatively in the milk that Sarah Peer had purchased.

The next person to give evidence was Mr John Marshall, the surgeon who attended the family on the evening of 21 March. He testified that he arrived at their house at about 8.45 p.m. and found Mr and Mrs Turner very ill, with symptoms such as would be produced by arsenic. He also said that he found Eliza ill and showing the same symptoms. The following morning, Mr Haldebart Turner showed Mr Marshall the dish the dumplings had been made in, which the surgeon washed out with a tea kettle of warm water. He let it stand and then decanted off the liquid in which he found half a teaspoon of white

powder which he determined was arsenic. It had been noted
that the knives the family had used at lunch were blackened.
Dr Marshall was asked, 'will arsenic if it is cut with a knife, will
it produce on the knife the colour of blackness?' To which he
answered, 'I have no doubt of it.' He examined the remains
of the yeast but found there was no arsenic in it. This was the
extent of the prosecution case against Eliza.

The forensic evidence of arsenic was scant at best, there
being no reliable means of detecting arsenic prior to 1836.

It should be remembered that there was no defence team
in those days and Eliza was not represented by counsel.
She simply made a statement to the court herself. She told
the judge, 'My lord, I am truly innocent of all the charges,
as God is my witness; I am innocent, indeed I am; I liked
my place, I was very comfortable; as to my master saying I
did not assist him, I was too ill. I had no concern with the
drawer at all; when I wanted a piece of paper, I always asked
for it.' She called four witnesses who testified to her previous good character.

The Newgate Calendar tells us that the Recorder summed
up to the jury as follows:

Gentlemen, you have now heard the evidence given on
this trial, and the case lies in a very narrow compass. There
are but two questions for your consideration, and these are,
whether poison was administered, in all, to four persons,
and by what hand such poison was given. That these persons were poisoned appears certain from the evidence of
Mrs Charlotte Turner, Haldebart Turner, Roger Gadsden,
the apprentice, and Robert Turner; for each of these
persons ate of the dumplings, and were all more or less
affected – that is, they were every one poisoned. That the
poison was in the dough of which these dumplings were
composed has been fully proved, I think, by the testimony
of the surgeon who examined the remains of the dough

left in the dish in which the dumplings had been mixed and divided; and he deposes that the powder which had subsided at the bottom of the dish was arsenic. That the arsenic was not in the flour I think appears plain, from the circumstance that the crust of a pie had been made that very morning with some of the same flour of which the dumplings were made and the persons who dined off the pie felt no inconvenience whatever; that it was not in the yeast nor in the milk has been also proved; neither could it be in the sauce, for two of the persons who were ill never touched a particle of the sauce, and yet were violently affected with retching and sickness. From all these circumstances it must follow that the poisonous ingredient was in the dough alone; for, besides that the persons who partook of the dumplings at dinner were all more or less affected by what they had eaten, it was observed by one of the witnesses that the dough retained the same shape it had when first put into the dish to rise, and that it appeared dark, and was heavy, and in fact never did rise. The other question for your consideration is, by what hand the poison was administered; and although we have nothing before us but circumstantial evidence, yet it often happens that circumstances are more conclusive than the most positive testimony. The prisoner, when taxed with poisoning the dumplings, threw the blame first on the milk, next on the yeast, and then on the sauce; but it has been proved, most satisfactorily, that none of these contained it, and that it was in the dumplings alone, which no person but the prisoner had made. Gentlemen, if poison had been given even to a dog, one would suppose that common humanity would have prompted us to assist it in its agonies: here is the case of a master and a mistress being both poisoned, and no assistance was offered. Gentlemen, I have now stated all the facts as they have arisen, and I leave the case in your hands, being fully persuaded that, whatever your verdict may be,

you will conscientiously discharge your duty both to your
God and to your country.

After a few minutes deliberation the jury returned a verdict
of guilty.

After her conviction, Eliza was returned to the female
Felons Side at Newgate where she wrote to her fiancé: 'They
have, which is the most cruellest thing in this world, brought
me in guilty.' She went on: 'I may be confined most likely six
months at least.' However, on the following day (the last day
of the Sessions), the Recorder sentenced her to be hanged by
the neck until she was dead. Journalists in court recorded, 'She
was carried from the dock convulsed with agony and uttering
frightful screams.' Eliza was taken back to Newgate and put
in the condemned hold. At this time many crimes, including
attempted murder, still carried the death penalty. However,
Eliza could have had her sentence commuted to transportation to the colonies. Attempted murder remained a capital
offence up to 1861.

While in Newgate, Eliza corresponded with another condemned prisoner, 24-year-old William Oldfield, a child rapist,
who she had presumably met at the end of the Sessions when
the prisoners were sentenced as a group.

There was considerable public disquiet over the verdict and
sentence, and various appeals were made for clemency to the
Prince Regent, the Home Secretary and the Lord Chancellor,
but all were rejected and the morning of Wednesday,
26 July 1815, was set for her execution. In 1815, William Hone
had started the *Traveller* newspaper, in which he campaigned
to save Eliza.

On Friday, 18 July, the Recorder made his report to the
Prince Regent in which he recommended execution for
Eliza. *The Examiner* newspaper that reported this also made
clear its doubts over her guilt and printed in full a letter she
had written thanking them for their support. On 24 July, Eliza

requested a meeting with the Turners, who accordingly visited her in Newgate. Here she effectively accused Charlotte of having an affair with Tom King and of knowing more about how the arsenic got into the dumplings than she did.

During the early hours of the Wednesday morning, the large portable gallows was brought out of Newgate and made ready outside the Debtor's Door. It was normal for prisoners to be hanged in groups for unconnected crimes, although this was to be the only triple hanging of 1815, a year in which twelve people were executed at Newgate. Long before eight o'clock, hoards of people were thronging the streets and jostling for the best positions from which to witness the executions. It was estimated that some 40–50,000 people witnessed the scene. The execution had to be delayed for half an hour due to the late return of John Langley, the hangman, from his trip to Ipswich for the execution of Elizabeth Wollterton the previous day.

Eliza was led from the condemned cell into the Press Yard soon after 8.30 a.m., where she exchanged a few words with William Oldfield, who asked her to pray. Her hands were pinioned in front of her with a cord and the noose put round her neck. She was dressed in a white muslin gown with a high waist and tied with a fashionable ribbon, a white muslin cap and a pair of high, laced, lilac boots. From the Press Yard, it was quite a walk to the steps of the scaffold, which she was the first to ascend. The Reverent Horace Cotton, the Ordinary of Newgate, accompanied her and asked her if she had anything to communicate to him in her final moments. She told him, 'Before the just and Almighty God, and by the faith of the Holy Sacrament I have taken, I am innocent of the offence with which I am charged.'

She proceeded up the steps of the gallows and the large crowd who had come to see her die fell silent. She stood calmly while the Reverent Cotton intoned prayers for her. John Langley threw the free end of the rope over the beam and tied it off. He attempted to draw the white cotton night-cap over her head, but he was unable to get it on over her cap. He then tried to bind a muslin handkerchief over her face but it proved too small. Then he pulled out his own dirty pocket handkerchief to tie over her face. This disgusted her. 'Pray do not let him put it on, Mr. Cotton!' she implored. 'Pray make him take it off. Pray do, Mr. Cotton!'

'My dear, it must be on. He must put it on,' Cotton told her. So she now stood silently, with her arms bound, while the dirty handkerchief was tied over her face.

She continued to wait stoically, pinioned and noosed, praying with the Ordinary while the other two criminals who were to hang with her, 51-year-old Abraham Adams, convicted of sodomy, and William Oldfield, who was 'guilty of an odious crime' – the rape of a 9-year-old girl, Eliza Willis – were prepared. Oldfield had apparently wanted to hang beside this Eliza and preferred death to transportation. As the noose was adjusted around his neck, Oldfield contin-ued to pray but seemed 'perfectly resigned to his fate' and smiled at the crowd. Again he spoke to Eliza, telling her that 'all was well in God' and to keep her spirits up. Just before the drop fell, she told Dr Cotton once again that she was innocent, saying, 'I know my situation, and may I never enter the Kingdom of Heaven, to which I feel confident that I am going, if I am not innocent.'

At around 8.40 a.m., the preparations were complete and Langley withdrew the pin releasing the trap, 'launching the prisoners into eternity' with a drop of about 12–18 inches. It was reported that Eliza died easily, 'almost without writhing'.

After her execution, the following paragraph appeared in a London evening paper:

We should deem ourselves wanting in justice, and a due respect for government, if we did not state that, in conse-quence of the many applications from the friends of this unhappy young woman who this day suffered the sentence of the law, a meeting took place yesterday at Lord Sidmouth's office, at which the Lord Chancellor, the recorder, and Mr Beckett were present. A full and minute investigation of the case, we understand, took place, and of all that had been urged in her favour by private individuals; but the result was a decided conviction that nothing had occurred which could justify an interruption of the due course of justice. So anxious was the Lord Chancellor, in particular, to satisfy his own mind, and put a stop to all doubts on the part of the people at large, that another meeting was held by the same parties last night, when they came to the same determination, and in consequence the unfortunate culprit suffered the penalty of the law.

Her father had to pay 14*s* 6*d* (72p) as 'executioner's fees' before he could obtain his daughter's dead body for burial. She was buried five days later, on the 31st in the churchyard of St George the Martyr in London, and her funeral was attended by several thousand people, such was the feeling of injustice done to her. A group of six girls in white dresses (as Eliza had worn) accompanied the coffin to the graveyard. It was noted that her face had not discoloured and looked peaceful in death. There was visible just a small rope mark under her chin.

On 28 July, Samuel Davis, one of the Principal Turnkeys (warders) at Newgate, gave a deposition under oath, in which he related a visit to Eliza by her father and how he told his daughter: 'Oh, my dear child, when you come out on the gallows, tell everyone that you are innocent, and then I can walk the streets, upright as a man, but if you say you are guilty, I shall never be able to hold my head among the public anymore.' The meeting was also witnessed by the Ordinary, the Rev. Dr Horace Cotton. If true, what effect did her father's entreaties have on Eliza?

Writing over 200 years after the event, even with the benefit of the trial transcript, it is difficult to know whether Eliza was guilty or not, especially as the evidence against her was purely circumstantial – a fact that even the trial judge acknowledged. What is interesting is that a lot of people at the time had serious doubts about her guilt, including, if the above report is to be believed, the Lord Chancellor.

Eliza was one of six women hanged nationally in 1815 so the execution of a woman was hardly a rare event. Four of these women were executed for murder and one for arson. Generally there did not seem to be any great public sympathy for women who had been sentenced to death. Admittedly, Eliza's looks and youth may have brought forth some, but many of the other women hanged at this time were young too. Newspapers were much more widely available by 1815 and adult literacy levels were also higher, so far more people could read about the case. The media and the public seemed to be polarised between condemning Eliza and supporting her. One newspaper article I have does its best to blacken her character and states that she was expelled from school at the age of 12 for 'lying and lewd talk'. It quotes a former employer, Mr Hardy in Lincoln's Inn Fields, of suspecting that she tried to poison his drink.

There was also a huge class divide at this time. Eliza, as a servant, was a member of the lower class. The Turner family, as home and business owners, were middle class. Sir John Silvester and the members of the 'Hanging Cabinet' were of the upper class, who would have had servants in their employ. They were mostly in favour of the execution of a servant who had, it seemed, tried to poison members of their class and was thus seen as a threat, whereas the lower classes felt that a member of their class was being unfairly victimised.

It seems that there was also a political element and divide. The Liberals and Reformists were against this execution, particularly as no one had died, whereas the Tories were more in favour of it. Remember that only householders had a vote in 1815 and thus the poor were excluded from the political process, as were women. It would be 103 years before the Reform Act of 1918 abolished the property-owning qualification for men and gave women some voting rights.

On the Wednesday, Thursday and Friday, after the execution, the Turners' home was besieged by protesters who had to be dispersed by the police.

As stated, the evidence against Eliza was circumstantial (as it usually was at this time) and principally given by people who were at least somewhat hostile to her.

It is unlikely that Eliza was having an affair with one of the apprentices (as alleged by Mrs Turner) as she was engaged and due to be married. Unless we accept that Eliza had a wish to take revenge on Mrs Turner for reprimanding her, by poisoning the family, what motive for the crime is left? Eliza risked her own life by eating a dumpling and also became ill; if she knew it contained arsenic, she almost certainly would not have known how much arsenic would be required to kill the family and not herself – how many people would?

Was Mrs Turner jealous of Eliza's good looks and did she want rid of her, for fear of her husband having an affair with her?

It has also been alleged that Robert Turner had become mentally unbalanced and decided to kill the whole family, but we have no proof of this.

Obviously, this far removed, we will never know for certain who put the arsenic in the dumpling dough. The pan in which they were made was not examined until the following day. Neither do we know whether the doctor was browbeaten into finding arsenic by Mr Turner senior to protect his son's reputation. Was Eliza simply a convenient scapegoat?

It is noteworthy that, since poisons have been very strictly controlled (from the 1920s onward), the number of murders by poisoning has reduced to virtually nil and it is now a very rare crime.

Only two more women were to hang for the crime of attempted murder. They were Ann Mary Chapman, also at Newgate, on 22 July 1829 and Sarah Chesham at Chelmsford on 25 March 1851. The last execution for this crime took place on 27 August 1861 when Martin Doyle suffered at Chester. The Criminal Law Consolidation Act of 1861 removed capital punishment for attempted murder.

Elizabeth Fricker
'Burglariously Breaking and Entering the Dwelling-House'

Once again this is a story of a servant who stole from her employer with the help of others, although on this occasion one of them was to hang with her.

Elizabeth Fricker was a thirty-year-old widow who worked as a maid servant in the household of Mrs Ann Ashworth, who lived in Berner Street in the Marylebone area of London. As in the case of Amelia Roberts, she let her accomplices into the house and between them they stole a considerable amount of silver plate. In the early nineteenth century, before the advent of expensive electronic consumer goods, the better-off had servants and seemed to spend a lot of money on silver tableware which was no doubt attractive to thieves because of its high value and the good demand for it.

The crime took place on the night of Sunday, 28 July 1816, which was Elizabeth's day off. She was not in the house much that day but came back in the evening. Elizabeth's behaviour seemed rather strange to Mrs Ashworth and also to her fellow servant, Hannah Holloway, who was the household's cook. Mrs Ashworth retired to her bedroom at about 11 p.m. and Elizabeth came in and tried to take the candle from the bedroom. Mrs Ashworth asked her why she was taking it and so she put it down and left it. A few minutes later she brought in a letter and told her mistress that she had to go out. She was told that she could not but persisted in her demand, as she said it was important. She left the bedroom and went out briefly, before returning and joining Hannah downstairs. Their work being finished for the day and having locked up the house, Hannah suggested that they go to bed but Elizabeth did not want to and seemed ill at ease. The two women went up to their shared bedroom, with Elizabeth suddenly remembering that she had left her book downstairs and going back down to fetch it. She then read for a bit before Hannah went to sleep. Hannah later testified that she had never seen her read a book before.

The next morning Elizabeth got up first and woke Hannah at about 6 a.m. Again this was unusual as normally Hannah had to wake Elizabeth. On going downstairs, Hannah discovered the break-in – the kitchen door was propped open with a wine bottle containing a candle and Mrs Ashworth's writing desk was on its side in the kitchen with some of its contents strewn around the floor. Hannah went upstairs and told her mistress what she had found. Mrs Ashworth came down and began checking around the property. She noticed that the sideboard door had been forced open – it was always kept locked at night – and that all of her silver plate was missing. She estimated the value of this to be over £400 – a considerable sum. It transpired later, at the trial, that on the Saturday prior to the robbery Elizabeth had asked to clean the silver, which Mrs Ashworth had thought was unusual.

The robbery was reported to the constable, Samuel Plank, who made a thorough examination of the house. He noted that there was no damage outside the property and that as there was no keyhole on the outside of the door, the lock could not have been picked, it could only have been opened from inside. Elizabeth drew his attention to one of the window shutters which was slightly ajar. Plank examined this, noting that there was a row of potted plants on the sill outside. There had been rain a few days earlier and the excess rain water had run down the outside of the pots and dried to a crust around the base of each one. When he looked carefully, he could see that the pots had not been disturbed, and if someone had removed them to gain access, they must have been inordinately careful in replacing them in their exact positions. He demonstrated this fact to Elizabeth, but she continued to assert that the burglars had come in through this window and not by any other route.

On the Monday afternoon Hannah made a trip to the butchers and returning to the house found Elizabeth in conversation with a man at the kitchen door. She was later to identify this man in court as William Kelly. Seeing Hannah, Elizabeth and William left the house, Elizabeth returning an hour or so later. Hannah asked her where she had been and Elizabeth told her that she told her that she had wished to 'vent her mind' on the man. She did not explain what she meant by this.

Plank was not satisfied with Elizabeth's story and arrested her on the Tuesday afternoon. Having taken her into custody he asked Elizabeth to let him see the contents of her box (servants typically owned a trunk in which they kept their belongings and which was convenient to move when they changed jobs). She let him see it and the only thing he found was a piece of flannel cloth – certainly no silver. He also questioned her about a man he had seen her talking to in the street. At first she was reluctant to tell him who the man was, but on being pressed by Mr Plant, claimed he was a tally man, named Finch, who sold items of drapery to people on tick, collecting the money in instalments. Elizabeth told the constable that she had owed Finch 8s for the best part of a year. During this interview the name of Kelly was not mentioned by either Elizabeth or the constable.

Elizabeth had been observed talking to her boy-friend William Kelly by John King who lived opposite Mrs Ashworth. He saw a tall man in Berner Street looking up at Mrs Ashworth's house and a few moments later Elizabeth emerged and got into conversation with this man. Mr King saw the man give her something although he was not able to see what it was. Knowing about the burglary he told his son to watch them and was able to attract Mrs Ashworth's attention and point the incident out to her. Mr King was able to get a good description of the man, which he later gave as evidence in court and which seemed to fit William Kelly closely. He also thought he had seen him outside the house before and Mr King's son Alfred was able to testify that he too had seen this man at least twice previously on the Tuesday.

On 29 August, Peter Kelly, William's father, went to the house of Hannah Compton and asked her if he could store a trunk there, telling her that it belonged to a friend of his who was looking for a new job. The trunk remained with Mrs Compton for nine days before an unidentified woman came and asked for it. Mrs Compton was not comfortable with this and went to Marlborough Street police station and got Constable William Craig to come and collect the trunk. The police broke it open in their office and found it contained a quantity of silver plate and various other items. This find led to the arrest of William Kelly and also his father. Elizabeth and William were charged with the burglary and Peter with receiving stolen goods.

The trial opened on Wednesday, 30 October 1816 at the Old Bailey before the Common Sergeant. Various witnesses were called to identify the accused, to give evidence of the crime and the relationship between Elizabeth and William. There was also evidence regarding the stolen goods which had initially been wrapped in some green baize and a tablecloth with a yellow border, both of which were later discovered in the trunk left by William. The prosecution had been able to build a strong case against the defendants who were now given the chance to speak in their defence.

Elizabeth made a straightforward denial of the charges but had no actual defence.

William offered a full confession, telling the court that he and he alone was responsible for the robbery and that the three other prisoners at the bar were entirely innocent. (A Mr Hitchen who had also been charged with receiving was acquitted.) William's father Peter simply told the court that he had no knowledge of what was in the trunk. All three were found guilty.

At the end of the Sessions Elizabeth and William were sentenced to death and Peter to transportation for fourteen years. All were returned to Newgate to await the execution of their sentences. Peter was in due course transferred to a ship bound for Australia.

Whilst awaiting her execution Elizabeth was visited by the great prison reformer Elizabeth Fry who endeavoured to offer her some comfort. She recorded the meeting in her diary and noted that she also saw six men waiting to be hanged and seven young children. One of the men had also been sentenced for burglary, two for robbery and three for forgery.

Elizabeth Fry was a Quaker who had been born in 1780. She worked tirelessly for prison reform, helping to found The Association for the Improvement of the Female Prisoners in Newgate. This group campaigned for better conditions for the female prisoners, a school for their children and a woman matron to look after them. Their activities spread to other towns and represented the first real attempt to treat criminals as human beings rather than vermin to be eradicated.

The Quakers generally, also campaigned against public executions. They did not approve of the morbid pleasure that the general public derived from watching them and of the rowdy and unsympathetic behaviour that they engendered.

It seems that Mrs Fry raised Elizabeth's case in the press and was very vigorously attacked for being a sentimentalist by the then Lord Chancellor, Lord Eldon, who said that if hanging was abolished for theft, the property of Englishmen would be left wholly without protection. Lord Eldon was noted for his rigid application of the law and his unwillingness to see it reformed.

Elizabeth was duly hanged outside Newgate on Wednesday, 5 March 1817, together with William and six other men. With them on the gallows were Andrew and Benjamin Savage who had both been convicted of forgery and uttering, Thomas Cann also convicted of forgery and James Gates and James Baker who had been sentenced to hang for robbery. The children whom Mrs Fry had met were not executed and were presumably transported.

Just after 8 a.m. the usual procession emerged from the Debtor's Door led by the City Marshall and the various officials. The eight prisoners were led up onto the platform and prayed with the Ordinary, Rev. Horace Cotton. John Langley prepared each of them in turn. Sometime around 8.15 a.m. the signal was given and the drop fell. There is no particular record of their deaths so it can be presumed that nothing untoward happened and that they all died quite quickly. Elizabeth's body was made available to relatives and friends for burial later in the day.

Amelia Roberts
The Last Woman to Die for Robbery

Amelia became the last woman in England and Wales to be hanged for robbery when she was executed at Newgate by James Foxen on Tuesday, 2 January 1827.

Thirty-two-year-old Amelia and her boyfriend, twenty-six-year-old Patrick Riley, were convicted of robbing the house of a wealthy gentleman by the name of Morgan Fuller Austin in

Red Lion Street, Clerkenwell, sometime around 9 August 1826. Amelia worked as a servant in the house and was regularly visited by Patrick, not a situation that met with Mr Austin's approval, who banned him from the house and threatened to dismiss Amelia.

Mr Austin had been at his country house and returned home on 10 August to find that Amelia had gone. She did not return and the following morning Mr Austin went to get some linen from the chest and began to realise that the house had been robbed. He found that all his silver tableware had gone together with his wife's jewellery and some of her clothes. In all, over £400 worth of goods had been taken, according to his later testimony.

Amelia and Patrick had ordered a Hackney cab to come to an adjoining street where Amelia loaded their haul into it. They asked to be taken to Picket Street in the Strand where they collected some more belongings before directing the cabbie to take them to Hounslow, which he did.

From Hounslow they took a coach to Newport in Monmouthshire where they took lodgings and passed themselves off as man and wife, she pretending that she was a milliner while he pretended to be a jeweller. They were arrested on 13 August by Mr Austin and his brother-in-law, in their lodgings. It is not clear how Mr Austin traced them but when he arrived Amelia was wearing one of Mrs Austin's dresses and Patrick had one of Mr Austin's silk handkerchiefs in his pocket. The majority of the stolen goods were discovered in the lodgings as they had not had time to sell them. Amelia and Patrick were taken into custody and duly returned to London to face trial.

They appeared at the Old Bailey before Barron Garrow (the Mr Garrow from previous cases seems to have been promoted to a judge by now), at the October Sessions on the 26th of that month. Mr Austin gave evidence to the court of the robbery and of the subsequent arrest and his goods were produced in court. The cabbie, John Harvey, described picking up the couple with their several boxes and the journey to Hounslow. Ann Watson, who was able to positively identify Patrick, also gave evidence of them being picked up in the cab, close to Red Lion Street. Andrew Lloyd, a constable, told the court how he had examined Mr Austin's house and was certain that there had been a robbery as the backs of the chests had been forced and the broken parts concealed under Mr Austin's bed. Mr Austin suggested in his evidence that Amelia had told him that she was glad she had been caught.

The defence of Patrick was a simple statement: 'I am quite innocent, and hope and trust the Almighty will bring me out of it'; plus the character statements of five of his friends. There was no defence offered by Amelia, but rather just a plea for mercy. Both were sentenced to death.

In accordance with the Recorder's recommendations to the Privy Council, Patrick's death sentence was commuted to transportation but Amelia was not to be so fortunate. This was probably due to two factors: the value of the goods stolen and the fact that she was in a position of trust in the house, a position which she had abused. Just two prisoners were not to be reprieved from those condemned at the October Sessions, the other being Charles Thomas White, a bookseller from Holborn, who had been quite separately convicted of arson.

In Newgate, awaiting her death, Amelia had paid great attention to the ministrations of Rev. Horace Cotton, the Ordinary, and ultimately came to accept her death as a release from a world of temptation. I am always inclined to take these reports with a pinch of salt, whether it really happened or whether it was what the broadside writers thought people wanted to hear we will never know. We are told that Charles White's behaviour was completely different and he resisted all attempts to bring him to religion. He became a nervous wreck at the thought of his imminent execution and continually schemed to somehow escape the noose.

The double hanging was set for the morning of Tuesday, 2 January 1827 and had attracted a particularly huge crowd. Just before 8 a.m. the pair were led out of Newgate. Amelia was allowed a seat in the space between the Debtor's Door and the steps of the gallows where she prayed with Mr Baker, the minister who attended her. She is said to have cried out 'Into thy hands, oh Lord, I commit my soul' and 'May God have mercy, save my soul'.

White appeared on the gallows first, accompanied by the sheriff's officer and Rev. Cotton. Foxen, the hangman, drew the white cap over his head but White continued to struggle against the cords that bound his arms and wrists and managed to get the cap off. He had to be held by two of Foxen's assistants who tried to tie a handkerchief over his face. Amelia was now brought up and prepared, a cord was tied around her legs once she was in position on the trap, the noose placed around her neck and a white cap pulled over her face. All should now have been ready and the Ordinary went to give the signal to Foxen to operate the drop. Just as he did so White was able to get his pinioned hands up to the rope and was thus did not drop correctly. The handkerchief fell, exposing his face which was contorted in agony with the tongue protruding as he writhed and squirmed. Fortunately Amelia died after only writhing for just a few seconds and hung limply beside the struggling White. Even the crowd were horrified by this display, according to the broadside published by J. Catanach.

Bell M'Menemy
Robbery with Violence in Glasgow

Isabella 'Bell' M'Menemy was born around 1803 in the County of Tyrone, Ireland, and had moved to Paisley, Scotland, in 1821 before going to live in Glasgow. Here she got to know Thomas Connor through a friend and also to know his mother. Up to this time, Bell had stayed out of trouble and had been employed at a steam loom factory. All this changed upon starting the relationship with Thomas and his mother. She quickly gained a conviction for stealing a watch, for which she had served a short prison sentence. She was described as a good looking woman, about twenty-three to twenty-five years old with a fair complexion and red hair.

Thomas Connor was about three years Bell's junior and had also been born in Tyrone. He had a criminal record stretching back to childhood. He had been banished from the county of Renfrew for stealing an anvil and a cart wheel from a blacksmith in Mearns. He had also been banished from Glasgow for theft. On 12 May 1826 he was tried at the Circuit Court for robbing a man but escaped with a verdict of Not Proven.

Bell and Thomas assaulted and robbed one Mr Alexander M'Kinnon (also given as McKennon) who had come to Glasgow from Tralee to sell eggs. The crime had taken place on 20 May 1828, sometime in the early hours of the Tuesday morning. Alexander had sold his eggs on the Monday and had some £8 in notes, a further £2 in silver and some coppers on him. He had decided to go for a drink at the end of the day and met Bell in a drinking house in Glasgow and got talking to her. She suggested that they went to another drinking house and on their way they met a night watchman who spoke to Bell. Towards the Aqueduct Bridge, they met a man that Bell claimed was her brother, but was in fact Thomas, and chatted to him for a few moments before Thomas grabbed Mr M'Kinnon and hit him on the head with a rock, knocking him unconscious. When he came round, he found his money had gone together with his shoes and the silver from the stocking he carried it in. Two policemen arrived at the scene and found a blood-stained shirt and the rock used to hit Mr M'Kinnon. Bell and Thomas and two others were duly arrested and charged with the then capital crime of assault and robbery.

Bell and Connor came to trial on Wednesday, 17 September 1828 at the Circuit Court of Justiciary in Glasgow before Lord Meadowbank, along with two other alleged accomplices, Hugh Richardson and Charles Hill, who were acquitted. Bell pleaded guilty and Thomas not guilty.

They were both found guilty by the jury who accepted Bell's confession and convicted Thomas on the evidence offered against him. On account of his youth, the jury recommended Thomas to mercy. Lord Meadowbank told Thomas that he would have thought getting off last time he was in court would have deterred him from further crime.

They were both sentenced to death and an execution date set for Wednesday, 23 October, between the hours of 8 and 10 a.m. The prisoners were then removed to the New Jail to await their fate.

In prison, as they were both Catholics, they were frequently visited by Bishop Scott and two other priests, Father McGrigor and Father McDonald. It is reported that they behaved with much propriety, and listened to the religious advice of these gentlemen with seeming penitence, especially Bell, who seemed from the questions she asked, to be an intelligent young woman. The judge's report went to London for consideration by the King and Privy Council. Petitions for a reprieve were got up for both of them on account of their age and sent to the authorities, but these were denied and the execution date confirmed. Bell was reported to have wept bitterly on being told there was to be no reprieve.

Bell had been given a new dress to wear for her execution by the Female Benevolent Society and Thomas had also obtained suitable clothing. Before she was led out, Bell was reported to have given her fellow prisoners a lecture on avoiding the wrong sort of friends and company, the need for keeping regular hours and associating with sober and industrious people and attending church regularly. Whether this really happened or whether it is just another example of the moralistic inventions printed in broadsides of the time we have no means of knowing.

The New Drop style gallows was erected in the square outside the New Jail, which was located in the Saltmarket area of Glasgow and a huge crowd had assembled behind the railings to witness the event. This was the first hanging of a woman in Glasgow since 1793, when Agnes M'Callum (also given as Agnes White) had been executed on 22 May for the murder of her bastard child. Bell and Thomas were to die at the hands of Thomas Young, who worked in Glasgow and elsewhere between 1815 and 1834.

Bell and Thomas emerged from the New Jail around 8 a.m. Thomas had to be supported while Bell reportedly faced her death with considerable courage, although she seemed somewhat fazed by the size of the crowd when she had mounted the gallows platform. As well as the prison officers, they were accompanied by the magistrates and at least one Catholic priest. A psalm was sung on the way out of the prison and another on the gallows. Unlike many couples in their position, they acknowledged and spoke to each other and shook hands with the officials.

They were then both prepared by Thomas Young and their heads covered with white hoods. After a few moments to allow for private prayer, the signal was given and the drop fell. Both struggled briefly before unconsciousness supervened. They were left to hang for the customary hour before being taken down and their bodies claimed for burial.

At least three companies printed broadsides purporting to have all the details of the crime, confessions, trial and execution of the couple and these were no doubt sold in large numbers amongst the crowd, at a price of 1*d*.

The next time Scotland was see to such a large crowd at a hanging, was on Wednesday, 28 January 1829, at the execution of multiple murderer and body snatcher William Burke in Edinburgh. Burke's hanging was attended by a crowd estimated at between 32 and 40,000 people. The last public execution outside the New Jail was on Friday, 28 July 1865, when Edward Pritchard was hanged for murder. After that, executions were carried out within Duke Street prison.

3

LATER GEORGIAN MURDERS

Elizabeth Godfry (or Godfrey)
Tragedy at an Execution

Richard Prince was a coachman by trade and was living with a woman named Emily Bisset in the Marylebone area of London in a house of 'ill repute', owned by their landlord Mr William Scott. Elizabeth Godfrey had taken the room adjoining theirs four days before Christmas 1806.

A quarrel had occurred between Richard and Elizabeth, apparently due to him having sent for William Atkins, the watchman, to arrest her for having a man (a customer?) in her room the day before, with whom she was arguing over money. It was alleged that Richard had cut Elizabeth's hand during this altercation. It seems that Elizabeth was quickly freed without any criminal charge being brought and returned to her lodgings. However this incident festered in her mind and she determined to take revenge on Richard.

Between 5 and 6 p.m. on Christmas Day 1806 she knocked on Richard and Emily's door and told Emily, who answered

her call, that she wanted to speak to Richard. Emily called him
but when he went to the door he did not see Elizabeth, so
he fetched a candle and returned. Elizabeth verbally abused
him for fetching the watchman and then stabbed him just
below the eye with a pocket knife, sending Richard reeling
back into the room, exclaiming 'Oh! I am a dead man.' He
pulled the knife from his face and threw it down. Mr Scott
was alerted by the commotion and came to see what had happened. Emily took Richard to the surgeon who decided that
he needed immediate hospital treatment for what was considered to be a dangerous injury. He was accordingly admitted to
the Middlesex Hospital under the care of a surgeon, Mr Barry.
Richard survived in hospital until Saturday, 18 January when
he finally died from the wound. John Foy, an officer from
Marlborough Street police station, was sent by the magistrate
to the hospital to enquire into the stabbing and took possession of the knife.

Elizabeth had been arrested and originally charged with
wounding, with the charge being upgraded to murder
after Richard died. She came to trial at the Old Bailey on
18 February 1807 before Mr Justice Heath. Emily Bisset, her
landlord William Scott and William Atkins the watchman gave
evidence for the prosecution. Mr Barry told the court that
he was certain that the cause of Richard's death was the stab
wound rather than other causes.

The case for the defence was that Richard had abused
Elizabeth and also given her a bad cut to the hand. She called
William Atkins to corroborate this. She also pointed out how
hard life was for a single woman with no man to protect her
and that she had not caused any trouble to Mr Scott on the
previous occasion she had lodged in his house. However she
had no real answer to the charge of stabbing Richard. It was
not possible to argue self-defence as the reported incidents of
his injuring her hand and of her stabbing him were separated
by a considerable passage of time. The jury found her guilty

of wilful murder and Elizabeth was returned to Newgate to await sentence at the end of the Sessions.

She was not the only person to have been convicted of murder at these Sessions. John Holloway and Owen Haggerty had murdered John Cole Steele. All three were duly sentenced to be hanged and their bodies delivered to Surgeon's Hall for dissection. Their executions were to take place three days later, on Monday, 24 February 1807.

The hanging of these three murderers attracted enormous public interest and it was estimated that up to 40,000 people had come to watch, with every inch of ground outside Newgate and the Old Bailey occupied. The sheer numbers and the pressure created by movements in the crowd quickly began to cause problems as people were being crushed and trampled even before the execution preparations commenced.

Just before 8 a.m. the prisoners were led out, accompanied by the Ordinary, Brownlow Forde. The first was Owen Haggerty who was already pinioned and had the halter around his neck. The rope was tied up to the beam and then John Holloway was brought out. Elizabeth was allowed to sit on a bench at the bottom of the stairs to the platform until the two men had been prepared. Haggerty said nothing on the gallows but Holloway made a short speech proclaiming his innocence until William Brunskill, the hangman, terminated it by pulling the white night cap over his face. Elizabeth was now brought up the stairs and must have been shocked to see the two hooded and pinioned men standing there. She was prepared in the same manner and all three continued to pray with Brownlow Forde who then gave the signal at around 8.15 a.m. to Brunskill to release the trap. The three hooded bodies dropped together, falling a short distance into the huge box-like structure of Newgate's gallows. Haggerty and Holloway became still almost immediately but Elizabeth writhed and struggled for some time after suspension, 'dying hard', as was the then expression. Little of her struggles would have been seen by the spectators; all they could typically see was her upper body and perhaps some convulsive movements in it.

As the three people died on the gallows above, more were being injured and dying in the crowd in the Old Bailey below. Women, children and men were crushed and then trampled as they fainted and fell. It is reported that there were cries of 'Murder, Murder' from some of the women. It was impossible for the small number of officials present to do anything to help the victims as they were so densely packed in.

The worst part of the crush was in Green Arbour Lane, nearly opposite the Debtors' Door where the gallows stood. A pie seller had placed his basket of pies on a stool which was pushed over by the surging crowd. The basket and upturned stool caused more people to fall and be trampled. A twelve-year-old boy by the name of Harrington, who had gone to watch the hangings with his father, was killed here, although his father survived and was taken to St Bartholomew's Hospital. A woman who was nursing a baby had the foresight to pass the infant over the heads of the crowd to a man who passed it on, finally enabling it to be rescued. Sadly the mother died a few moments later.

Elsewhere a cart onto which spectators had crowded collapsed and some of these people died in the ensuing panic, in which everybody was trying to save themselves.

It was only after the bodies of the three murderers could be taken down and the gallows removed back inside Newgate that officials were able to clear the street and begin to attend to the casualties. There were a total of twenty-seven bodies recovered and some seventy or so casualties requiring treatment. The site was strewn with hats, shoes and other personal effects of the dead and injured.

Most of the dead were taken to St Bartholomew's Hospital where a temporary mortuary was set up to enable relatives to come and identify their loved ones. An inquest into the tragedy opened at the hospital the following day which concluded on the Friday with a verdict 'That several persons came by their death from compression and suffocation.' Hardly helpful! It is not clear what, if any, action was taken by the authorities to prevent a recurrence of the tragedy but no similar problems were reported subsequently.

Mary Bateman
'The Yorkshire Witch'

It might seem incredible to us today that a relatively uneducated woman who was a career criminal could successfully convince a large number of people that she possessed supernatural powers and healing abilities, but Mary Bateman succeeded in doing so in Leeds in the late eighteenth and early nineteenth centuries. Mary was born Mary Harker around 1768 to a farmer at Asenby, some 4 miles south of Thirsk in North Yorkshire, and even as a child exhibited criminal tendencies. Like many girls of her era she went into domestic service as a teenager, initially working for a family in Thirsk, but was soon sacked for stealing from them. She continued her criminal career with a series of minor thefts and scams and by 1778 had moved to Leeds as she had become too well known locally.

In 1782, after knowing him for just three weeks, she married John Bateman who was a wheelwright but marriage did not curtail her activities and the couple had to move regularly to avoid arrest. They had four children, including a son also christened John. By 1799 Mary was living in Marsh Lane, Leeds. She started dressmaking and also took to telling fortunes, claiming to have supernatural powers which she used to great effect. She made and sold potions that were supposed to cure various ailments and ward off evil spirits. There was still a popular belief in the power of witchcraft at this time and Mary found she could cash in on it. It was probably far

more profitable and certainly less risky that stealing, a crime
for which she could easily be hanged.

It is generally thought that Mary poisoned three people in
1803 although she was never tried for or convicted of these
murders. The victims were two Quaker sisters who lived above
their draper's shop with their mother in St Peter's Square in
Quarry Hill, Leeds. Mary sold them medicines that were in
fact poison mixtures and, having killed them, she robbed the
house and shop. When the neighbours asked why the three
women had died she told them that they had caught bubonic
plague. Amazingly there was little suspicion as to the cause of
death and no inquest into them. So Mary just walked away
from the crime with her booty.

Mary frequently used a 'Mrs Moore' to help her in her
scams. This non-existent lady was the initial fount of all Mary's
'wisdom' and was always consulted on behalf of Mary's clients.
They were told that money she took from them was of course
to go to Mrs Moore. In 1806 Mary invented a new alter ego
called 'Mrs Blythe' to help her in her plans.

Living in the Bramley area of Leeds at this time was a com-
fortably-off but childless middle-aged couple, William and
Rebecca Perigo. Rebecca was suffering from a fluttering in
the breast whenever she lay down and was also having psy-
chological problems, claiming to be haunted by a black dog
and other spirits. She was told by her doctor, one Dr Curzley,
that she was under some sort of spell and that he was unable
to help her. At Whitsun 1806 the Perigos were visited by their
niece who suggested obtaining help from Mary Bateman who
she said would be able to rid her aunt of the spirits that were
possessing her. As a result a meeting was arranged between the
Perigos and Mary outside the Black Dog pub. Mary asked for
an item of underclothing which she would send to Mrs Blythe
in Scarborough who would be able to help. William Perigo
took a flannel petticoat to Mary who promised to send it to
Mrs Blythe and told William to come and see her the fol-

lowing week. This he did and Mary showed him the letter from Mrs Blythe. The imaginary Mrs Blythe directed that Mary should go to the Perigos' house and sew four guinea notes and some gold coins which she had sent, one into each corner of Rebecca's bed, where they were to be left for eighteen months. William was to give Mary four guinea notes in exchange to return to Mrs Blythe. The notes were duly sewn into her bedclothes and William was instructed to visit Mary regularly to receive further instructions from Mrs Blythe. The next instruction was that William should nail two horseshoes to the door. William was soon to receive a letter from Mrs Blythe instructing him to take Mary a further two guinea notes and to purchase a cheese to be sent to her by Mary. The letter was to be burnt after it had been read. The next letter requested a small quantity of china and silverware be sent to her, together with some tea and sugar. Again the letter was to be burnt. A further request was for a bed and bedclothes as Mrs Blythe was unable to sleep in her own bed due to the battle she was having with the spirits that had taken over Rebecca. Again the letter was to be immediately burnt after it had been acted upon.

The next letter predicted an illness in the Perigo house affecting one or both of them. It instructed Rebecca to take half a pound of honey to Mary who would mix into it some special medicine that Mrs Blythe had made. Also the Perigos were to eat puddings for six days into each of which they were to mix a daily marked packet of powder that Mary would give them. Rebecca went to see Mary who did as the letter instructed and she left with the honey and the packets of powder.

On 5 May, another letter arrived instructing the Perigos to begin eating the puddings on 11 May. Interestingly it said that only sufficient pudding was to be made for each day, nobody else was to be allowed to eat any of it and that if there was any left over it must be immediately destroyed.

It also said that should William or Rebecca become ill they were not to get the doctor because he would be unable to help. Unsurprisingly this letter, like its predecessors, was to be burnt. So the scene for the final act was now set. The Perigos would poison themselves and kindly destroy all the evidence of Mary's involvement.

To begin with eating the puddings produced no ill effects but on the sixth day they tasted different and caused William and Rebecca to have severe stomach cramps and vomiting. As directed a doctor was not consulted and Rebecca, who continued to eat the honey, died on 24 May 1807. William did consult a doctor who suspected that Rebecca could have been poisoned but no post-mortem was carried out. William slowly began to recover somewhat as he was no longer eating the puddings. Mary had been very clever up to this time. Through Mrs Blythe she continued to demand items of value from the Perigos but not more than she assessed that they could afford, in view of William's successful business. Her real problem was that William had lived rather than died as planned.

William decided at length to examine the little silk purses that contained the guinea notes and gold coins that Mrs Blythe had asked to have sewn into Rebecca's bed clothes, surely they should still contain the notes and coins that had been placed in them. Instead they contained cabbage leaves and copper coins. Now it seems that the penny had finally dropped with William. He arranged a meeting with Mary on the pretext of buying another bottle of medicine and took assistance with him, in the form of Constable Driffield. Mary had brought with her a bottle of liquid containing oatmeal and arsenic with which she presumably hoped to silence her principal accuser. As soon as she saw the constable she tried to make out that it was William Perigo who had bought the bottle for her. He was not impressed by this charade. Mary was now taken into custody and when the constable searched her house and was able to recover many of the items that had been sent to Mrs Blythe by the Perigos.

She appeared before the magistrates the following day charged with Rebecca's murder. They committed her for trial at the Yorkshire Lent Assizes of 1809 which opened at York Castle on Friday, 17 March before Judge Sir Simon Le Blanc.

Evidence of the handwriting on Mrs Blythe's letters being identical to Mary's was given as well as how Mary had sent the letters to Scarborough and had them mailed back so that they would bear the correct postmark. A thorough search by constables in Scarborough had revealed, predictably, that there was no Mrs Blythe. Forensic evidence was provided by a Mr Chorley who had analysed the remains of the honey and found that it contained mercuric chloride which was extremely poisonous and this was consistent with the symptoms displayed by the Perigos.

Mary's defence was straightforward denial of any involvement with the death.

Sir Simon Le Blanc summed up and told the jury that to bring in a guilty verdict they had to satisfy themselves on three points. These were that Rebecca had died from poisoning, that the poison had been administered with the knowledge and contrivance of Mary and that it had been done in the expectation of causing Rebecca's death. He went on to remind them that although there was a strong case against Mary for having systematically defrauded the Perigos this did not make her automatically guilty of murder.

The evidence of criminality and murder was so overwhelming that it did not take the jury long to deliver its verdict. In accordance with the usual procedure Mary was asked if she had anything to say as to why sentence of death should not be pronounced on her. Breaking into floods of tears she pleaded her belly (claimed to be pregnant). As a result the judge ordered the court doors to be locked and immediately empanelled a jury of matrons to examine her. They found her not to be pregnant and so he proceeded to sentence her to be hanged and afterwards dissected on the following Monday. She was forty-one at this time and had an infant child with her in prison up until the time she was condemned.

Over the weekend Mary wrote a letter to her husband in which she enclosed her wedding ring and asked him to give it to their daughter. She admitted some of her crimes but continued to deny the murders. It was reported by the *Leeds Intelligencer* newspaper that she continued her criminal habits even in the condemned cell, telling the fortune of one of her female attendants for a guinea. On the morning of execution she was up at 5 a.m. for a communion service in the chapel.

Mary was executed on Monday, 20 March by William 'Mutton' Curry the Yorkshire hangman, alongside Joseph Brown who had been convicted of the murder of Elizabeth Fletcher. Curry was nicknamed 'Mutton' as he had twice been convicted of sheep stealing and reprieved on both occasions, the last on condition that he remain prisoner in the castle and carry out the executions there, which he did from 1802 to 1835. The New Drop gallows was set up in the area behind the castle and some 5,000 people came to watch Mary die. Despite the best efforts of the chaplain, Rev. George Brown, Mary persisted in her denial of the murder(s) and her other criminal activities to the end, dying as one report put it 'with a lie on her lips'. It seems though that many still believed she had supernatural powers and there was some sympathy for her. It was reported that some of the spectators really thought that she would be saved from death by some divine intervention at the last moment, but this was not to be. A broadside was published detailing the crimes and execution of Mary and Joseph Brown.

After execution Mary's body was sent to the Leeds Royal Infirmary for dissection and afterwards put on display. The public paid 3*d* each to view her body and £30 was raised for the hospital. Strips of Mary's skin were sold as curios.

Her skeleton was used initially for anatomy classes and afterwards, together with a plaster cast death mask of her skull put on display. It can still be seen in the Thackray Museum in Leeds, to whom it was loaned by the Infirmary.

Mary was always stealing from and defrauding people and was well known as a thief so why wasn't she informed on by the people of Leeds? It is probable that they feared her witchcraft more than her predations. It would be easy to brand William Perigo as totally naive for allowing himself to be so completely taken in by Mary but no doubt he was desperate to save his wife's life and when the doctor could offer no hope he looked elsewhere for assistance. Sadly he found one of the most criminal women of the time.

Edith Morrey
A Cheshire Love Triangle

Edith was born Edith Coomer and married George Morrey, a farmer's son on Tuesday, 18 April 1797 at St Chad's church in Wybunbury in southern Cheshire. She was then about nineteen years old and the daughter of a well-to-do farmer. Initially the marriage was happy and they settled in the Cheshire town of Nantwich. George opened a grocery there and the couple made a reasonable living over the next four years. They returned to the village of Hankelow to take over George's father's farm in early 1801 when he retired. They were blessed with seven children, three boys and four girls, although one of the girls died in infancy. George tended the farm whilst Edith made cheese for sale locally and looked after the family.

The Morreys were wealthy enough to have servants and by Christmas 1811 they had a maid, Hannah Evans, who had been with them nearly a year and a twenty-year-old farmhand called John Lomas who had just joined them. At this time

Edith was once again pregnant but was to have a miscarriage in February 1812.

We have no means of knowing Edith's emotional state at the time, so soon after a miscarriage, but it was quite possibly rather fragile. For whatever reason, Edith quickly fell for John and they began having an affair. Over the next two months or so Edith started to think in terms of marrying this young man, some fifteen years her junior; however there was one obvious impediment – George. No doubt Edith was not prepared to give up her children and comfortable lifestyle by simply running away with John, nor was she willing to face the social disgrace that this course of action entailed at the time. So another way had to be found to keep John's affections and rid themselves of George. Edith determined that John should kill George and afterwards they could be together.

On Saturday, 11 April 1812 George had been to Witton Wakes, a major fair in Northwich and did not return home until midnight. Edith and Hannah Evans were still up at this time and George had supper before he and Edith retired to bed. Hannah went a little later after she had cleared away the supper. Hannah was soon awakened though, by the sounds of a commotion from inside the house. She and John Lomas ran to the house of a neighbour to raise the alarm. The pair then returned to the farm with a couple of neighbours, Thomas Timmis and John Moores. The two men found Edith sitting by the fireplace and then opened the door into George's bedroom where they made a grim discovery. George was laying face down on the floor with an axe handle projecting from underneath him. He had several wounds from this but in addition had had his throat cut, so there was blood everywhere. Timmis and Moores decided that George's brother, Jem, should be sent for and told Lomas to go to his house. Returning with Jem, John Lomas told him that the house had been burgled with £150 missing from George's desk and that his master had been killed by the intruders. However, aspects of this story did not ring true. John was wearing a clean shirt on the Sunday morning which raised suspicion and there were no signs of any forcible entry into the house. When questioned on this John showed, unconvincingly, how easy it was to open the front door from the outside. Unconvincingly because it relied upon the nail that was the bolt not being fully inserted.

The police arrived in the shape of William Dooley, the Parish Constable and John Groom who was a special constable and also a solicitor. John Groom questioned Edith and got the same story that John Lomas had given. He also noticed that John had dried blood on his nose and on his wrist. He asked John to produce his dirty shirt and John refused, saying that he had worn the present one all week. Groom began a search of the house now that it was getting light outside and they could see a little more. As they got to the bottom of the stairs they noticed a handprint in dried blood and, looking carefully, were able to follow a trail of blood spots which went back through the kitchen to John's room. The constables examined John further and noticed blood stains on the cuffs of his jacket. They then demanded that John open his box which he kept in his room. They all went to his room only to find Edith already there and were in time to see her take something from the box and attempt to conceal it. This was of course the blood-stained shirt. Constable Dooley now arrested John on the strength of this evidence. John told the constable that the shirt had been bloodied due to having to bleed George's mare at the blacksmiths earlier in the week. Dooley took John back to his house in Audlem where he made a confession and implicated Edith as the principal in the killing, telling the constable that she had given him the signal to enter his master's bedroom when she was sure that George was asleep and handed him the axe. She held a candle for him whilst he struck the blows and passed John the razor when it became clear that George was still alive. William Dooley asked how long Edith and John had been planning the murder and he told the constable that it had been some time.

Back at the farmhouse Constable William Hall from Hankelow, having heard John's confession and allegations against Edith, decided to arrest her. He told her that he was taking her into custody and she asked to be allowed to get ready, which he allowed. She slipped into another room and moments later returned with blood pouring from a razor wound to her throat. Fortunately the local surgeon was on hand having come to view George's body for the inquest and he managed to staunch the flow of blood and sew up the wound before Edith bled to death.

Constable Dooley had a full search made of the premises and as part of this drained the pond which revealed the murder weapon. Lomas had closed the blade before throwing the razor into the pond and it was seen to have blood and hair on it. Edith was placed under the guard of Richard Thursfield, who was Constable Dooley's deputy and he had been told to record anything Edith said when she came to. She told him she wished she had not lived and that she had not been in her right mind of late.

As was usual at the time the inquest on George was held at the village pub, The White Lion, on the Monday afternoon following the killing, before Chester Coroner Mr Faithful Thomas. Also as normal, witnesses were called to give their accounts of the murder, a practice which tended to prejudge any subsequent trial. Edith and John were both declared to be guilty of murder and committed for trial. George's body was buried on 15 April at St Chad's, Wybunbury. John was taken to Chester Castle to await trial and Edith transferred there on 4 May when she was sufficiently recovered from her suicide attempt.

Chester was part of the Welsh Circuit and thus its assizes were known as the Great Sessions. The court sat at the Shire Hall in the outer bailey of Chester Castle. Edith and John stood trial on Friday, 21 August before Chief Justice Robert Dallas and Francis Burton, a more junior judge. They were both charged with Petty Treason rather than murder, as the deceased was the husband of one defendant and the master of the other. The prosecution was led by Samuel Benyon, assisted by David Jones. Edith was represented by John Cross and John Hill, John being represented by John Lyons.

The evidence and witness testimonies from the inquest were repeated, lasting some four hours. John Cross questioned Hannah Evans as to the state of the Morreys' marriage and as to whether she had noticed any impropriety between mistress and servant. She confirmed that she thought her employers were happily married and that she had not seen any intimacy between Edith and John and that there seemed to be no tension in the house when George returned home on the Saturday night. John Cross also tried to introduce the jury to the possibility that burglars had killed George rather than the defendants. John Lyon suggested that William Dooley had put pressure on John Lomas to make a confession but he refuted this and assured the court that he had neither bought pressure upon John nor promised him leniency in return for his confession.

The jury returned a verdict of guilty against both prisoners after just a few minutes discussion. Judge Dallas then addressed both of them, suggesting that although he believed that John had actually carried out the killing it was Edith whose guilt was the greater for planning and organising the destruction of her husband. Asked if he had anything further to say before he was sentenced, John told the court that he deserved his execution and hoped to be quickly forgotten. On Edith's behalf, John Cross told the court that she was pregnant and thus could not be sentenced to death at this time. A panel of matrons were sworn in from the married women in the court at the time and they were taken with Edith to the house of Matthew Hudson, the governor of the county gaol at Chester

Castle, where she was examined and determined to be 'quick with child' to use the contemporary expression. She was about five months pregnant.

Robert Dallas proceeded to pass the death sentence on them both and John was removed to the condemned cell to spend his last three days. Edith was respited until after she had given birth and also housed with the County Gaol in the Castle. The governor of the gaol allowed Edith and John to meet twice over the weekend before he was hanged and even allowed them a final embrace.

Uniquely in Britain, Cheshire county executions were not carried out at the county gaol at all, but rather at the Chester City Gaol which had opened in 1808, under the jurisdiction of the Chester Sheriff. On the morning of execution John had thus to be transferred to the City Gaol where the gallows was erected on the flat roof of the gatehouse. John's hanging took place there on Monday, 24 August 1812. He spent some time with the chaplain, Rev. William Fish, before being led out up to the roof for his appointment with hangman Samuel Burrows. A large crowd had gathered to witness the event and the usual broadsides were sold. John made a short speech from the gallows warning others not to follow his example. His body was dissected after death by Owen Titley at the infirmary next door to the gaol.

Edith remained in the County Gaol and gave birth on 21 December 1812 to a healthy male child who was taken from her a week later for adoption. By law Edith could now be hanged within a month but in fact this was not to be so. Her execution warrant was signed by Robert Dallas, her trial judge, at the next Great Sessions on Wednesday, 21 April 1813 and her hanging was scheduled for two days later on Friday the 23rd. Edith slept quite well on the Thursday night and got up at 5 a.m. on the Friday morning. She dressed in her least valuable clothes, as these would afterwards be the property of the hangman, and drank a little coffee but refused any breakfast. She went to a service in the prison chapel at 8 a.m. which lasted nearly an hour. Matthew Hudson, the Governor, then had her taken into his parlour to await the arrival of the under sheriff. He arrived a little before noon and Hudson personally led Edith out to the cart waiting to take her to the City Gaol. She was accompanied by John Robinson, one of the turnkeys, in the cart which was flanked by constables for the short journey of around 100yds between the two prisons.

On arrival at the City Gaol she was taken in through the gatehouse and then up onto the flat roof where the New Drop gallows was waiting for her. Here she ascended the platform without assistance and knelt in prayer with Rev. Fish before submitting herself to Samuel Burrows. He tied her wrists and arms and also tied a cord round her legs before placing the noose around her neck. Chaplain Fish exhorted her 'to dismiss all worldly thoughts and fix her whole being on the Redeemer'. Edith thanked John Robinson for the kindness he had shown her. She was given a handkerchief to drop by Samuel Burrows as the signal for him to release the bolt before he pulled a white night cap down over her face. She duly gave the signal just after 1 p.m. in the afternoon and the drop fell, plunging her through it to knee level. For whatever reason the black screens that usually surrounded the platform were not erected for Edith's execution so everyone was able to witness her struggles over the next two and a half minutes or so as she fought her losing battle against the noose. At length her body became still and was left on the rope for an hour before being removed for dissection. Her hanging had attracted a crowd estimated at 10,000 people.

Edith's dissection was carried out the next morning by Owen Titley. He only opened her thorax and abdomen and removed her heart for preservation. After having done so her body was sewn back up and left on display for a short while before being taken for burial.

Edith's baby was adopted by her parents, William and Edith Croomer and christened Thomas. At the age of twenty he was convicted of theft and sentenced to transportation to Australia for seven years.

One wonders how Edith's miscarriage affected the balance of her mind and her judgement in early 1812. She seemed to be on good terms with George even on the Saturday evening but what were her true feelings for John Lomas, her junior and in every way her inferior? In those days the miscarriage would not have been considered a factor in her defence and there were no psychiatrists to examine her and bring forward expert testimony. One may remember that much was made of the miscarriage that Ruth Ellis suffered in 1955 and the effect upon her mind and subsequent actions.

Catherine Kinrade
A Love Triangle on the Isle of Man

Nineteen-year-old Catherine was having an affair with her brother-in-law, John Camaish, who was nine years her senior. She was described as having 'uncommonly interesting and rather handsome features'. John had married Catherine's older sister, but had always harboured feelings for Catherine. They plotted to murder Mrs Camaish, who was pregnant at the time, so as to get her out of the way and allow their relationship to become permanent. To this effect Catherine put some of the arsenic powder into her sister's porridge which, although it caused vomiting and severe stomach cramps, did not have the desired result. John then purchased some more arsenic from a shop in Ramsey, telling the chemist that he intended to use it to kill vermin. He persuaded his wife to take the arsenic on the basis that it would cure her of some unspecified illness. She died very quickly after this second dose. It should be noted that arsenic is a cumulative poison and builds up in the body, so that there would still have been a residue present from the previous attempt.

Suspicions were aroused as to the cause of the untimely death of Mrs Camaish, due to the behaviour of Catherine and John. An inquest was therefore held which found she had died from arsenic poisoning, rather than a severe attack of gastroenteritis that had similar symptoms and was a common cause of death. Catherine and John were arrested and charged with the killing, he as principal and she as an accessory to murder. They came to trial in late March 1823 before the Deemster, as Manx high court judges are known at Castle Rushen, Castletown. The jury returned a verdict of guilty and the pair were sentenced to be hanged and their bodies to be dissected afterwards and not to be permitted a Christian burial, in accordance with Section 53 of the Manx Criminal Code of 1817. They were returned to the island's then main prison within the castle to await their fate. The prison within the castle had been sub-stantially upgraded in 1815 to provide accommodation for both debtors and criminals.

In the Isle of Man the coroner of the sheading in which the crime occurred was responsible for carrying out death sentences, whereas in England it was the sheriff of the county. As in England it was normal to appoint a hangman, but no one volunteered for the job and so the coroner of Ayre sheading ended up having to perform the execution himself. (Ayre is one of the six sheadings, which are administrative areas, this one forming the northern tip of the island. Each one has a coroner whose role nowadays might be likened to that of the leader of a council.)

It was reported that Catherine was so poorly educated that she was unable to pray when she was first committed to prison and had to be taught how to do so by the chaplain. Once she had mastered prayer she spent many hours doing so and was judged to be fully penitent by the time of her execution. This, of course, was considered to be most important for her spiritual salvation. She also confessed to her part in the murder.

John, in contrast, showed no remorse until four or five days before he was to die. He then began to become increasingly desperate, shaking constantly and refusing food. He made a confession on the morning of his death and admitted buying both lots of poison.

Catherine asked to see John on that morning and this was allowed. She told him that they should forgive each other which they did and then they shook hands before being returned to their cells. This is quite unusual, as often when a couple were to be executed for the same crime there was animosity between them at the gallows, each blaming the other for their fate.

On the morning of Friday, 18 April they were brought out from their separate cells to be pinioned and have the nooses placed around their necks before being loaded into the cart for the journey from the Castle to the place of execution. They were accompanied by ministers of religion to the execution ground.

An immense crowd of spectators had gathered around the gallows by the lake near Castletown to await the arrival of the prisoners. It was reported that every vantage point was covered with people of both sexes and all ages, as hangings were rare events on the island.

The cart was backed under the gallows, similar to Tyburn executions in London, and the ropes tied up to the beam. The Rev. Mr Kewley than recited prayers for the condemned couple for several minutes and when he had finished he embraced Catherine and shook hands with John. He and the other officials got down from the cart and the order was given for the horse to move forward, leaving the prisoners suspended, at least in John's case. Catherine was less fortunate because the rope slipped and her feet were able to touch the ground.

As a consequence of this, while John expired very quickly, Catherine struggled for some time before succumbing.

They were left hanging for half an hour before being taken down and placed back into the cart to be taken back to the castle, prior to being sent to Douglas for dissection. It appears that this part of their sentence was not actually carried out and their bodies were returned to their friends for burial. A broadside was published by John Muir of Glasgow and sold widely at the execution and afterwards, both on the Isle of Man and on the mainland.

These hangings were two of only seven to be carried out on the Isle of Man in the nineteenth century. Catherine Kinrade was the only female to be hanged there in the nineteenth or twentieth centuries.

The Isle of Man is a self-governing British dependency, which did not finally abolish the death penalty until 1993.

Jane Scott
Patricide in Preston

Jane was the wayward daughter of John and Mary Scott who were shopkeepers in Bridge Street in Preston, Lancashire. By the age of sixteen Jane had become pregnant and her parents stood by her, despite the fact that she also stole from them to fund her lifestyle of drinking and debauchery with her friends. Her child died at an early age of what was thought to be natural causes. She had a further pregnancy and this child also died suddenly in March 1827. Although child deaths were commonplace there was a degree of suspicion raised over this second death. However no formal investigation was carried out into it.

On Monday, 14 May 1827 Jane prepared some porridge for her parents' supper as a result of which they both became violently ill. They were attended by a local doctor,

Dr Brown, who was unable to do much for them. Mary died in the early hours of Tuesday morning and by dawn Jane's father had also succumbed. Dr Brown testified later that he had instructed Jane to keep the pot in which the porridge had been made for examination but when he returned for it he found that Jane had cleaned it thoroughly, removing all trace of the contents. Dr Brown informed the authorities and an inquest was held that concluded that the Scotts had died from arsenic poisoning, administered by their daughter. Jane was therefore arrested and sent to Lancaster Castle to await trial at the next assizes.

The *Preston Chronicle* of 19 May ran the story under the headline 'Patricide – man and wife poisoned by arsenic supposed to have been administered by their own daughter'.

Jane duly came to trial only on the charge of murdering her father before Mr Justice Bayley at the Lancashire Summer Assizes of 1827, which opened on 29 August. The evidence against her was strong but the failure to attend of the doctor giving the medical evidence of poisoning led to her being acquitted because the prosecution had failed to prove that the John Scott had died from poisoning. It was therefore decided to proceed with the second charge, that of the murder of her mother Mary and to defer this to the Lent Assizes of 1828. Jane therefore remained in prison in the castle for a further six months awaiting this and in that time became very weak.

The Lent Assizes were formally opened at about 5 p.m. on Saturday, 8 March by Baron Hullock, the Civil Judge. He was joined at Lancaster the following day by Mr Justice Bayley, who was the judge for the criminal list and who had presided over Jane's first trial.

The proceedings began on Monday, 11 March, and all the criminal cases were concluded by Thursday, 20 March. Jane asked the judge not to allow anyone from Preston to sit on the jury. We do not know if this request was complied with. Various witnesses were called including a chemist from Preston who identified Jane as a person that he had sold arsenic to, purportedly for killing rats, on three separate occasions, the last being a few days before her parents died. Dr Brown, who attended John and Mary on the fatal night, reiterated how he had told Jane to preserve the saucepan with the remains of the porridge and how she had defied him by cleaning it out. George Richardson, a boyfriend of Jane, told the court that a week or so before her parents' deaths, Jane had suggested that they got married and that he had told her that he was in no financial position to do so. She replied that she would soon be able to provide for them both and that her parents would give them whatever they needed.

Jane's defence attempted to use the acquittal on the charge of murdering her father as a reason for the jury to return a not guilty verdict but this line was not permitted by the judge.

It took the jury just twenty minutes to find Jane guilty. When asked if she had anything to say as to why sentence of death should not be pronounced upon her, Jane appealed to the judge for mercy and asked that he reduce her sentence to transportation. This in law, he was unable to do. Instead he donned the black cap and sentenced her to death, telling her that 'she was to be taken to the place from where she came and from there to the place of execution on Saturday next, and there hang by the neck until dead, and afterwards the body to be taken down and dissected and anatomised'. Jane sobbed as her sentence was pronounced and had to be helped down from the dock to the cells below. At this time the provisions of the Murder Act of 1752 were still in place, mandating execution within forty-eight hours followed by dissection of the prisoner's body.

In the condemned cell Jane was attended by the chaplain and confessed to the murders of her parents and her two children and also to the many thefts from her parents.

Her execution was set for midday on Saturday, 22 March and attracted a huge crowd with many coming from her native Preston to watch. It was said to be one of the largest gatherings ever at Lancaster for an execution.

In the period from 1800 to 1865, Lancaster executions were carried out at 'The Hanging Corner', a small round tower on the east side of the castle. The balcony style gallows was erected the previous afternoon and consisted of two uprights that were seated into holes cut into the flagstones of the courtyard. A heavy cross-beam ran between the uprights with a platform containing the trap doors beneath it at the level of the bottom of the French windows leading from the 'Drop Room', the platform being draped in a black cloth to hide the legs of the prisoner. High railings surrounded the drop area and the spectators were allowed up to these, within a few feet of the gallows. Many more crowded onto the opposite bank to get a good view of the proceedings.

Jane was brought into the Drop Room from the condemned cell where her hands and arms were pinioned, but as she was so weak it had been decided to wheel her onto the gallows seated in a specially modified office chair, which in those days was rather like a child's high chair. She was therefore wheeled forward through the inward-opening French windows straight onto the platform. On the drop she was taken out of the chair and held up by two female warders, one on either side, whilst the unidentified hangman made the final preparations and the chaplain read from the burial service. Jane seemed barely conscious and was almost oblivious to what was going on around her. When all was ready the trap was released and she dropped a short distance quickly becoming unconscious. After her body had hung for an hour it was taken off the rope and taken in through the small lower window. Jane's body was sent for dissection in accordance with her sentence. The chair is still on display within the Drop Room of the castle.

Thus ended the criminal career of a real 'bad girl'.

Mary Ann Burdock
The Bristol Poisoner

Mary was born in Ross-on-Wye in 1805 and moved to Bristol as a teenager to find employment 'in service' as domestic work was known at the time. Her first job was as a housemaid to a Mr Plumley who lived in St Nicholas Street for whom she worked for eighteen months before being sacked for petty theft.

She now found a boyfriend, a tailor by the name of Agar, whom she soon married and equally soon left for another man. She then spent some time in a relationship with a wine merchant before forming another with a Mr Wade who was a ship's steward. The couple opened a lodging house in the St Phillips area of the city and this seemed to do quite well initially. Mr Wade died and Mary married for the second time to Mr Burdock who was one of the lodgers. Another of Mary's lodgers was an elderly lady of about sixty, called Clara Smith whom Mary and her maid servant, Mary Ann Allen (also given as Alien), looked after. Clara was quite wealthy but did not trust early banks and kept her money in a locked box in her room. It is thought that the box contained some £3,000 which had been left to Clara by her husband who had been a successful ironmonger. This was indeed a great deal of money at the time.

Mary's finances were stretched by 1833 and she decided that the easiest way to top them up was kill Clara and help herself to the money. As usual arsenic was the cheapest and most readily available means to achieve this. Clara died on 26 October 1833 after exhibiting the typical symptoms of stomach cramps and vomiting. The cause of death was given as 'natural' and Clara was buried in St Augustine's churchyard. Mary's lifestyle seemed to suddenly improve after the death of her elderly lodger.

Clara's relatives were suspicious when Mary told them that she had left very little money and in due course reported their suspicions to the police. It was not until the autumn of 1834, fourteen months after Clara's burial, that the police actually took any real interest and interviewed Mary Allen who had helped to look after Clara. Mary Allen told the officers that she had seen Mary Ann Burdock administer a yellow powder to Clara. As a result an exhumation order was obtained from the coroner and Clara's body was removed for examination. The autopsy took place at the Bristol Royal Infirmary on 22 December before several of its leading surgeons. It was immediately noticed how well preserved the body was. Clara's internal organs were sent to the Bristol Medical School, where William Herapath was able to confirm that her stomach contained a large amount of arsenic. He appeared as an 'expert witness' at the subsequent trial. William Herapath had a very high reputation as an analyst and was one of the founders of the Bristol Medical School.

Mary was arrested and charged with Clara's murder, being remanded in custody to await trial at the Bristol Sessions of Gaol Delivery for the City which were held in April 1835.

Mary came to trial at the Guildhall before Sir Charles Wetherell on Friday the 10th of that month, the proceedings lasting three days and concluding on the following Monday. The prosecution was mounted by three Crown lawyers, Mr Smith, Mr Rogers and Mr Cooke, the defence being handled by a Mr Payne, assisted by Mr Stone. The evidence of Mary Ann Allen and William Herapath were crucial in obtaining a conviction.

On Monday, 13 April 1835, Mary Ann was sentenced to be hanged two days later on the Wednesday. She impressed the governor and matrons who looked after her in the condemned cell with her courage.

A huge crowd estimated at some 50,000 had assembled to watch her die and there was the usual carnival atmosphere. Mary's was to be the first female execution on top of the gatehouse of the New Gaol in Cumberland Road. The gallows had been erected the night before. Mary dressed in her best black silk dress for the occasion. She had asked that the prison carpenter line her coffin with flannel and the matron to have her body wrapped in a warm shroud. Due to the passing of the Anatomy Act a year earlier Mary's body did not have to undergo the indignity of public dissection but was to be buried within the precincts of the New Gaol.

The usual procession consisting of the governor, under sheriff, chaplain, turnkeys, the hangman and Mary herself ascended the internal stairs of the gatehouse and appeared on the roof. The crowd became silent as Mary was prepared and the hood and noose applied. Mary held a handkerchief in her hand which she was to drop when she was ready for the hangman to release the trap door. When she had finished her prayers she dropped the handkerchief and the trap fell. Her suspended body could now be seen by the crowd.

Mary's was the first female execution in Bristol for twenty-two years. The previous occasion was when Maria Davis and Charlotte Bobbett were hanged together on 12 April 1802 for the murder of Maria's son, fifteen-month-old Richard Davis.

4

INFANTICIDE AND THE MURDER OF BASTARD CHILDREN

One of the most common female capital crimes was the 'murder of her bastard', as it was called, or infanticide as we would call it now. Looking carefully through the records most cases seem to be genuine murders rather than stillbirths or deaths from natural causes in the first few days of life. Babies were poisoned, had their throats cut, were battered to death, drowned in streams and rivers or even in the privy.

The offenders were typically young women who had got pregnant outside of wedlock and were quickly abandoned by the father. Bear in mind that there was no effective contraception until the early part of the twentieth century.

Such concepts as post-natal depression were not recognised in law until much later nor was the sheer desperation of young women often already living in abject poverty, finding themselves pregnant and then giving birth without any means of support, either financial or moral. There was also the considerable social stigma of single parenthood.

Some seventy-nine women were hanged for this crime between 1735 and 1799 and a further nineteen between

1800 and 1834. The last was twenty-four-year-old Mary Smith who went to the gallows at Stafford on 19 March 1834. It is not always possible from surviving records to know whether a child murder fell into this category or not. Large numbers of women and girls continued to be sentenced to death after 1840 for killing their infant children but were all reprieved.

It wasn't until the Infanticide Act of 1922 that the killing of a newborn baby by its mother was no longer classed as a capital crime. Eleven years later the 1922 Act was amended to remove the death penalty altogether for women who killed their babies in their first year of life.

In some cases it was possible to show that a baby had not been born alive and the mother could then be charged with concealment of the birth but this did not carry the death penalty.

Three cases of the murder of bastard children are examined in this chapter.

Elizabeth Harrard
An Extremely Sad Case

The recovery of the body of a tiny baby boy was carried out by the Beadle of Isleworth, Mr John Thackery, on Saturday, 14 July 1739. He had been summoned to the bank of the Powder Mills River by a local farmer, one Mr Ions who had discovered the baby floating in the river. Mr Ions had taken the baby from the water and placed it on the grass beside the bank. The Beadle examined the corpse and noted that it had only been in the water a short while and was not bloated. He also noted that the little boy had received a severe blow to the left side of the head and that there was congealed blood around the wound. John Thackery took the child to the Stock House and the Middlesex coroner, Mr Wright, was informed of the death. Whilst there Mr Thackery was told that there was a suspicion that one Elizabeth Harrard of Isleworth was the mother of the baby and he duly investigated this. Elizabeth was detained by the Overseers of the Poor for neighbouring Teddington and bought back to Isleworth. She was in a very weak condition and Thackery was ordered to get her a bed as she was too ill to be sent to Newgate Prison.

After Elizabeth's arrest a Mrs Elizabeth Nell examined the prisoner in her capacity as a midwife. Elizabeth told Mrs Nell that she had given birth to a baby, claiming that it had been born on the previous Monday in a field and that she had been disturbed by some men and left the baby. Mrs Nell replied that she did not believe this story and Elizabeth told her that the child was stillborn. Again Mrs Nell said she did not believe this as she could tell from the corpse that the baby had been born alive. It seems that Elizabeth did not realise that Mrs Nell was a professional midwife and when this was pointed out to her, Elizabeth gave another version of events. She now told Mrs Nell that the baby had been born alive and had survived for just fifteen minutes. Elizabeth was resting by the river bank after giving birth and had the child on her lap when it rolled off and fell into the river. Mrs Nell persisted with her questioning and the story changed a little, with Elizabeth now saying that the baby had lived for thirty minutes and that she wrapped it in part of her apron and threw it into the river after it had been dead for an hour. Mrs Nell had examined the corpse after it was recovered and noted that there was no water in it, in other words it had not drowned and felt that the cause of death was a severe blow to the head.

The Inquest was held on Wednesday, 18 July and the coroner directed Mr Thackery to show the body to Elizabeth. She begged him not to saying "tis my own child, born of my own body.' Thackery asked her how she could tell that it was her child without seeing it. Elizabeth continued to insist that it was her child and implored the Beadle not to open the coffin.

The coroner's court found that the child had been murdered by its mother and Elizabeth was committed for trial at the Old

Bailey. This took place on 6 September 1739 and evidence was brought against her by John Thackery and Mrs Elizabeth Nell, with Samuel Goodwin giving evidence for Elizabeth. John Thackery related the above story to the court.

Mrs Thackery, the Beadle's wife, also gave evidence against Elizabeth. Her husband had initially taken Elizabeth to a pub called the Sign of the Bell after her arrest and had asked his wife to look after her. She told the court that she had asked Elizabeth if she was the mother of the baby that had been found and Elizabeth agreed that she was. She also named the father as one John Gadd whom she had lived with for some time but who had deserted her when she became pregnant. She had also had a previous pregnancy by him which had miscarried. Elizabeth confessed to Mrs Thackery that the baby had been born alive and that she had put it into the river. She told Mrs Thackery that she was very poor indeed and had nothing to wrap the baby in, other than an old piece of apron.

In her own statement Elizabeth told the court that on the day the baby died she had walked to Richmond to seek work and had to rest because she had gone into labour. The Beadle of Richmond came to her and refused to get a woman to help her, instead threatening her and telling her to leave the parish immediately. She was similarly treated by Beadle of Twickenham and left in the field by the river to sort out her problems by herself. She told the court that she was in a very poor physical condition by this time and that she did not know whether the baby was dead or alive. Mrs Nell confirmed that Elizabeth had told her of the Beadle of Richmond refusing her any form of assistance.

The only witness for the defence, other than Elizabeth herself, was Samuel Goodwin. He told the court that he had seen Elizabeth with John Gadd on several occasions and that she had told him that Gadd had taken the apron from her after the baby was born, torn off a piece of it and wrapped the baby in it before taking it away. He implied that it was therefore Gadd who had thrown it into the river and not Elizabeth. Against the rest of the evidence this was not really convincing and the jury returned a verdict of guilty against Elizabeth.

She was returned to Newgate to await sentence at the end of the Sessions and was duly condemned to hang. The Recorder did not recommend leniency in Elizabeth's case and so she was scheduled for execution on the next 'hanging day' which was to be Friday, 21 December 1739. With her in the carts that morning were John Albin, John Maw, William Barkwith, James Shields, Charles Spinnel and Thomas Dent, all of whom had been convicted of highway robbery, Richard Turner who was to hang for stealing in a dwelling house and Edward Goynes for the murder of his wife. The usual procession set off for the two-hour journey to Tyburn where the prisoners were prepared by John Thrift and his assistants before all ten were launched into eternity together as the carts were drawn from under them. After they were suspended Susanna Broom was led to a stake that had been set up near the gallows and strangled and then burned for the Petty Treason murder by stabbing of her husband, John.

Elizabeth was one of seven women who were hanged nationally in 1739, and one of four to die for the murder of her bastard child.

It is impossible in this day and age to imagine the mental and physical condition that Elizabeth was in at the time the baby died. She was totally destitute, abandoned by her boyfriend, in great pain, very weak from having just given birth and denied assistance of any kind by the authorities. If indeed she did kill her baby it is not hard to understand the total desperation that led her to do so. However none of these factors, all of which were either known to the court at the time, or were basically self-evident facts, were seen as an excuse for her crime in 1739.

Ann Statham
A Case of Post-Natal Depression?

Ann Statham was an unmarried twenty-eight-year-old woman who had lived with her mother near Wichnor (nowadays spelt Wychnor) between Lichfield and Burton-on-Trent in Staffordshire. Thomas Webster drove the Mail Coach between Birmingham and Derby and had got to know Ann who lived just a few yards from the main road that he traversed each journey. They formed a relationship and she moved to Birmingham to be with him. They had been living together for some ten months at the time of the crime and Ann had quickly become pregnant by him. Unlike some men of the time it seems that Thomas was happy to support Ann and the baby.

In June 1816, the now heavily pregnant Ann moved to Derby where her baby boy was born. She returned to Wichnor aboard Thomas' coach on 23 July, when the baby was five weeks old. She stopped off at nearby Burton-on-Trent on the way back and went to visit John Mason who was a constable in the town. John saw that Ann had a baby with her and heard it cry although he was later to tell her trial that he could not identify the baby as he did not see its face which was covered by a shawl. On the following Saturday John took Ann to the Three Tuns public house in Wichnor and noticed that she did not have the baby with her. He enquired after it and was told by Ann that it had died suddenly, she thought from a fit. She said that she was going to bury the baby at Walton and John offered her money to help with the funeral expenses, which she told him she didn't need.

On the evening of Tuesday, 29 July, Ann was walking along the tow path of the Trent and Mersey canal and was seen with the baby by a bargeman named John Deakin. He testified at her trial that the bank was in poor condition and very muddy.

The wife of the landlord of the Three Tuns, Mrs Thompson had spoken to Ann on the Tuesday evening and she had told her that she had suffered a fit whilst walking along the tow path and dropped the baby, who had fallen into the canal. This surprised Mrs Thompson, as she had known Ann for some years and had never known her have a fit.

The body was recovered by another bargeman, Thomas Wooton, on Sunday, 28 July who spotted a small bundle in a white bed gown and cap floating in the water. He took it to the Three Tuns where it was placed in the store room. First thing on the Sunday morning the body of a baby was viewed by John Mason and it seemed to be about the same age as Ann's baby. John sent for Charles Nicholls, another constable from Burton and he went to Ann's mother's house where she was eating breakfast with her mother and questioned her. When he asked her where her baby was she became agitated and she told him that it was in Derby. He persisted with the questioning, reminding her that she had been seen with the baby near the Three Tuns on the Tuesday evening. Ann simply repeated that the baby was in Derby, an answer that in no way satisfied Constable Nicholls who arrested her. William Challinor, a butcher from Burton, had also seen Ann with the baby when she had visited the town a few days earlier and had been able to see its face so was able to positively identify the dead baby as hers.

Mr Enoch Hand, the coroner who performed the inquest on the corpse, asked Ann if the child had been christened and she told him that it had, as William Statham. Death was found to be due to drowning and it was recorded that there were no marks of violence on the body.

She was taken to Burton and was committed by the magistrates to stand trial at Stafford Assizes, charged with the baby's murder. Charles Nicholls was in charge of Ann for the journey to Stafford Gaol on Tuesday, 8 August and told the court that she had said to him 'Do you think I shall be hung? They cannot hang me for nobody saw me.'

Ann had to wait nearly nine months until the Staffordshire Lent Assizes of 1817 for her trial which took place on Wednesday, 19 March of that year before Mr Justice Park. The prosecution was led by a Mr Dauncey and the various people mentioned above gave evidence against her. Mr Justice Park pointed out the various contradictions in Ann's story to the all-male jury and they returned a verdict of guilty.

Before passing sentence the judge told Ann that the crime of murder of an infant was a particularly heinous one, especially as at one moment it appeared that she had been breastfeeding the little boy and the next she had dropped him into the canal and left him to drown. There was no apparent motive for the crime. Thomas Webster, the father, was happy to support them both and all her friends knew about the pregnancy and birth.

He then passed sentence on her, telling her that 'she was to be taken to the place from whence she came and that on Friday next' she was to be taken from there to the place of execution where she was to be hanged by the neck until she was dead and that afterwards her body was to be delivered to the surgeons for dissection. Ann would become the first woman to be executed at Stafford Gaol.

Ann had now just two days left to live in accordance with the provisions of the 1752 Murder Act. As was customary at many prisons at this time, the gallows was set up over the imposing main entrance of the gaol on the flat roof of the gatehouse, as this location was much easier to guard and afforded the many spectators a good view of the proceedings. On the Thursday the gallows was erected in preparation for the following day. In the condemned cell Ann seemed resigned to her fate and had confessed her guilt to the chaplain. The execution was set to take place between 11 a.m. and noon and a large crowd had assembled in Gaol Square. Soon after 11 a.m. Ann was duly led up onto the gatehouse roof in a procession with the under sheriff, the chaplain and several turnkeys. She ascended the few steps onto the platform of the New Drop style gallows and knelt in prayer with the chaplain. It is reported that the structure collapsed at this point sending Ann, the chaplain, the hangman and the turnkeys into a heap on the roof below. The gallows was quickly repaired enabling the execution to take place an hour or so later. By this time Ann was, unsurprisingly, in a great state of agitation and had to be supported on the drop by two turnkeys whilst the preparations were made. The bolt was released by the unidentified executioner and Ann paid the ultimate price for her crime. Her body was left to hang for the normal hour, before being taken back into the Gaol. It seems that she was not actually dissected but that her body was symbolically cut several times before it was returned to her friends for burial.

If one accepts the evidence against Ann, which is difficult to question 190 years later, it is clear that there was no recognition of the possibility that she was suffering from post-natal depression at the time. Could this explain her actions? As stated earlier it appears that the father was willing to support Ann and the baby and that she was not stigmatised by her friends or in danger of losing her job as the result of her pregnancy and William's subsequent birth. In 1817 she was simply seen as evil and a murderess; now she would be viewed quite differently and be examined by psychologists to determine her motives and her responsibility for her actions.

Strangely the *Staffordshire Advertiser* newspaper makes no mention of the gallows' collapse nor does it give any real details of her execution. However Ann was the last prisoner to be hanged on top of the gatehouse lodge at Stafford. From here on executions were performed on a portable gallows, similar in pattern to the one used at Newgate, drawn out in front of the gatehouse. This arrangement was used for the execution of Edward Campbell for uttering forgery on 16 August 1817, who was the only other person to be hanged in the county that year. Ann was one of seventeen prisoners condemned at the Lent Assizes but the only one to be executed. Only three more women were executed at

Stafford. They were twenty-four-year-old Mary Smith for the murder of her bastard child at Bloxwich who was hanged on Wednesday, 19 March 1834; Ann Wycherley for child murder on 5 May 1838 and finally Sarah Westwood for poisoning her husband with arsenic who was executed on Saturday, 13 January 1844. Male executions continued to be carried out at Stafford until 1914 when part of the prison was turned over to the military during the First World War. Staffordshire executions from hereon took place at Winson Green prison in Birmingham.

Hannah Halley
A Horrible Murder in Derby

Hannah Halley found herself in a seemingly impossible situation. She murdered her newborn infant because she could not keep her job and nurse a baby, and without the job she could not afford to support the child. Thirty-one-year-old Hannah worked at the Darley cotton mill in Derbyshire and gave birth to the baby on Tuesday, 14 August 1821 at her lodgings in Brook Street, Derby.

Earlier that day her landlady and a friend of the landlady had noticed that Hannah looked very unwell and she agreed that she felt ill. She went up to her room where she gave birth a little later and the two women heard the cries of a newborn baby and went up to offer assistance. When they entered the room Hannah denied that she had given birth and was seen putting a jug under the bed which she had previously been trying to conceal under her clothes. Hannah continued with the denial so one of the women threatened to get the local constable and left the room to do so, followed by Hannah. The other woman was then able to recover the jug and was horrified to see the baby inside, dreadfully scalded but still alive. It seems that Hannah had pushed it into the jug and poured boiling water over it. The constable was sent for and arrested Hannah at the house and she was taken to Friar Gate Gaol to await trial for the murder. Amazingly the poor little baby lived until the following Saturday.

It transpired that Hannah had had a child five years earlier so she did know that she was pregnant. It is not known what became of this child.

Hannah had to wait to come to trial until the following March when the next Derbyshire Assizes opened. Her case was heard before Mr Justice Best on Friday the 22nd of that month. She was charged with the wilful murder of her infant and evidence was given against her by the two women, the constable and a doctor. A very clear case was presented to the jury proving not only the act but also the intent to kill, as evidenced by Hannah's frequent denial of her pregnancy. Consequently they had no difficulty in reaching a guilty verdict. Mr Justice Best sentenced Hannah to death and she was taken back to Friar Gate Gaol and lodged in the basement condemned cell for the last two days of her life. Having been sentenced on a Friday and Sunday being a '*Deis non*', the execution was to take place on Monday, 26 March 1822.

The gallows was erected on the pavement outside the main door in preparation. As was normal Hannah received the support and ministrations of the prison chaplain over the weekend and spent much time in prayer with him. It is recorded that she slept only fitfully and appeared almost prostrate with fear and grief. However when the time came she seemed to find reserves of courage and climbed the steps of the gallows with a surprisingly firm step watched by a large crowd. She submitted herself to the necessary preparations and prayed with the chaplain. When all was ready the drop fell and Hannah reportedly died with very little struggle. Her body was afterwards sent for dissection in accordance with her sentence.

Hannah was the last woman to be executed at Derby and one of only two to be hanged outside Friar Gate Gaol. Oddly both were called Hannah, the other being Hannah Bocking three years earlier, who was one of the youngest girls hanged in the nineteenth century. (See Chapter 7 for details of her case.)

Two other women had been hanged in Derby in the period 1735-1799. They were Mary Dilke for the murder of her bastard on 1 January 1754, Mary being executed on Saturday, 23 March 1754 and Ann Williamson who suffered on Friday, 1 August 1755 for picking the pocket of George White at Ashbourne Fair. These executions had been carried out at Nun's Green which was the previous execution site.

5

THE EARLY VICTORIAN PERIOD: 'NOTHING LIKE A GOOD HANGING!'

Queen Victoria ascended to the throne in 1837 at the age of eighteen and her reign saw a great deal of change in the penal system. For the first thirty-one years of it executions were a very public event enjoyed by the masses. People would come from far and wide to witness the spectacle and in some cases special trains were even laid on. Broadsides were sold at many executions giving the purported confessions of the prisoner and there was considerable press interest, particularly when the criminal was female.

Thirty women and two teenage girls were to be executed in England and Scotland in the thirty-one-year period from May 1838 to the abolition of public hanging in May 1868. Of these, twenty-one had been convicted of poisoning (two-thirds of the total). Sarah Chesham was actually executed for the attempted murder of her husband but was thought to be guilty of several fatal poisonings as well. Attempted murder ceased to be a capital crime in 1861 under the provisions of the Criminal Law Consolidation Act of that year. Mary Ann Milner would have made the total thirty-three had she not hanged herself in Lincoln Castle in the early morning the day of her scheduled execution on 30 July 1847. There were no female executions in Wales during this time but a further ten women were hanged in Ireland during the period, all for murder.

Sarah Chesham's case prompted a House of Commons committee to be set up to investigate poisoning. This found that between 1840 and 1850, ninety-seven women and eighty-two men had been tried for it. A total of twenty-two women were hanged in the decade 1843-1852 of whom seventeen had been convicted of murder by poisoning, representing 77 per cent of the total. There were no female executions in the years 1840-1842 in England. This rash of poisonings led to a Bill being introduced whereby only adult males could purchase arsenic. Poisoning was considered a particularly evil crime as it is totally premeditated and thus it was extremely rare for a poisoner to be reprieved whereas it was not unusual for females to be reprieved for other types of murder, such as infanticide. One of the few poisoners to be reprieved was Charlotte Harris in 1849 who had murdered her husband but who was pregnant at the time of her trial.

Five cases are looked at in this chapter.

Sarah Dazley

Sarah was born in 1819 as Sarah Reynolds in the village of Potton in Bedfordshire, the daughter of the village barber, Phillip Reynolds. Phillip died when Sarah was seven years old and her mother then embarked on a series of relationships with other men.

Sarah grew up to be a tall, attractive girl with long auburn hair and large brown eyes. However she too was promiscuous and by the age of nineteen had met and married a local

man called Simeon Mead. They lived in Potton for two
years before moving to the village of Tadlow just over the
county border in Cambridgeshire in 1840. It is thought that
the move was made to end one of Sarah's dalliances. Here
she gave birth to a son in February 1840, who was christened Jonah. The little boy was the apple of his father's eye,
but died at the age of seven months, completely devastating
Simeon. In October Simeon too died suddenly, to the shock
of the local community. Sarah did the grieving mother and
widow bit for a few weeks, before replacing Simeon with
another man, twenty-three-year-old William Dazley. This
caused a lot of negative gossip and considerable suspicion
in the village. In February 1841, Sarah and William married
and moved to the village of Wrestlingworth 3 miles away
and 6 miles north-east of Biggleswade in Bedfordshire.
Sarah invited Ann Mead, Simeon's teenage daughter to live
with them. It seems that all was not well in the marriage
from early on and William took to drinking heavily in the
village pub. This inevitably led to friction with Sarah which
boiled over into a major row culminating in William hitting
her. Sarah had other men in her life throughout both her
marriages and confided to one of her male friends, William
Waldock, about the incident telling him she would kill
any man who hit her. Sarah also told neighbours a heavily embroidered tale of William's drinking and violence
towards her.

William became ill with vomiting and stomach pains
a few days later and was attended by the local doctor,
Dr Sandell, who prescribed pills which initially seemed to
work, with William being looked after by Ann Mead and
showing signs of a steady recovery. Whilst William was still
bedridden, Ann not entirely realising what she was seeing at
the time, observed Sarah making up pills in the kitchen.

Sarah told a friend of hers in the village, Mrs Carver,
that she was concerned about William's health and that she

was going to get a further prescription from Dr Sandell. Mrs Carver was surprised to see Sarah throw out some pills from the pillbox and replace them with others. When she remarked on it, Sarah told her that she wasn't satisfied with the medication that Dr Sandell had provided and instead was using a remedy from the village healer. In fact the replacement pills were those that Sarah had made herself. She gave these to William who immediately noticed that they were different and refused to take them. Ann who had been nursing him and had still not made any connection with the pills she had seen Sarah making, persuaded William to swallow a pill by taking one too. Inevitably they both quickly became ill with the familiar symptoms of vomiting and stomach pains. William vomited in the yard and one of the family pigs later lapped up the mess and died in the night. Apparently, Sarah was able to persuade William to continue taking the pills, assuring him that they were what the doctor had prescribed. He began to decline rapidly and died on 30 October, his death being certified as natural by the doctor. He was buried in Wrestlingworth churchyard. Post-mortems were not normal at this time, even when a previously healthy young man died quite suddenly.

As usual Sarah did not grieve for long before taking up a new relationship. She soon started seeing William Waldock openly and they became engaged at her insistence in February 1843. William was talked out of marriage by his friends who pointed to Sarah's promiscuous behaviour and the mysterious deaths of her previous two husbands and her son. William wisely broke off the engagement and decided not to continue to see Sarah.

Suspicion and gossip were now running high in the village and it was decided to inform the Bedfordshire coroner, Mr Eagles, of the deaths. He ordered the exhumation of William's body and an inquest was held on Monday, 20 March 1843 at the Chequers Inn in Wrestlingworth High Street. It was found that William's viscera contained traces of arsenic and an arrest warrant was issued against Sarah. Sarah, it seems, had anticipated this result and had left the village and gone to London. She had taken a room in Upper Wharf Street where she was discovered by Superintendent Blunden of Biggleswade police. Sarah told Blunden that she was completely innocent and that she neither knew anything about poisons nor had she ever obtained any. Blunden arrested her and decided to take her back to Bedford. What would be a short journey now required an overnight stop in those days and they stayed in the Swan Inn, Biggleswade. Sarah was made to sleep in a room with three female members of the staff. She did not sleep well and asked questions about capital trials and execution by hanging. This was later reported to Blunden and struck him as odd.

The bodies of Simeon Mead and Jonah had also now been exhumed and Jonah's was found to contain arsenic, although Simeon's was too decomposed to yield positive results.

On 24 March 1843, Sarah was committed to Bedford Gaol to await her trial and used her time to concoct defences to the charges. She decided to accuse William Dazley of poisoning Simeon and Jonah on the grounds that he wanted them out of her life so he could have her to himself. When she realised what he had done she decided to take revenge by poisoning William. Unsurprisingly these inventions were not believed and were rather ridiculous when it was William's murder she was to be tried for. In another version William had poisoned himself by accident.

She came to trial at the Bedfordshire Summer Assizes on Saturday, 22 July before Baron Alderson, charged with William's murder, as this was the stronger of the two cases against her. The charge of murdering Jonah was not proceeded with but held in reserve should the first case fail.

Evidence was given against her by two local chemists who identified her as having purchased arsenic from them shortly before William's death. Mrs Carver and Ann Mead told the court about the incidents with the pills that they had witnessed. William Waldock testified that Sarah had said she would kill any man that ever hit her after the violent row that she and William had. Forensic evidence was presented to show that William had indeed died from arsenic poisoning, it being noted that his internal organs were well preserved. The Marsh test, a definitive test for arsenic trioxide had only been available for a few years at the time of Sarah's trial. Arsenic trioxide is a white odourless powder that can easily pass undetected by the victim when mixed into food and drink.

Since 1836 all defendants had been legally entitled to counsel and Sarah's defence was put forward by a Mr O'Malley based upon Sarah's inventions. He claimed that Sarah had poisoned William by accident. Against all the other evidence this looked decidedly weak and contradicted the stories Sarah had told the police. It took the jury took just thirty minutes to convict her. Before passing sentence Baron Alderson commented that it was bad enough to kill her husband but it showed total heartlessness to kill her infant child as well. He recommended her to ask for the mercy of her Redeemer. He then donned the black cap and sentenced her to hang. It is interesting to note that Baron Alderson had, at least in his own mind, found her guilty of the murder of Jonah even though she had not been tried for it.

During her time in prison, Sarah learnt to read and write and began reading the Bible. She avoided contact with other prisoners whilst on remand, preferring her own company and accepting the ministrations of the chaplain. In the condemned cell she continued to maintain her innocence and as far as one can tell never made a confession to either the matrons looking after her or to the chaplain.

There was no recommendation to mercy and the Home Secretary, Sir James Graham, saw no reason to offer a reprieve. The provision of the Murder Act of 1752, requiring execution to take place within two working days had been abolished in 1836 and a period of not less than fourteen days substituted. Sarah's execution was therefore set for Saturday, 5 August 1843. A crowd variously estimated at 7,000–12,000 assembled in St Loyes Street, outside Bedford Gaol to watch the hanging. It was reported that among this throng was William Waldock.

The New Drop gallows was erected on the flat roof over the main gate of the prison in the early hours of the Saturday morning and the area around the gatehouse was protected by a troop of javelin men. William Calcraft had arrived from London to perform the execution.

Sarah was taken from the condemned cell to the prison chapel at around 10 a.m. for the sacrament. The under sheriff of the county demanded her body from the governor and she was taken to the press room for her arms to be pinioned. She was now led up to the gatehouse roof and mounted the gallows platform, accompanied by the prison governor and the chaplain. She was asked if she wished to make any last statement which she declined, merely asking that Calcraft be quick in his work and repeating 'Lord have mercy on my soul'. He pinioned her legs, before drawing down the white hood over her head and adjusting the simple halter-style noose around her neck. He then descended the scaffold and withdrew the bolt supporting the trap doors. Sarah dropped some 18in and her body became still after writhing for just a few seconds. Sarah was left on the rope for the customary hour before being taken down and the body taken back into the prison for burial in an unmarked grave.

It was reported by the local newspapers that the crowd had behaved well and remained silent until Sarah was actually hanged. Once she was suspended they carried on eating, drinking, smoking, laughing and making ribald and lewd remarks. Copies of broadsides claiming to contain Sarah's confession and her last dying speech were being sold among the crowd, which amazingly people bought even though she had made neither.

The 1840s were a time of great hardship nationally and yet Sarah, whilst hardly wealthy, did not seem to suffer from this and it was never alleged that she was unable to feed her child or that she was destitute. Extreme poverty in rural areas did appear to be the motive in some murders at this time, especially of infants. Sarah's motive seems to be a much more evil one – the elimination of anyone who got in the way of her next relationship.

Sarah's was the first execution at Bedford since 1833 and she was the only woman to be publicly hanged there. In fact Bedfordshire executions were rare events and there were to be only two more in public, Joseph Castle on 31 March 1860 for the murder of his wife and William Worsley on 31 March 1868 for the murder of William Bradbury.

Sarah Westwood

Sarah and John Westwood had been married for some twenty years by 1843 and lived in the parish of Burntwood near Lichfield in Staffordshire, the parish in which this book was written.

John was a nail maker and was assisted in his small business by his son, seventeen-year-old Charles. It seems the family were fairly poor. The household, by 1843, comprised Sarah, John, Charles and four younger daughters. Three older children had already left home. Additionally there was a lodger named Samuel Phillips who had lived with the Westwoods for some seven years and whom Sarah was believed to be having an affair with. There had certainly been quarrels between John, Sarah and Samuel. One of these took place on 2 September in the street and was witnessed, the two men fighting and rolling around on the ground while Sarah watched. John is alleged to have screamed at Samuel 'Damn your eyes, what was you doing at her when I knocked you down?' Sarah was shouting at Samuel to kill John. When the fight subsided Sarah threatened to leave John. Another violent quarrel was witnessed by John's brother, Robert Westwood, at his home.

On Thursday, 9 November John and Charles returned home to lunch as normal and John had some gruel, bread and meat for his meal. He was in the habit of reading a few pages from the Bible after lunch and then having a brief nap before returning to work. On this afternoon he rapidly complained of stomach pains and soon began vomiting. Charles came home from work later in the afternoon and heard his mother ask John if he wanted her to get the local surgeon in to see him. For whatever reason, he refused this and died later in the evening.

John had been in generally good health prior to this day and so his death was regarded as suspicious and a post-mortem was ordered. This was carried out by Mr Charles Chevasse of Lichfield who found a large quantity of arsenic in John's stomach so an inquest was therefore held. This took place before the Staffordshire coroner, Mr Thomas Philips, and returned a verdict of poisoning against Sarah who was arrested on Monday, 20 November by Inspector John Raymond from nearby Shenstone police station. Sarah complained to the inspector that she could not obtain bail. He told her that bail would be out of the question on a murder charge to which she replied that no one could prove she had murdered John.

The police investigated the source of the arsenic and were able to trace the purchase of it to Heighways Chemists in Walsall, some 10 miles away, on 1 November. Sarah had gone to the shop with Hannah Mason who was Samuel's mother and known locally as 'a wise woman'. Hannah made a special remedy for a common complaint known as 'the itch' which contained four ingredients, hellebore, red precipitate, white precipitate and arsenic. Hannah mixed up the ingredients in the shop. On 8 November Sarah returned alone to Heighways where she was able to purchase a further supply of the chemicals, as they remembered her having come in a few days previously with Hannah whom they trusted. This time the chemicals were left in their separate packets.

Although there were normally only two assizes a year at Stafford when there were large numbers of criminals awaiting trial a third could be organised and this took place on Thursday, 28 December 1843. Baron Rolfe was the presiding judge, Mr Corbett led the prosecution and Mr Yardley the defence. Various witnesses were called by the prosecution, including ten-year-old Eliza Westwood, who recounted asking her mother what the white powder was in her father's gruel. Both she and her brother Charles also told the court that none of the children suffered from 'the itch' which was the alleged reason for buying the chemicals. Hannah Mason told of the shopping expedition to Walsall at the beginning of November.

The forensic evidence was presented and as usual evidence to show that John had been in good health immediately before lunch on the day of his death. In his submission to the jury Mr Corbett suggested that Sarah wanted to be rid of John so that she could have Samuel Philips and that this was the motive for the murder.

Mr Yardley addressed the jury for some three hours in Sarah's defence and did all he could to show that she may not have been guilty. He reminded them that Sarah had asked John if she wanted her to send for the doctor but that it was he who had refused medical attention. He suggested that John may have committed suicide as he had been depressed since the early summer. His efforts were to no avail and it took the jury just fifteen minutes to find Sarah guilty. They made a recommendation to mercy, but when the foreman was asked why by Baron Rolfe he could offer no reason for doing so. Sarah continued to protest her innocence and then claimed she was pregnant. A panel of matrons was sworn in and within an hour they declared her not to be with child.

Sarah was visited in Stafford Gaol by her son Charles and daughter Harriet but Samuel Phillips was not permitted to see her which caused her much distress.

The Home Secretary, Sir James Graham, found no reason to intervene in the case, so an execution date of Saturday, 13 January 1844 was set.

Sarah received the sacrament from Rev. George Norman on Friday the 12th but was so weak that she had to be carried to and from the prison chapel. Despite his entreaties she resolutely refused to make a confession.

She was reported to have slept little on the Friday night but to have managed two cups of tea and some bread and butter on the Saturday morning. Sarah had to be carried to the gallows by two warders and once on the platform was allowed to sit on a stool while George Smith, who was Stafford's usual hangman, made the preparations. She was attended on the gallows by the usual officials, the under sheriff, the governor and the chaplain. Her last words were reported as 'It's hard to die for a thing one's innocent of'. At 8 a.m. Smith released the trap doors and Sarah and the stool dropped. The execution was witnessed by a large crowd, comprising a majority of woman. It would seem that her sufferings were quickly over.

She was the last woman to suffer at Stafford and her body is buried within the precincts of the gaol.

Maria Manning
'The Bermondsey Tragedy'

Maria Manning was born in Switzerland in 1821, her maiden name being de Roux. She emigrated to Britain and worked in London as a lady's maid to the wealthy Lady Blantyre, who was the daughter of the Duchess of Sutherland. Here she

developed a taste for a luxurious lifestyle, amid the elegance
of her employer's homes and general finery. She dreaded the
idea of poverty, a very real state for so many at this time in
history and resolved that she would never live like that. Lady's
maids, if they worked for a good employer, could enjoy a
life way beyond that of ordinary girls of the time. My own
grandmother was one in the early twentieth century and
travelled much of Europe at a time when most people had
seldom been further than the next town. So it was that in
1846 Maria went across the Channel on the boat to Boulogne
with her employer and met Patrick O'Connor, a fifty-year-
old Irishman who worked as a customhouse (customs) officer
in London's docks. Patrick was a man of independent means
and his wealth immediately attracted Maria.

Maria was also involved with Frederick George Manning,
who worked as a guard on the Great Western Railway, not a
very well-paid job. Both men proposed to her, the problem was
deciding which one would make the better husband. Frederick
was the same age as her and was the weaker character. Patrick
was much older and also a heavy drinker. Frederick promised
Maria that he was soon to come into money via an inheritance whereas Patrick seemed already to be well off and had
told Maria that he had a large amount of money invested in
foreign railway stocks. In the event, Frederick won the day and
the couple married in St James' church, Piccadilly, in May 1847.

They were able to afford a fairly stylish home in Miniver
Place, in London's Bermondsey area. However, Maria had
realised by now that Frederick was not going to get the promised inheritance. She still kept in contact with Patrick and was
probably having an affair with him, with the apparent acquies-
cence of Frederick. Maria felt she had married the wrong man
but was determined that she would have Patrick's money, if
not his person, and hatched a plan to kill him.

She purchased some quicklime and a shovel and on
8 August 1849 invited Patrick to dinner. He duly arrived but

had brought a friend with him which scuppered Maria's plan. So she invited him again for the following evening, telling him to come alone so that they could be more intimate with one another. When he arrived the next evening, Maria suggested that he may wish to wash his hands before dinner and as he stood at the sink to do so, she shot him in the head with a pistol. The bullet wound did not kill him and Frederick had to finish Patrick off by battering his head in with a ripping chisel (crowbar). The two of them then buried the body in a pre-dug grave below the kitchen flagstones, covering it with plenty of quicklime, which was thought to speed decay of the flesh, and was ironically what they too were to be buried in.

The following day Maria went to Patrick's lodgings and managed to con her way into his rooms where she systematically went through his belongings, taking everything of value including his share certificates. She paid a further visit the following day to see if there was anything she had missed. Two days later the Mannings got a nasty fright when two of Patrick's colleagues came to their house looking for him as he had told them he was eating there on the evening of the 9th. Maria admitted that he had eaten with them on the 8th but denied having seen him since. They went away leaving Maria and Frederick thoroughly unnerved. The couple suspected that the men were in fact detectives, so they decided to leave London immediately. Maria sent Frederick to try and sell their furniture and as soon as he had gone, packed everything of value that she could carry and ordered a cab to take her to King's Cross railway station where she caught a train to Edinburgh. Frederick decided to leave the country and went by train and ship to Jersey.

Patrick's colleagues had by this time reported him missing to the police and expressed their suspicions about the Mannings. The police decided to visit Miniver Place and while carrying out a thorough search of the premises noticed that the mortar between two of the flagstones in the kitchen was still damp. The flagstones were lifted revealing the battered and bloody body of Patrick. A manhunt was commenced to find the Mannings. The cabman who had driven Maria came forward and described how he had taken her to one station, where she deposited two trunks, before taking her on to King's Cross. Superintendent Haynes of Scotland Yard, who was in charge of the investigation, was able to find out that Maria had bought a ticket for Edinburgh and telegraphed the information to his Scottish counterparts. They had in fact already arrested her for trying to sell some of Patrick's railway stock to a firm of Edinburgh stockbrokers who had heard about their theft in London and were suspicious of Maria's French accent. Thinking that they were about to be the victims of fraud they sent for the police. She was duly brought back to London and charged with Patrick's murder, being remanded in custody at Horsemonger Lane Gaol.

Frederick was arrested a week later in Jersey where he had been spotted by a man who had known him in London and who had read about the murder in the papers. On his return to London, the man went to the police and a Scotland Yard detective, Sergeant Langley, was sent out to make the arrest as he happened to know Frederick. He was traced to a rented room in St Laurence and was found asleep in his bed on 21 August. Once in custody he told police that it was Maria who had shot Patrick. He also told the police, 'I never liked him so I battered his head with a ripping chisel'. He was brought back to London, charged with the murder and also remanded at Horsemonger Lane Gaol.

It seems clear that Maria's motive was purely greed, although she was willing to grant Patrick sexual favours, she was really only interested in his money. Whether Frederick conspired with her in this to boost his parlous financial situation is unclear; or whether he just finished off Patrick out of dislike for the man whom he saw as his rival for Maria's attentions and out of fear that if Patrick survived, he would betray them to the police. At this time, attempted murder was still a capital crime and it was probable that Maria at least, and quite possibly both of them, would have been hanged just for trying to kill Patrick. So it was clearly better to kill him and dispose of the body as quickly as possible in the hope of escaping detection.

For geographical convenience the couple were moved from Horsemonger Lane to Newgate Prison for the two-day trial which opened at the Old Bailey on Thursday, 25 October before Chief Justice Cresswell. Both were represented by counsel and the respective lawyers tried to shift responsibility for the killing from their client to the other's client. It seemed that both Frederick and Maria expected the other to shoulder responsibility but neither would. At the end of the trial, it took the jury forty-five minutes to convict them. Maria lost the composure she had shown during the trial and screamed at the jury, 'You have treated me like a wild beast of the forest.' She continued to rave at the judge as he tried to pass sentence on her. They were taken back to Newgate and then across London to Horsemonger Lane Gaol to await their executions. She is said to have asked the warders escorting her how they had liked her performance in court.

Horsemonger Lane Gaol was built between 1791 and 1799 in Southwark, South London, as the county prison for Surrey, being renamed the Surrey County Gaol in 1859. The Mannings were to spend just over two weeks in its condemned cells. Maria was considered a suicide risk by the authorities and was guarded by teams of three wardresses who slept in the cell with her, much to her disgust. She was able to lull them into a false sense of security and had let her fingernails grow long. While they were asleep, she tried to strangle herself and puncture her windpipe with her own hands and it took the combined efforts of all three to stop her.

Maria had written a letter to Queen Victoria, whom she had met as a servant to Lady Blantyre, asking for a reprieve which was, of course, denied. It is said the Queen did study Maria's letter and took an interest in the case but concluded that her guilt was proven. It is also said that Maria wrote to Frederick while awaiting execution, exhorting him to take the sole blame for Patrick's death. This he refused to do. He did, however, make a confession stating that Maria had shot Patrick and that he had finished him off. This was probably about the truth of the matter.

Their executions were set for the morning of Tuesday, 13 November 1849 and were to attract one of the largest crowds ever to attend a public hanging. It is estimated that between 30 and 50,000 people came to see it and it was equally popular with the upper classes as with the poor. Every available space was filled with spectators and several hundred policemen were on hand to marshal the crowd. Many fashionable ladies had come to watch and were fascinated and later infuriated by what Maria had chosen to wear for the occasion.

The gallows was erected on the flat roof above the main gate at Horsemonger Lane. It was described as 'a huge, gaunt and ominous looking structure.' William Calcraft officiated and Maria became the twentieth woman that he would put to death.

Their execution was fully reported in *The Times* newspaper as follows:

> At a quarter past eight Manning and his wife entered the prison chapel. The Sacrament was administered to them when the governor appeared and said that time pressed. Calcraft also came forward and the wretched pair were conducted to different parts of the chapel to be pinioned. The operation was performed on the male prisoner first and he submitted to it with perfect resignation. In the pinioning of Mrs. Manning a longer time was occupied. When

the cords were applied to bind her arms her great natural strength forsook her for a moment, and she was nearly fainting, but a little brandy brought her round again, and she was pinioned without any resistance. She drew from her pocket a black silk handkerchief and requested that she might be blindfolded with it, a request that was acceded to. Having had a black lace veil fastened over her head, so as to completely conceal her features from the public gaze, she was conducted to the extremity of the chapel, where the fatal procession was at once formed and in a slow and solemn manner moved forwards towards the drop, the prison bell tolling.

The procession passed along a succession of narrow passages, fenced in with ponderous gates, side rails and chevaux de frise of iron. In its course a singular coincidence happened. The Mannings walked over their own graves, as they had made their victim do over his. Mrs. Manning walked to her doom with a firm, unfaltering step. Being blindfolded she was led along by Mr. Harris, the surgeon. She wore a handsome black satin gown.

At last nine o'clock struck and shortly after the dreadful procession emerged from a small door in the inner side of a square piece of brickwork which rests on the east end of the prison roof. To reach this height a long and steep flight of stairs had to be climbed, and it only wonderful that Manning, in his weak and tottering state, was able to ascend so far. As he ascended to the steps leading to the drop his limbs tottered under him and he was scarcely able to move. When his wife approached the scaffold he turned round with his face towards the people, while Calcraft proceeded to draw over his head the white nightcap and adjust the fatal rope. The executioner then drew the nightcap over the female prisoner's head and all the necessary preparations now being completed the scaffold was cleared of all it occupants except the two wretched beings doomed to die. In an instant Calcraft withdrew the bolt, the drop fell, and the sentence of the law was fulfilled. Frederick died almost without a struggle while Maria writhed for some seconds. Their bodies were left to hang for the customary hour before they were taken down and in the evening buried in the precincts of gaol.

Scarcely a hat or cap was raised when the drop fell and the bodies of the murderers had hardly ceased to oscillate with the momentum of their fall before the spectators were hurrying from the spot.

It is claimed that Maria and Frederick made up on the gallows and that she kissed him before they were executed as a sign of forgiveness for not taking all the blame. Whether this is true or not we will never know.

Charles Dickens attended the execution and wrote a letter to *The Times* expressing his revulsion at the proceedings. Dickens was one of a number of influential people who campaigned against public hangings at this time.

The case attracted enormous public interest, especially because of the sexual intrigue and scandal element, which was much rarer and much more shocking then. Maria was perceived as the dominant partner in the marriage and the prime mover in the murder, two other unusual features of the case. Most murders, then as now, were simple and sordid affairs with little of real interest in them. There were the attempts at escape and the brutal nature of the crime to add to the interest. By 1849 newspapers were far more available and the case made the headlines.

It was convenient too that Maria was Swiss-born and therefore a foreigner. As one witness to her execution remarked in a letter to *The Times*, 'Thank God she wasn't an English woman' – in other words the reputation of England was unsullied by the crime.

One feels that Charles Dicken's indignation was far more due to the attitude of the crowd towards the hanging than through any concern for the Mannings and their sufferings. People thoroughly enjoyed a 'good hanging' and when the prisoners were a husband and wife from reasonable circumstances, it was an added bonus. Some of the wealthier spectators had paid a lot of money to get good vantage points overlooking the gallows, and fashionable ladies were using opera glasses to get a better view. It is probable that many in the crowd were disappointed by the fact that both of them died without any real struggle. This was certainly the case at the execution of the famous poisoner, Dr William Palmer, hanged at Stafford in 1856, who became still almost immediately to the disgust of the crowd. Victorian England was full of hypocrisy and publicly expressed disgust at this sort of prurience while privately enjoying it immensely. Public hangings were a perfectly legal form of sadistic and voyeuristic entertainment and after all, the victims were murderers so one could justify going to watch their punishment as it was a good moral lesson. It is unlikely that many in the crowd felt any sympathy for the Mannings in their final moments but rather just a morbid fascination with the 'show'. Even the 'stars of the show' often entered into the spirit of the event somewhat, by wearing their best clothes. What Frederick wore was not recorded but it was probably a smart suit. Maria chose the fashionable black satin dress and veil, to ensure she presented a good appearance at the end. Black satin, as a dress material, promptly went out of fashion and stayed so for nearly thirty years as a result.

Maria also made it into Madame Tussaud's Chamber of Horrors, and it is probable that Calcraft sold them the dress. Tussaud's would most likely have sent an artist to court to draw her face to be sure of getting a good likeness. An amazing 2.5 million broadsides were printed for this execution.

The Stackpooles
A Family Affair

Twenty-year-old James Stackpoole was due to receive an inheritance of £65 a year from the estate of a deceased uncle when he came of age (twenty-one) in May of 1853, an amount that would have made him the wealthiest member of his family at the time. Under the terms of the will his uncle, Thomas, would receive this inheritance in the event of James' death.

A plot was hatched by James' relatives, sister Honora and cousins Richard and Bridget, who were married to each other, together with uncle Thomas to kill James. Accordingly the young man was invited to Thomas' home in Blanealiga, near Miltown Malby in Southern Ireland on Saturday, 18 September 1852. James had retired to bed and was asleep when the four relatives entered the room and dragged him out of bed and began battering him with fire tongs and brass candlesticks. James pleaded for his life and offered his uncle the price of four cows to spare him. However the murderous onslaught continued, all four beating him and finally dragging him downstairs to the kitchen where Richard killed him with two axe blows to the head. Thomas made one of the servants, John Halpin, strike James with a candlestick to prevent him incriminating the family by making him part of the crime. Bridget and Honora disposed of the remains which were discovered the following day by eleven-year-old Michael Mulqueeny, at Belford Bridge (also referred to as Swallow Bridge). James' hat and boots were left with the body. Michael reported the find to a Mrs Morony who alerted the police in the form of Constable May. On the Monday morning Bridget and Honora laundered the blood-stained clothes that they had been wearing the previous night. They made little attempt to remove all the blood spatters from the house though and these were later spotted by Constable May.

At the house the constable arrested Bridget, Honora and her husband Tom, John Halpin and a servant girl, named Flanagan. He and Magistrate Mr Morony arrested Richard Stackpoole the next day. Mr Morony cautioned Richard to say nothing to incriminate himself but Richard wanted to talk and said: 'I will tell you, I may as well tell the truth; I hear they are [metaphorically] hanging each other; I will save my own neck.' Mr Morony told him he could not offer him a plea bargain and that he could make any statement he wanted at the inquest but that anything he did say could be used in evidence against him.

The coroner, Mr Francis O'Donnell, held a formal inquest on James which returned a verdict of murder and placed the responsibility for the crime on the four family members, who were committed for trial.

Their cases were heard by the Crown Court on Wednesday, 23 February 1853 before the Honourable Justice Perrin at Ennis. Richard Stackpoole was tried first before a twelve man jury with a Mr Herrick leading the case for the prosecution. The jury heard evidence from Michael Mulqueeny who discovered James' body, John Halpin, the servant and eleven-year-old Anne Stackpoole who also was able to give the court a detailed account of the murder, as she was present in the house at the time. Constable May described the details of the arrest which were corroborated by Mr Morony the magistrate who described the statement Richard gave to him.

Mr O'Hea led Richard's defence and cross-examined the various witnesses. He made an eloquent closing speech to the jury before Mr Justice Perrin summed up. The jury retired for about an hour returning to find Richard guilty of wilful murder. He seemed completely unmoved by the verdict. Bridget and Honora were tried the following day on the same evidence and both convicted. Thomas was too ill to face trial with the others at this time and his trial was deferred to the next assizes.

All three were sentenced to death at the end of the assizes on Saturday, 26 February and transferred to Ennis Gaol to await execution. Here they were attended by Roman Catholic clergymen and began to take interest in religion and acknowledge the gravity of their crime.

The executions took place on Friday, 29 April 1853 and attracted a large crowd. The gallows was erected early on Friday morning outside Ennis Gaol and a large number of local people had turned out to witness the hangings. The gallows was only big enough for a double execution and it was decided that Richard and Bridget would be hanged first as they had expressed a wish to die together.

At about 12.30 p.m. they were brought out from the Gaol accompanied by officials and clergymen and mounted the platform where they prayed together. The usual preparations were made and the drop fell at around 12.40 p.m. According to the report in the *Clare Journal & Ennis Advertiser*, Bridget died without a struggle while Richard 'lingered' for a few minutes. Their hooded bodies were left to hang for an hour. At 1.45 p.m. Honora was led to the gallows to undergo the ultimate punishment of the law. She too died without a struggle, becoming the last woman to be publicly hanged in Ireland.

All three bodies were buried within the prison later in the day.

Thomas Stackpoole was initially reported to be recovering from the illness that had prevented his trial but relapsed and later died in prison before the start of the next assizes.

This seems to be a crime of pure greed typified by almost reckless stupidity. The murder was committed in the presence of the servants and the children and little or no effort was made to destroy the evidence of a particularly brutal crime.

Strangely the previous female execution at Ennis had many similarities. Thirty-two-year-old Bridget Keogh was hanged with one of her brothers, Patrick Howe, for the axe murder of Arthur O'Donnell on 27 July 1850. Her other brother, John Howe, was too ill to be tried. Again the motive was robbery.

Elizabeth Martha Brown(e)
The Inspiration for *Tess* of the *D'Urbervilles*

Elizabeth Martha Brown was an ordinary woman of humble birth who worked as a servant. It is thought that she was born in 1810 or 1811 and that her maiden name was Clark. Not much else is known about her early years. She became the last woman to be publicly hanged in Dorset, and is remembered as the inspiration for Thomas Hardy's famous novel *Tess of the D'Urbervilles*. She had been married to Bernard Bearn, who died in 1841.

Elizabeth was eighteen years older than her husband, John Anthony Brown, and they had met in 1848 when she was housekeeper to a farmer and he a farmhand. She came into a small inheritance and used this for marriage on 24 January 1852 and to open a shop. They lived at Broadwinsor in Dorset.

It was claimed at the time that he had married her for money, as well as for her looks. He was a waggoner who owned a horse and wagon. On 5 July 1856, he left home with his wagon for a trip to Beaminster, a distance of some 2 miles, and did not return until around midnight. John came home drunk and without his hat. Elizabeth remonstrated with John over the loss of the hat and he responded by hitting her with his horse whip and kicking her. This was the last straw for Elizabeth, who retaliated by hitting him over the head with the wood-chopping axe, smashing his skull and killing him sometime between 2 and 3 a.m. on 6 July. Elizabeth suspected her husband was having an affair with one Mary Davis for about twelve months. It seems that jealousy was the principal motive, together with revenge for his ill treatment of her.

She was arrested but claimed that her husband's death had been caused by being kicked in the head by a horse. The police did not believe this and thus she was charged with murder on 7 July 1856.

Elizabeth came to trial at Dorset Summer Assizes at Dorchester on 21 July 1856 before Mr Justice Channel. The jury did not believe the horse story either and brought back a guilty verdict after a lengthy deliberation. The mandatory death sentence was passed and she was returned to Dorchester Gaol to await her execution some three weeks later. Elizabeth would have been treated very well in prison, where she would have been looked after by two matrons and received the ministrations of the chaplain, Dacre Clemetson.

There were obvious mitigating circumstances, which led to substantial agitation for a reprieve. Reprieves for murder, although rare, were by no means unknown. There was, however, much public sympathy for her in view of the abuse she had suffered at the hands of her husband. The Home Secretary, however, refused a reprieve even in view of the evidence of obvious provocation, perhaps because Elizabeth had made the fatal mistake of maintaining, virtually to the last, the lie that her husband had died from a horse kick. Elizabeth became 'locked into' this lie as so many have before and since. Ultimately, in the condemned cell, on the eve of her execution, she confessed that she had killed John with the axe and, therefore, was responsible for his death. She accepted her fate with great courage. Diminished responsibility was not a defence open to her in 1856; it would be another 101 years before it was recognised in English law. Elizabeth made a full confession to the murder on the Thursday before her execution:

My husband John Anthony Brown, deceased, came home on Sunday morning, 6 July at 2 am in liquor and was sick.

He had no hat on. I asked him what he had done with his hat. He abused me and said 'what is it to you, D...n you?' He then asked for some cold tea. I said that I had none, but would make him some warm. He replied 'Drink that yourself, and be D...d'. I then said 'What makes you so cross? Have you been at Mary Davis's?' He then kicked out the bottom of the chair that upon which I had been sitting.

We continued quarrelling until 3 am, when he struck me a severe blow on the side of my head, which confused me so much that I was obliged to sit down. Supper was on the table and he said 'Eat it yourself, and be d...d'. At the same time, he reached down from the mantlepiece a heavy horse whip with a plain end and struck me across the shoulders with it three times. Each time I screamed out.

I said 'If you strike me again I will cry murder.' He retorted 'If you do, I will knock your brains through the window'. He also added 'I hope I shall find you dead in the morning'. He then kicked me on the left side which caused me much pain, and he immediately stooped down to untie his boots.

I was much enraged and in an ungovernable passion, on being so abused and struck, I directly seized a hatchet which was lying close to where I sat and which I had been using to break coal with to keep up the fire and keep his supper warm, and with it (the hatchet) I struck him several violent blows on the head, I could not say how many.

He fell at the first blow on his head, with his face towards the fireplace. He never spoke or moved afterwards. As soon as I had done it I wished I had not, and would have given the world not to have done it. I had never struck him before after all his ill-treatment but when he hit me so hard at this time, I was almost out of my senses and hardly knew what I was doing.

Signed Elizabeth Martha Brown.

Strangely, if Elizabeth had told the truth in the first place she may well have only been convicted of manslaughter and received a prison sentence.

The under sheriff of Dorset was responsible for Elizabeth's execution, appointing William Calcraft as the hangman. Calcraft was Britain's principal executioner from 1829 to 1874, the longest serving hangman of all. The execution was set for 9 a.m. on Saturday, 9 August 1856. Calcraft travelled to Dorchester by train and arrived at the prison the day before.

The gallows was erected on the roof of the gatehouse of Dorchester prison the evening before. The prison chaplain, Dacre Clemetson, was so overcome with emotion that he declared himself unable to accompany Elizabeth on her final journey and asked her parish priest, Henry Moule to deputise for him.

A crowd of between 3,000 and 4,000 had gathered. To add to the public interest Elizabeth was an attractive woman, who looked younger than her years and had lovely hair. She was also incredibly brave in the face of death – so much so that Henry Moule regarded it as a sign of callousness. She had chosen a long, tight-fitting thin black silk dress for her hanging. She climbed the first flight of eleven steps where William Calcraft, a forbidding figure in his black clothes and bushy white beard, pinioned her arms in front of her before leading her up the next flight of nineteen steps, across a platform and on up the last flight of steps to the actual trap. Here he put the white cotton hood over her head and the halter noose around her neck. He then began to go down below the trap to withdraw the bolts (there was no lever on the platform), when it was pointed out to him that he had not pinioned Elizabeth's legs. He returned to her and put a strap around her legs, outside of her dress to prevent it billowing up and exposing her as she hanged. While this was going on, Elizabeth stood stoically on the trapdoors, supported by a male warder on each side just waiting to die. The rain made the hood damp and it clung to her features, giving her an almost statuesque appearance. It must also have made it hard for her to breath through the damp cloth.

Once again, Calcraft went below and pulled the bolts thus releasing the trapdoors with a resounding thud. Elizabeth fell a distance of about a foot. Death was certainly not instantaneous and she struggled hard for a few moments before losing consciousness as the rope constricted the major blood vessels and put pressure on the nerves in her neck. She was left to hang for the regulation hour before being taken down and buried within the prison in a plain elm coffin at one o'clock. Her execution caused a leading article in the *Dorset County Chronicle* advocating the abolition of the death penalty.

Thomas Hardy was a boy of sixteen when he went to watch this spectacle with a friend and was able to secure a good vantage point in a tree very close to the gallows. He noted 'what a fine figure she showed against the sky as she hung in the misty rain, and how the tight black silk gown set off her shape as she wheeled half round and back', after Calcraft had tied her dress close to her body. It made an impression on him that lasted until old age, he still wrote about the event in his eighties. It seems possible that Hardy found something erotic about the execution and particularly her body and facial features through the tight dress and rain-soaked hood.

James Seale became the last person to be publicly hanged in Dorset when he was executed for the murder of Sara Guppy. He went to the gallows two years later, on 10 August 1858, an event also witnessed by Hardy.

6

VICTORIAN CHILD MURDERS

The cases of nine women who murdered children are examined in this chapter.

Ann Wycherly
Her Child was an Encumbrance

Ann was a twenty-eight-year-old mother of two illegitimate children who in December 1837 was living with the children in the workhouse at Drayton (now Market Drayton) in Shropshire, just over the Staffordshire border. She would have been described at the time as a dissolute young woman. The older of her two children was a girl of three, also called Ann, who was not well treated by her mother according to the witness testimony of another of the workhouse's inmates. The younger child was an infant whom Ann had conceived with her then lover, Charles Gilbert.

Ann left the workhouse with her two children on Thursday, 14 December and the three were recognised early in the afternoon by a James Freeman. By 6 p.m. Ann was exhausted and knocked on the door of the cottage of one Sarah Newbrook, asking her if she could rest there for a while. Sarah allowed her to do so and noted that she only had the infant child with her.

On Friday, 22 December William Poole, a farm labourer saw something floating in a pit on his employer's land near Chipnal. He went and informed the farmer, Mr Butters, and between them the two men were able to pull the small object out of the pit and onto the bank where they were no doubt horrified to see it was the body of a little girl.

An inquest was held at the Noah pub and William Crutchley the governor of the Drayton workhouse identified the body as that of Ann Wycherly. The inquest found that the cause of death was drowning but noted that the girl's body and head had several bruises. William Crutchley obtained an arrest warrant from the local justices of the peace and went in search of Ann. He found her soon after in service at Baldwin's Gate where, assisted by two local constables, he arrested her. He showed Ann the girl's body and noted her reluctance to look upon it and even greater reluctance to touch it. He asked Ann why she had killed the girl and she told him that she would not have done so had Charles Gilbert not persuaded her to do so. According to Ann, Gilbert had helped get the poor girl into the pit and had then thrown tiles at her. This would account for the bruising found on her. Ann was remanded to Stafford Gaol by the local magistrates to await her trial.

She was tried at the next assizes which took place on Wednesday, 14 March in the courtroom of the imposing Shire Hall in Market Square, Stafford, which can still be visited today. Her case was heard by Baron Alderson with the prosecution led by Mr Corbett. William Crutchley gave evidence against her and told the jury how she had left his workhouse with the two children and of her confession to him. Catherine Biffen, another girl from the workhouse, told the jury about

Ann's mistreatment of her daughter and Mr Hopkins, the surgeon from Drayton, gave evidence of the cause of the little girl's death.

In his summing up Baron Alderson told the jurors that even if someone else had been the instigation for Ann to carry out the murder, that did not in anyway diminish her guilt or responsibility for the crime. The jury did not even retire before finding Ann guilty.

Baron Alderson now proceeded to sentence Ann to death and asked if she had anything to say. She told him 'she was with child'. He therefore ordered the courtroom doors to be locked and empanelled a jury of matrons from the women in the public gallery to see if she was pregnant. Ann and the other women were sent off to the Grand Jury room where after close examination that took best part of an hour she was declared not to be quick with child. Before he left Stafford, Baron Alderson decided to respite Ann until 5 May just in case the matrons had been mistaken. As they hadn't been Ann was to suffer her punishment on that day. Her execution was set for 9 a.m. on that Saturday, instead of the usual 8 a.m. to enable the London Mail coach to arrive, in case there was a reprieve.

After the problems experienced with the collapse of the gallows at Ann Statham's hanging in 1819 a new portable gallows had been built, of similar pattern to the one used at London's Newgate prison. This was wheeled out in front of the prison in the early hours.

In the condemned cell Ann had told the Governor, Thomas Brutton, that she was not afraid to die and again implicated Charles Gilbert in the killing. On the Friday the gaol chaplain, the Rev. Buckeridge gave her the Sacrament.

A few minutes before 9 a.m. on the Saturday the usual procession emerged from the main gate of the prison to the solemn tolling of the prison bell. It was headed by the sheriff of the county, Thomas Brutton, followed by Rev. Buckeridge, Ann, two turnkeys and the hangman. Ann was able to climb the steps up to the platform unaided where she prayed with the chaplain before being pinioned, hooded and noosed. As the chaplain read the burial service the drop was operated and Ann fell a short distance into the box-like structure. According to the local newspaper she struggled for less than a minute before hanging still. At 10 a.m. her body was taken down and moved into the prison for burial in the small graveyard that was adjacent to the solitary confinement cells. Unusually this execution only drew a small crowd as it was thought a reprieve was likely.

It seems that the motive for the killing was that the child was an encumbrance to the new relationship and neither Ann nor Charles Gilbert wanted her.

Ann was one of two women and two men who were condemned at the same assizes but the other three were all reprieved. The other woman was fifty-nine-year-old Hannah Heath who had also been convicted of killing a child. It was reported that Baron Alderson was surprised by the jury's guilty verdict in her case and obviously recommended a reprieve.

Harriet Parker
Murder for Revenge

New Year's Day 1847 was to be the last day that Amina and Robert Henry Blake would ever see. They were brother and sister aged eight and five respectively and were suffocated in their father's bed by his jealous partner, thirty-eight-year-old Harriet Parker.

Robert Blake senior had begun a relationship with Harriet two years previously and had left his wife Esther and moved from Birmingham to London to live with her.

On New Year's Eve Robert had been drinking heavily and came home in the afternoon and demanded that Harriet make him something to eat and boil some water for him to wash in before he went to the 'Stump' in Old Street to meet a another woman, probably a prostitute. Harriet followed Robert out but he told her that he was determined to meet the woman. She stayed with him and they met up with a friend of his, Stephen Hewlett. They arrived at the Stump and Robert again said he was going to meet the other woman there and kissed the post. A row erupted and Robert punched Harriet in the mouth. They then went into a pub called the Duke of Bedford where Robert managed to lose Harriet. She was alleged to have told Stephen 'that it was a good job you didn't go out with him. He'll repent in the morning and I'll die like a strumpet at Newgate'. She continued 'I'll have my revenge on the children if I can't have it on him'. Stephen was concerned by Harriet's threats and followed her home to Cupid's Court. He had noticed that she had a heavy object wrapped in her handkerchief with which she had presumably meant to use on Robert. He asked if she was all right and Harriet responded that she had something very black on her mind and that she would stop it before long. 'You will hear of me before you see me.' Stephen accepted these strange comments and left. A little later Harriet put the children to bed and when she was sure that they were both asleep she suffocated them one at a time with the bedclothes.

At 4 a.m. the next morning Harriet woke her neighbour Mrs Moore to tell her what she had done and to pour her heart out to her over her treatment by Robert the previous evening. The local constable, Constable Fowler, was called and having seen the bodies of the two children he arrested Harriet, who told him that she had been intending to kill them for ten months. She also told him that 'I knew well what I was about'. Amina had a small abrasion on her throat and it was clear that both she and Robert had been suffocated.

Harriet was charged with both murders and remanded to Newgate to await trial. She appeared at the Old Bailey on Friday, 4 February 1848 and as was normal in multiple murder cases, the prosecution only proceeded with one of the two charges, that of the killing of Amina. Robert Blake gave evidence which largely confirmed Harriet's version of the New Year's Eve events. He also told the court of his unfaithfulness towards Harriet on previous occasions. The jury deliberated for ten minutes before finding her guilty but recommended Harriet to mercy on the grounds of Robert Blake's provocation. This was rejected by the judge who reminded them that it was not Robert Blake that she had killed but rather his defenceless children. The judge asked Harriet if she had anything to say before he sentenced her to death and she shouted out 'God forgive you Blake! You have bought me to this.'

Harriet acknowledged the heinousness of her crimes and went to great lengths to avoid prison staff from touching her in Newgate because she feared that they be contaminated by her. Through the ministrations of the Ordinary she seemed to have become truly penitent whilst waiting for her fate and read the Bible a great deal. In fact she wanted to send Robert Blake the Bible with a personal inscription in it.

With the help of the Ordinary, Harriet wrote a letter to Robert Blake on 7 February saying:

Dear Robert,

This is the last time you will ever receive advice from me. My days are numbered. This day fortnight I shall be silent in the grave. Take, therefore, these few lines into consideration; never again trifle with a woman as you have with me. Promise to forsake all others and cling once again to her who ought to hold the only place in your heart – the wife of your bosom. This, Robert, is what I sincerely wish. I have deeply injured her and so have you. Let her, then, after this have your best and purest affections. I deserve my awful fate and God give me strength to go through it all. I freely forgive you for all your wrongs to me. Be warned, Robert, and remember that those who break the sacred tie pledged at the altar of God will never prosper; more than

one within these walls can testify to the truth of this by
bitter experience.

She went on a little further asking him to settle several small
bills for her.

Harriet was hanged outside Newgate at 8 a.m. on
Wednesday, 23 February 1848 by William Calcraft. The
under sheriff claimed her body from the governor and she
was led from the condemned cell to the Press Room where
her hair was cut short to avoid fouling the noose and her
arms and hands pinioned. She was then led out through the
Debtor's Door and here thanked the governor and her jailers
for their kind treatment, before ascending the gallows with
a firm step, preceded by the Ordinary. She was positioned
on the trap and Calcraft placed the hood over her head and
the noose around her neck while she prayed fervently. The
trap was released and Harriet dropped a foot or so, writhing
and convulsing at the end of the rope for some moments
before becoming still. She was taken down after an hour and
buried within Newgate under the flagstones in the passage
that connects the prison to the Old Bailey in a cheap pine
coffin with quicklime sprinkled over her corpse. Her initials
were later carved into the wall above her resting place to
enable identification of the grave.

The execution was widely reported in the press and a broadside was sold at her hanging which was attended by what one
newspaper described as 'a dense mass of human beings' who
shouted, hooted and whistled at her.

Was Harriet temporarily insane through jealousy and Blake's
abuse of her at the time of the killings? It seems a reasonable
proposition. The McNaughten Rule as a legal test of sanity
had been introduced five years earlier in 1843 and classified a
prisoner as insane if they did not have sufficient mental capacity to understand the nature of their acts or that such acts were
wrong. Against this definition Harriet could have no defence

of insanity as she clearly did know what she was doing and that it was wrong. Although the court might have accepted a defence of provocation if she had killed Robert Blake it was not really possible to extend this to the killing of the children as the judge pointed out to the jury.

Eliza Joyce
Children Are Such Troublesome Things

William Joyce was a gardener who lived in Boston in Lincolnshire with his two children, William and Emma, from his first marriage. He remarried in 1840 to twenty-seven-year-old Eliza, who was to bear him another daughter, christened Ann, at the end of 1842. The marriage appeared to be happy one and they were not living in abject poverty, as were so many at this time. Sadly Emma had died of apparently natural causes in October 1841 and Ann in early 1843.

Fifteen-year-old William had been ill for some time and was visited by Dr Smith on 13 September 1842. His treatment seemed to help and William had recovered somewhat by Friday the 16th. Eliza went into town and purchased some arsenic that day for killing vermin, or so she told the chemist who was reluctant to supply the poison. The chemist happened to see William Joyce senior the following day and told him that Eliza had bought arsenic from him. William immediately returned home and collected the poison and took it back to the chemist who noted that some of it was missing. Dr Smith called at the house later that day and found William junior had deteriorated considerably. His father told the doctor about the arsenic and a sample of William's vomit was analysed and found to contain it. He began to recover and was well enough to make a sworn statement before the mayor in which he alleged that it was his stepmother who had administered the arsenic to him. William died at Christmas time 1842 and as a result Eliza was charged with his murder, coming to trial at the Lincolnshire Spring Assizes. The indictment against her was thrown out because the name of the victim had been wrongly given as Edward William Joyce. Indictments had to be absolutely correct.

Eliza remained in prison until 18 July 1843 when she returned to court to face a charge that had now been reduced to attempted murder. Up to 1861 attempted murder still carried the death penalty so this might have been less of a relief than it seems. However it could not be proved that William's death was attributed to the arsenic that Eliza had given him the previous September. Although there was no doubt that Eliza had bought arsenic she claimed that she had dropped some of it on the floor and used a teaspoon to pick it up with. Later she had used the same spoon to give William his medication. The jury believed this and Eliza was found not guilty.

William Sr, who did not share the jury's view, had by now separated from Eliza over the strange deaths of his children. She was forced to go into Boston Workhouse to support herself. Here she made a confession to the overseer, Mr Sturdy, that not only had she poisoned William but had also murdered both the other children, Emma and Ann. Emma had died of apparently natural causes in October 1841 but according to the confession had actually been poisoned with laudanum. Laudanum is an opiate that was cheap and widely used during the nineteenth century as a pain killer and sleeping draught, but like all opiates it is dangerous in excess. Eliza told Mr Sturdy that she had given Emma two teaspoonfuls and that the girl had died very quickly afterwards. Baby Ann was born on New Year's Day 1842 and on 21 January 1843, Eliza gave her a dose of laudanum which caused her death the following day. Dr Ingram, the family's doctor, who attended both girls, certified the deaths as having been due to convulsions. Eliza was asked by Mr Sturdy why she had killed the children and she is said to have replied 'I don't know, except I thought it was such a troublesome thing to bring a family of children

into this troublesome world.' Ann was once again arrested and
committed to Lincoln Castle to await trial. This took place
on Thursday at the Assize Court within the castle grounds
18 July 1844 and lasted less than an hour. Eliza's confessions
were read to the court and she acknowledged the validity of
them. She was duly condemned and her execution set for
Friday, 2 August 1844.

From 1817 the New Drop pattern gallows at Lincoln was
erected for each execution on the roof of Cobb Hall, a large
tower forming the north-east bastion of the castle and visible from the street below. It was accessed by the prisoner and
officials via a spiral stone staircase within the tower leading
up to the roof level. When Eliza woke on her final morning
she looked out of the window of her cell and was horrified
to be able to see the gallows. She was described as being in
'a state of considerable self-possession' when she first woke
but somewhat overcome by what she saw from the window.
However she soon recovered her composure and reportedly
discussed the procedure for her execution with the matrons
guarding her.

Four to five thousand people came to watch the hanging
at noon. The castle bell was tolling and at five minutes before
the hour Eliza was brought out onto the roof of Cobb Hall by
two gaolers, accompanied by the under sheriff of Lincolnshire,
Mr Williams, the governor, Captain Nicholson, the chaplain,
the Rev. W.H. Richter and William Calcraft the hangman.
Eliza was wearing the typical long black dress, as worn by
most condemned women of the period and was carrying a
small prayer book. As was not unusual she was not pinioned
at this stage. It is recorded that she took a final look over the
city before she climbed the last few steps up onto the platform of the gallows where Calcraft strapped her arms, wrists
and legs and removed her bonnet before he applied the hood
and noose. Exactly at noon Calcraft released the trap and Eliza
fell a short distance through it, dying without a struggle. She

dangled on the rope for an hour and then was taken down and buried the following morning within the Lucy Tower.

Her execution was reported by the local papers of the time.

The previous female execution at Lincoln was that of Elizabeth Warriner on Thursday, 26 June 1817 who had also poisoned her stepson. Eliza was the last of five women to be hanged in public at the castle during the nineteenth century, all for murder.

It seems that Eliza's death did not have the deterrent effect that the authorities had hoped for because three years later another woman, Mary Ann Milner, was to be hanged at Lincoln for administering arsenic to her sister-in-law. It is thought that she also murdered her mother-in-law and her niece. Mary Ann's execution was scheduled for 21 July 1847 but she hanged herself in her cell that morning, to the great disappointment of the assembled crowd. Her suicide led to the practice of guarding condemned prisoners round the clock and never leaving them alone in their cells.

Ann Lawrence
She Killed for Revenge and out of Jealousy

Strangely the last two women to be publicly hanged in Britain both died in front of Maidstone Gaol some sixteen months apart, each for the murder of a child.

Twenty-nine-year-old Ann Lawrence was separated from her husband, Stephen, by whom she had a four-year-old son, Jeremiah, known as Jesse. Mother and son were living with Ann's boyfriend, Walter Highams, in their terraced cottage at No.2 Ebury Cottages in Tunbridge Wells in Kent.

In the early hours of Saturday, 14 April 1866 Ann killed Jesse and attempted to murder Walter. John Allen was passing the cottage on his way to work when he was startled by the door opening and a blood-stained woman running out shouting 'murder!' and 'go for a policeman – I'll give myself up.' Mr Allen did as he was bid and went to fetch the constable. He sent another neighbour, Edmund Cavey, back to the cottage to find out what had happened. Mr Cavey arrived at the cottage to find Ann still attacking Walter Highams. Mr Cavey went for to get some more help and with two other men was able to rescue Walter from Ann. Walter staggered next door where his neighbours looked after him and treated his wounds until he could be taken to hospital where he had two fingers amputated. In the meantime Constables Henley and May arrived and took charge of the situation. They took Ann back into the cottage and she told them that Walter had killed her child. The police soon made the grim discovery of the little boy, lying on his bed in an upstairs room with his throat deeply cut and the razor still in the wound. Ann began screaming 'I want my child' and the policeman told her that he was dead. She persisted and told them that her child was alive and well, as indeed it was when they went back upstairs and discovered a nine-month-old baby.

Initially she told the constables that Walter had killed Jeremiah, who was his stepson and that this had caused her to attack him with a billhook (a small chopper with a hooked blade that is used for chopping firewood). She claimed that she acted in self-defence as she thought Walter intended to kill her too.

Superintendent Embery arrived on the scene at about 6.30 that morning and began questioning Ann about the events. She still persisted in the story that Walter had murdered Jeremiah and that she had attacked and had intended to kill him. Embery decided to arrest Ann and take her to Tunbridge Wells for further questioning. Enough evidence was unearthed to be able to charge her with both the murder of Jeremiah and the attempted murder of Walter.

Ann came to trial at Maidstone on 20 December, her case occupying two days. She was arraigned before Sir W.F. Channell on two counts, murder and attempted murder but the latter was not proceeded with. She pleaded not guilty to the charge of Jeremiah's murder.

The prosecution case was opened by Mr Sergeant Parry Q.C. and Ann was skilfully defended by Mr Ribton and Mr Ormerod who probed every avenue to try to get an acquittal for her.

The court heard evidence from Walter Highams, who described the frenzied attack on himself but had not witnessed the actual murder as he was asleep at the time. Evidence was given by the two constables and the neighbours. Dr Richard Davy, the House Surgeon at Tunbridge Wells Infirmary, who had examined the body of Jeremiah and afterwards the clothes Ann was wearing at the time of arrest, explained to the jury that the pattern of blood stains he had found on the dress was consistent with what he would expect from slitting the throat of a child and the severance of the main arteries. The jury deliberated for three hours before reaching a guilty verdict. Before Ann was sentenced to death she was asked, as was customary, if she had anything to say and she said that she wished to make a statement. Once again she affirmed her innocence of the murder and told the court that her conscience was clear. The judge then passed sentence on her and she was taken back to Maidstone Gaol to await execution.

Another murderer was also convicted at this assize, twenty-year-old James Fletcher, a Derbyshire miner, who had battered to death prison warder James Boyle with a hammer in Chatham Prison part-way through serving a seven-year sentence. Although Ann and James had been convicted of separate offences they were to hang together, which was still normal practice and remained so up to 1875 when Elizabeth Pearson was hanged at Durham alongside two men convicted of unrelated murders. Up to the end of 1903 female prisoners were hanged with co-defendants of either sex, but the practice ceased after this.

Ann was to be the first woman to hang at Maidstone Gaol. The last female execution in Kent having taken place over sixty years earlier when Elizabeth Barber suffered for the murder of John Daly at the old execution site at Penenden Heath on 25 March 1805. As was now usual when a woman had been sentenced to death, a petition had been got up by well-meaning local people to save her but the Home Secretary was unmoved by this and had to take into account the violence of the crimes.

Death warrants were received for both prisoners on Saturday, 5 January and these were read to them by the governor of Maidstone Prison, Major Bannister. Ann told the governor that she hoped her execution would be carried out.

The gallows was erected outside the main gate in County Road during Wednesday. The structure comprised a platform supported by heavy beams, containing the trapdoors, and surrounded by a railing. In the centre there was a simple gallows consisting of two uprights and a cross-beam with two iron chains for attachment of the ropes. The drop was reached by a short flight of steps and the lower portion beneath the platform was draped with black cloth to prevent the crowd seeing the legs and lower body of the prisoners. This gallows was to be used the following year for the execution of Francis Kidder.

It is recorded that Ann slept well on the Wednesday night prior to her execution and ate a good breakfast. She particularly asked that her baby not be given to Walter after her death and arrangements were made for it to go into Maidstone workhouse at Coxheath.

William Calcraft arrived at the prison around 11 a.m. on the Thursday, 10 January 1867 and made his preparations. Both Ann and James Fletcher were given the sacrament in the prison chapel during the morning by the Rev. W. Fraser and then taken to reception cells which were close to the gallows. Calcraft pinioned their wrists in these cells before they were led out just before noon. James was brought out first and when Calcraft had him positioned on the trap he was hooded and noosed. Ann was led onto the gallows, accompanied by a warder and knelt for some time in prayer before being led onto the trap besides James. A white cotton hood was drawn down over her head and the halter-style noose adjusted around her neck. Although she appeared faint she was able to retain a considerable degree of composure until the end and could be heard repeatedly saying 'Jesus, have mercy' whilst the final preparations were made. As the drop fell a woman in the crowd let out a shriek. Ann died quite easily for the time and did not appear to struggle for long. As usual broadsides were sold among the crowd at the execution.

Ann's husband, Stephen Lawrence, had tried to gain admittance to the prison and had to forcibly removed by the police. It is not known whether he joined the crowd to watch his estranged wife die. It was estimated that some 4,000 to 5,000, including a large number of women, had assembled in County Road to do so.

On the Sunday before her execution Ann had asked to see the governor, Major Bannister, to whom she gave a full confession and accepted responsibility for the murder. She told him that she could not remember how she had done it because she was so enraged at the time. She also told him again that she hoped that she would not reprieved and that she wanted her death. She also apologised for having tried to incriminate Walter Highams.

Her motives began to unfold and she related that the main reason for both crimes was jealousy over Walter's affairs with other women and her wish to avenge herself on him for them.

Ann had been working as servant when she first met Walter, who after his wife had left him in 1864, had invited Ann to live with him. She decided to leave her husband, Stephen Lawrence, for Walter soon after Jeremiah was born. The couple often rowed and it was usually over Walter's other relationship.

Prior to Ann going to live with him he had been having an affair with a young woman, one Miss Eaglington in the nearby village of Town Malling, whom he had got pregnant. He continued to see her after the relationship with Ann had started and a second pregnancy ensued. This led to a physical fight between Ann and Miss Eaglington in January 1866. Four days before the murder Walter had sent Ann up to London to buy produce for his fruit and vegetable shop in Tunbridge. Thinking that she would be away overnight he again went to see Miss Eaglington but Ann returned on the Wednesday evening and found out where he had gone which led to a major row the following day, culminating with Ann hitting Walter on the head. On the Friday Walter took Jeremiah out with him delivering and the child had a fall and got his clothes dirty. This led to further friction between them. Ann thus went to bed that night consumed with jealousy and rage and sadly poor Jeremiah was the principal victim.

It would seem that Ann was genuinely sorry for what she had done and that her execution bought her closure, rather than having to live in prison for twenty or more years with her conscience.

Frances Kidder
The Last Woman to Hang in Public

Frances Kidder made history by becoming the last woman to be publicly hanged in Britain, when she was executed at Maidstone at midday on Thursday, 2 April 1868.

Twenty-five-year-old Frances had been born in 1843 to John and Frances Turner of New Romney in Kent. She married William Kidder in 1865 as she was pregnant by him and she gave birth to the baby daughter they named Emma before the marriage. What Frances did not know at the time was that William had two children by a previous relationship with a woman called Staples. The younger child was sent to live with relatives after its mother died but his daughter, Louisa, who was about ten years old, came to live with Frances and William at Hythe in Kent. From the outset things did not go well between Louisa and Frances. Although corporal punishment in the home was considered normal in the 1860s, Frances inflicted wanton cruelty on the little girl who turned from being a typical lively ten-year-old into a withdrawn and sullen girl over the next two years. Frances beat the child with anything that came to hand, made her wear rags and often deprived her of food. She was also frequently excluded from the house, irrespective of the weather, or was made to sleep in the cellar with old sacks for bedding. Such was the abuse that their next-door neighbour, William Henniker, reported William and Frances to the police who charged Frances with cruelty for which she was fined. Louisa was sent to live with a guardian. However William did not make his regular maintenance payments to the guardian and Louisa was returned to them. Louisa's presence rekindled France's resentment and the abuse of the little girl resumed. William and Frances began to quarrel over her treatment of his daughter and at least once he threw Louisa out of the house.

Frances helped William in his work as a potato dealer and in July 1867 was quite seriously injured in an accident when she was thrown from their horse and cart due to the horse bolting. The accident may have caused brain damage. In any event she took some time to recover from it and it did nothing to reduce her enmity towards Louisa. On 24 August 1867, she had taken Louisa to visit her parents in New Romney and also took her own daughter, Emma, with her. She was to tell her parents' neighbour, Mrs Evans, of her feelings towards Louisa and that she intended to get rid of her before returning to Hythe.

On the Sunday Frances told her parents that she was ill and would not be going out for a walk with them, preferring

to stay at home with the children. Once they had left she
suggested to Louisa that they visit a nearby fair and told her
that it would be sensible to change into their old clothes
before going. This they did and then started out on foot
for New Romney. They came to Cobb's Bridge and it was
here that Frances grabbed Louisa and forced her into the
stream that ran under the bridge. She held the girl's face
down in the stream and drowned her in less than a foot of
water. Frances' father and her husband who had come to
collect his wife and daughter started searching for them.
Frances got back to her parents' house just before William
returned and he immediately noticed that Louisa was not
with her. Neither William nor his mother could get a satisfactory explanation from Frances as to Louisa's whereabouts.
She ran upstairs to her bedroom and was discovered by her
father, having changed into dry clothes. He found her previous clothes which were very wet and muddy but could get
nothing out of her regarding Louisa. In view of the history
of violence towards the girl, he and William decided to go
to the police. Constable Aspinall returned with her father
and husband and took Frances into custody on suspicion of
Louisa's murder. The constable questioned her and she told
him that Louisa had fallen into a ditch after being frightened
by passing horses near Cobb's Bridge. A search was organised
and little girl's body was soon discovered. It was removed to
the Ship Inn to await an inquest and Frances was charged
with murder. The coroner's inquest opened the next day
and heard various witness testimonies which led to a verdict that Louisa had been murdered by her mother. She was
thus taken before the magistrates for a committal hearing
who remanded her in custody to appear at the Kent Spring
Assizes at Maidstone. She was transported to Maidstone
Prison the following day, suffering fits during the journey
and having to stop at Ashford Police Station until they subsided. She remained on remand for over six months and was

ministered to by the chaplain, Rev. W. Fraser, who managed to teach her to read and get some grasp of religion. William did not visit her on remand and it was rumoured that he had started a new relationship with Frances' younger sister who had been helping him look after Emma.

Frances' trial took place at Maidstone on 12 March 1868 before Mr Justice Byles and was to last six hours. She had a court appointed barrister, Mr Channell, to defend her. The prosecution brought in evidence of the widespread abuses of Louisa and of previous threats to kill her. A local doctor who had examined Louisa at the Ship Inn told the court that the girl had died from drowning but that he had found no marks of violence on her body. Mr Channell suggested to the jury that some of the witness evidence against Louisa, whilst not actually lies, may well have been exaggerated, but made little of the injuries sustained in the accident with the horse and cart and the effect of them on her mental and physical health, nor of the doctor's findings of no marks of violence on Louisa's body. Frances clung to her defence of the two of them being frightened by the horse and of Louisa falling into the water, from where she claimed she had tried to rescue her. Mr Justice Byles made a careful summing up and told the jury that they were to give Francis the benefit of the doubt if they were not wholly satisfied with the largely circumstantial evidence against her. All of this was rejected by the jury after just twelve minutes of deliberation. Francis had shown an interest in the proceedings and particularly in the judge's summing up but was calm when she was sentenced to death and walked unaided from the dock.

In the condemned cell, she confessed the murder to Rev. Fraser. She was visited twice by William whilst here and on both occasions they quarrelled over his relationship with her younger sister, which he strongly denied at the first meeting although he admitted it at the second. She was also visited by her parents and Emma. She frequently became hysterical while awaiting her death and this behaviour continued until the moment she was hanged.

The execution was set for midday on Thursday, 2 April and William Calcraft again officiated. The gallows that had been used to execute Ann Lawrence the year before was again erected for the hanging outside the main gate in County Road.

Around noon the under sheriff of the county, the chaplain, Calcraft and the other prison officers formed up outside her cell and Calcraft went in to pinion her, with a strap around her body and arms at elbow level and another around her wrists. She was then led out across the yard to the main gate which opened to reveal the gallows. Frances had to be helped up the steps onto the platform and held on the trapdoors by two warders where she prayed intently while Calcraft made the final preparations. Her last words were 'Lord Jesus forgive me'. With that Calcraft released the trap and she dropped some 18in, struggling hard for two or three minutes, writhing in the agonies of strangulation. A well behaved but quite small crowd estimated at 2,000 people, a lot of them women, had come to watch her final moments although they could only see the top half of her body above the platform. Her body was left hanging for an hour before being taken down and buried in an unmarked grave within the prison. There was some sympathy for Frances in the press and amongst the public. *The Times* commented on the way William had treated her and the fact that he had deserted her in prison and taken up with her sister. It was reported that an effigy of him was burned in Hythe after the execution.

On 29 May 1868 Parliament passed the Capital Punishment (Amendment) Act ending fully public hanging. Six more men were to die in public before this Act came into force. The last of these was Michael Barrett who was hanged at Newgate on 26 May for his part in the Fenian bomb outrage in Clerkenwell.

Mary Anne Barry
'An Accessory Before the Fact'

Although after 1868 the law required that executions be carried out within prisons, these early non-public executions were by no means private and some forty to fifty people were present in the prison yard at Gloucester on the morning of Monday, 12 January 1874 to witness the execution of two men and one woman. They were Charles Edward Butt, Mary Anne Barry and Edwin Bailey. Curiously both their victims had died on the same day – Sunday, 17 August 1873.

Edward Butt, aged twenty-two, had shot and killed twenty-year-old Amelia Selina Phipps out of jealousy because she would not have a long-term relationship with him. They were near neighbours on adjoining farms at Arlingham. Amelia was friendly towards Edward but simply did not want him, a fact that he seemed unable to accept. They had at least two violent quarrels and in the end he blasted her with a shotgun. He was duly arrested and charged with the crime, coming to trial at Gloucester Assizes on Christmas Eve 1873. The jury rejected his contention that the shooting had been an accident.

Mary Anne Barry aged thirty-one was employed by Edwin Bailey, who was a year older than her, to clean his shop but there may well have been more to the relationship than this. Edwin owned a shoe shop in the Clifton area of Bristol and was a married man with a disabled wife who lived in London. He was known as a bit of a menace to young girls and some of the local servant girls would not go into his shop to take repairs.

Seventeen-year-old Mary Susan Jenkins (known as Susan) worked as a servant in Clifton and had accused Edwin of sexually assaulting her in his shop, although she did not report the matter to the police. Strangely she continued to visit the shop after this incident and had some sort of relationship with Edwin, as a result of which she became pregnant. She gave birth to a baby daughter named Sarah on 23 October 1872. Edwin denied paternity and Susan was forced to obtain a court order for maintenance, which he resented. The court fixed a sum of 5s a week and it was paid over to the local constable, Constable Critchley in Stapleton. Susan took the baby to live with her parents in Stapleton just on the outskirts of Bristol. She returned to work in Clifton in December 1872, leaving her mother in charge of Sarah.

In late December of 1872, Mary Anne, just going by the name of Ann, started to visit Susan's mother and seemed to take to the baby.

Susan met Ann for the first time in the early New Year of 1873. Mary Anne brought Sarah little gifts and claimed that the ladies of the Dorcas Society, a Christian charity, had taken an interest in the child. The visits continued and in May Susan asked Ann if the Dorcas Society had forgotten about her as she had heard nothing from them.

Sarah began teething and Ann recommended the use of Steedman's Soothing Powders. These were not something the Jenkins family could afford, however. On 13 August 1873 Susan Jenkins received a letter apparently from the Cotham Dorcas Society, signed by Jane Isabella Smith, and containing three packets labelled 'Steedman's Soothing Powders'. On 17 August, Susan unsuspectingly gave one of the powders to little Sarah who quickly went into convulsions and died, her body rigid and arched. A doctor who arrived after the baby's death was shown the two remaining packets of powder and examining the contents immediately became suspicious. The police were called and Constable Critchley took charge of the powders, the letter and envelope that they had come in. He had had dealings with Edwin Bailey over the maintenance payments for Sarah and noticed that the handwriting on the letter and envelope were just like Edwin's.

A post-mortem was carried out on the baby, which con-cluded that she had been poisoned by the contents of the packets. The packets were genuine but their original contents had been removed and replaced by a rat poison containing strychnine, a fact that was confirmed by the county analyst.

An inquest was opened at the Volunteer Inn in Stapleton on 18 August and adjourned until 5 September. Edwin was present at the second hearing and heard Constable Critchley's evidence regarding the similarities of the handwriting. He was bound over to be present at the next hearing scheduled for a week later but did not show up for it.

Meanwhile the police had been making enquiries about the woman 'Ann' who had been visiting the baby which led to the arrest of Mary Anne Barry at her lodgings in Bristol on 14 September. Mary Anne was really Anne Salmond but had taken her common-law husband's name of Barry. She made a statement to the police in which she said that Edwin sent her on errands including visiting the Jenkins to try and find out who Sarah's father really was, as he absolutely denied he was. Nothing she said incriminated Edwin or helped her own position however.

Edwin had gone to London to visit his wife, having made preparations to leave the country immediately afterwards, but she persuaded him to stay and they returned to Bristol where he was arrested at his shop.

Edwin and Mary Anne were tried together before Mr Justice Archibald at Gloucester Assizes on Tuesday, 23 December 1873, the day before Edward Butt. Mr Justice Archibald told the jury that 'Edwin Bailey and Mary Anne Barry are accused of causing the death of Sarah Jenkins by poison, or rather I ought to tell you that the prisoner Bailey has been committed as principal in the offence and Mary Anne Barry as an accessory before the fact.'

The paper of the letter purporting to come from the Dorcas Society was traced to Edwin and the handwriting matched his according to handwriting expert Mr Charles Chabot, who appeared for the prosecution. No evidence was offered by the defence counsel. It took the jury an hour to reach a verdict of guilty against both defendants and they were accordingly condemned to death. The jury made a recommendation to mercy for both of them. Presumably the trial judge did not support this and did not make a similar recommendation to Robert Lowe, the Home Secretary. Petitions for a reprieve were got up locally but no reprieve was to be forthcoming and an execution date of 12 January 1874 was fixed.

William Calcraft was not available for this hanging due to ill health, so instead the job was offered to Robert Anderson (Evans) from Carmarthen in Wales, by the under sheriff of Gloucestershire. Anderson suggested that the platform of the gallows be mounted over a pit to make it level with the prison yard and this modification was done. The platform was enclosed by a 4ft-high black calico screen.

The hangings took place at 8 a.m. and when the prisoners had been pinioned in their cells they were led out in a procession, headed by the chaplain. Edward Butt and Edwin were wearing suits and Mary Anne a long print dress. She was accompanied to the gallows by the matron of Gloucester Gaol, whilst Edwin was accompanied by the governor, Captain H.K. Wilson. The rest of the party comprised the deputy governor, the chaplain, the prison doctor and several warders.

The three condemned prisoners knelt on the platform and recited the Lord's Prayer with the chaplain before submitting to the final preparations. Mary Anne was placed between the men on the trap, their legs were tied and the white hoods placed over their heads, followed by the nooses. The chaplain and the hangman shook hands with each prisoner and then Anderson withdrew the bolt releasing the trap doors and causing the prisoners to drop below the level of the calico screen. The two men died almost without a struggle but Mary Ann Barry suffered longer and Anderson had to press down upon her shoulders to quicken her death.

A black flag was hoisted over the prison to show that the executions had been carried out and after the formal inquest their bodies were buried wearing the clothes they were hanged in, in unmarked graves in the execution yard, with quick lime thrown into the coffins.

The chaplain revealed that both Edwin and Mary Anne had confessed their guilt to him and Anderson said that Mary Anne had whispered to him on the gallows that she had dreamt she would die like this.

Mary Anne Barry became the last woman to suffer death by the short-drop method of hanging in Britain and the last woman to be executed at Gloucester Gaol.

We are left wondering what her motive was in helping with the baby's murder and whether she was trying to save Edwin, if indeed he was her lover, although we have no clear evidence of that.

Frances Stewart
The Murderous Grandmother

Fanny Stewart, as she was known, was the first woman in England to be hanged by the newly introduced 'long-drop' method when she was put to death in the execution shed at London's Newgate prison on Monday, 29 June 1874 by William Marwood, who succeeded William Calcraft.

Frances was a forty-three-year-old widow who was convicted of drowning her one-year-old grandson, Henry Ernest Scrivener, after a quarrel with her son-in-law. She lived with her daughter Henrietta and Joseph Scrivener at Lordship Place, Chelsea in London. Joseph had accused his mother-in-law of breaking the door of the hen house, which she denied and this led to an acrimonious quarrel, with Joseph telling Frances that either she would have to go or they would. On the evening of Tuesday, 28 April Frances did leave and took young Henry with her. She went to the house of a friend, a Mrs Sparville, who put them up for the night. Frances left with the baby the following morning telling Mrs Sparville that she had not decided whether to return to Lordship Place. In the event she did not and wandered the streets all day instead. She went back to Chelsea in the evening and met a Mrs Ireland who knew both her and Henrietta. Mrs Ireland took the exhausted Frances to her home and then went out to get some beer for them. She asked Frances to take the baby home to his mother before she left later in the evening. Frances told her that the baby was all right and that he loved his granny and she loved him.

Joseph Scrivener received a highly disturbing letter on the same evening suggesting that Frances had drowned herself and the baby. The letter read 'Joe, I have left Mrs Sparville, if you or your wife had come there you would have found the child. It is the only thing I can do to make your heart ache as you have made mine so long.' Joseph immediately went to the police with the letter.

Frances however was still alive and was seen on Friday, 1 May in Great Queen Street where she pushed a note through the letterbox of the house where her younger daughter Caroline worked. The note read 'Come at once as I have done murder and I want you to give me into the hands of justice.' Later Frances went to the door and spoke to Caroline who had not seen the note. Caroline sent for the police and Frances told them that she had taken the child.

She was arrested and taken before a magistrate who committed her for trial and remanded her to Newgate. However there was no body at this point to show that a murder had occurred, only Frances' partial confession.

The body of Henry was found a week or so later in the River Thames. There were no external injuries and the cause of death was drowning.

Frances was visited by her daughter in Newgate who told her more of the circumstances of the boy's death. She said that she had been crossing Albert Bridge over the River Thames but could not find anywhere to sit down. She lent against the bridge parapet and lost her grip on Henry, who fell into the river below.

Her trial, held at the Old Bailey on Wednesday, 10 June was a relatively brief affair and the jury quickly convicted her. However in view of her age, her recent widowhood, her known love for the baby boy plus the provocation of her son-in-law, they added a recommendation to mercy. Once again this was not apparently endorsed by the trial judge, even though he was reported as saying that she 'had committed the act under some perversity of mind'. Sir Richard Asheton Cross, the Home Secretary, saw no reason to interfere with the course of the law in this rather sad case.

After the ending of public executions some prisons had constructed execution sheds within one of the prison's yards as was the case at Newgate. Frances was to be the first woman to be hanged within this shed and the first woman to be hanged by William Marwood. On the morning of her death she was pinioned in the condemned cell and then led in a procession of two matrons, the under sheriff and the chaplain to the gallows. Here Marwood made the necessary preparations and operated the trap doors. According to a report from the *Echo* newspaper he bungled the execution by not tightening the noose sufficiently and she struggled somewhat. Whether this is actually true we cannot know. Reporters were not actually allowed inside the shed and had to watch the proceedings from outside. The entrance to the shed had two pairs of half doors and only the upper pair were left open after the prisoner and officials had entered. Thus, with a long drop, all that would be seen was a taut rope hanging down from the beam, the prisoner's body would have been completely below the level of the trap doors.

The body was still left on the rope for an hour to ensure total death, before being taken down for inquest and burial within the prison.

This case did not attract great publicity at the time and Madame Tussaud's did not feel the need to make a wax effigy of Frances for the Chamber of Horrors as they did with more heinous murderers.

Elizabeth Berry
A Classic Murder for Gain

Elizabeth Berry has the odd distinctions of being the first woman to be hanged at Walton Prison in Liverpool which had facilities for female inmates and, as far as I know, the only woman to be hanged by a man with the same surname as herself. She was executed by James Berry in 1887 and even more strangely they had actually met and even danced together. This had occurred in August 1885 at a police ball in Manchester. James presumably had attended this ball on his own because it is doubtful that his wife Sarah, whom he had married in 1874, would have approved of him dancing with an attractive woman two years his junior. They clearly made some impression on each other though, because both of them remembered the other when they next met nearly eighteen months later.

Elizabeth was a thirty-one-year-old widow who worked as a nurse in Oldham workhouse for which she was paid £25 per annum. Out of this sum she paid £12 a year to her sister-in-law who looked after Elizabeth's daughter, eleven-year-old Edith Annie. One assumes that this burden put a considerable strain on Elizabeth's finances and was probably the motive for murdering her daughter. She had lost her husband, son and mother over the preceding five years and there was a strong suspicion that they too had been poisoned by her. In each case

Elizabeth had received an insurance payment for the death. These deaths were not investigated further and it was doubtful after that length of time that anything could be proved from exhuming and autopsying their bodies.

Edith was invited to spend a few days with her mother at the workhouse and she and one of her school friends duly arrived on Wednesday, 29 December 1886. They were both lively, healthy children who played together in the wards. However by the Saturday, which was New Year's Day 1887, Edith had begun to feel unwell and had severe vomiting. Elizabeth was observed giving the child some milky liquid from a glass. She took Edith to see the workhouse doctor, Dr Patterson, that lunchtime and told him that Edith had a stomach upset from something she had eaten at breakfast that morning. He prescribed some suitable medication and Edith began to recover a little. Dr Patterson saw her again the following day. Elizabeth showed the doctor a towel with blood as well as vomit stains on it at this meeting and while examining these, the doctor noted an acidic smell coming from them. He decided to give Edith some bicarbonate mixture but needed the key to the dispensary, which Elizabeth kept. Whilst in the dispensary he noticed that the bottle of medical creosote was empty and wrote out a prescription for some more which he handed to Elizabeth. Edith's condition worsened on the Sunday evening and Dr Paterson noticed there were red marks around her mouth. He consulted another doctor and the pair agreed that it looked as if Edith had ingested a corrosive poison. Edith's condition began to deteriorate rapidly during Monday and she sadly passed away in the early hours of Tuesday. Dr Paterson had his suspicions as to the cause of death and must have realised that he himself had prescribed the poison that killed her when he wrote out the order for the replacement creosote. He refused to sign a death certificate and requested a post-mortem. As expected this showed that Edith had indeed been poisoned and therefore a warrant was issued for Elizabeth's arrest.

She came to trial at Liverpool Assizes in the famous St George's Hall on 21 February before Mr Justice Hawkins, the proceedings lasting for four days. Expert medical evidence was presented as to the cause of death. The jury were also told about two insurance policies. One was for £10 on Edith's life with a burial society, which were popular at the time as they meant that the loved ones would get a proper Christian burial. The other policy was a joint life one which paid £100 to either Elizabeth or Edith on the death of the other. In view of the fairly overwhelming medical evidence and a strong motive, Elizabeth was found guilty of the wilful murder of her daughter. She received the mandatory death sentence and was taken back to Walton to await execution.

At this time the two Liverpool prisons, Kirkdale and Walton, shared a gallows which was transported from one to the other as required. This meant that there was quite a lot of noise as it was re-erected. At Walton it was housed in the prison van shed which had a brick lined pit in the floor. The van shed was close to the Female Debtor's Wing where Elizabeth was being held and she enquired what the cause of all the noise was. She was then moved to another cell further away until the construction was finished, later returning to the condemned cell. She was attended by three sets each of two female warders working in three eight-hour shifts and was regularly visited regularly by the chaplain.

Her case was considered by the Home Office but the Home Secretary, Henry Matthews, saw no reason for a reprieve and her execution was set to take place on the morning of Monday, 14 March 1887.

James Berry was required to be at the prison on the Sunday afternoon. When he arrived the governor said to him 'I did not know you were going to hang an old flame, Berry.' James was aware of the prisoner's name but did not apparently realise who she actually was. However Elizabeth knew the name of Britain's then chief hangman and had told the governor about their meeting. As was normal Berry went to look at the prisoner to assess the correct length of drop for her and to see how she was bearing up or otherwise under the strain. He immediately recognised Elizabeth's auburn hair, even though it had been cut very much shorter than when he last saw her. Having been given her weight he decided on a drop of 6ft 6in and went to the van house to set the rope accordingly. Unsurprisingly Elizabeth passed a restless last night, as did most people in her position.

The following morning James entered her cell and bade her good morning. Elizabeth came to him, her hand held out in greeting, saying 'Good morning, Mr Berry. You and I have met before.' James pretended he had forgotten but she reminded him of the occasion. Some further conversation ensued and Elizabeth begged James to be quick and not hurt her. Being a very religious man James asked her if she had made her peace with God but she declined to answer this so he told her to make good use of the few remaining minutes of her life. Just before 8 a.m. he returned and pinioned her wrists in front of her with a leather strap before she was led from the condemned cell in a procession consisting of the governor, the chaplain, the under sheriff, at least two warders and James Berry for the 60yd walk to the gallows. There was still snow on the ground that March and so sand had been sprinkled on it to prevent an accident. Initially Elizabeth was able to walk quite well with a warder supporting her on either side but nearly fainted when she turned the corner and saw the noose waiting for her. She recovered somewhat and exclaimed 'Oh God forbid, God forbid.' She required help in getting onto the platform and again fainted, having to be held up by the two warders whilst James made the necessary preparations. He fastened a leather strap around the bottom of her skirt above the ankles. Elizabeth had again recovered a little and her last words were 'May God forgive me' as James pulled the white hood over her head and adjusted the Italian silk hemp noose around her neck, with the metal eyelet positioned under the angle of her left jaw, held in position by a leather washer. The free rope was allowed to loop down her back. James did not have an assistant and so was required to undertake all the preparations. As all was now ready he pushed the lever, her body disappearing from view with a crash. Death was certified by the prison doctor as having been 'instantaneous'.

One of the wardresses present is alleged to have said to James afterwards 'There goes one of the coldest blooded murderers – the worst species of woman kind to carry out the deeds she has carried out.'

Outside the prison a crowd estimated at 800 people had gathered, although they saw and heard nothing other than the bell tolling and the black flag hosted over the prison to show that the execution had taken place. Elizabeth's body was taken down and after a formal inquest, buried within the precincts of the prison. Berry took the opportunity to cut a small lock of hair from her head to keep as a souvenir. Although the press were not allowed to watch Elizabeth die, they were permitted to attend the inquest. The *Oldham Chronicle* regaled its readers with an account of the scene, reporting that Elizabeth's corpse was covered by a white sheet that came up to her chin and was tucked up under her left ear (to hide the mark left by the eyelet of the noose). It noted that the body had been washed and that the hair was still damp and had not been combed. However her face was at peace and her expression did not give the impression that she had suffered a violent death.

James recorded that he hated hanging women and that he was pleased to get out of Walton as quickly as he could because he was feeling unwell afterwards. Elizabeth was the third of four women that he hanged, the other two being Mary Lefly in 1884, Mary Ann Britland in 1886 and Mary Eleanor Pearcey in 1890.

It is interesting to compare this execution to the later twentieth-century ones where rarely a word was spoken, never mind a full conversation between executioner and prisoner. James Berry would certainly not have been allowed to visit a prisoner and talk with them in later times.

There was to be only one more female execution at Walton, that of fifty-three-year-old Margaret Walber, who was hanged by James Billington on Monday, 2 April 1894 for murdering her husband. However the prison was to be the site of one of the last two executions in Britain, carried out simultaneously on the 13 August 1964 when Peter Anthony Allen was hanged for his part in the robbery and murder of John Alan West, at the same time his accomplice, Gwynne Owen Evans.

Louise Masset
'Orrible Murder at Dalston

Louise Josephine Masset was the first person to be executed in Britain in the twentieth century. She was hanged at Newgate prison on Tuesday, 9 January 1900 for the murder of her son. (Her name is also given as Louisa.)

Louise was an attractive thirty-three-year-old who was half-French (on her father's side) and half-English. She was described as a 'cultured' woman. In 1896, she gave birth to an illegitimate son called Manfred and felt forced to leave France due to the stigma attached to illegitimate births in those days; it was considered 'quite scandalous'. She came to England and settled at 29 Bethune Road, Stoke Newington in London. It does not seem that she was very maternal and soon placed Manfred in foster care with a Mrs Helen Gentle who lived in Tottenham. Mrs Gentle looked after Manfred from a baby and was paid 37s a month, which allegedly came from the child's natural father in France. This arrangement enabled Louise to work as a day governess for a wealthy family. She also gave piano lessons. Playing the piano was a popular form of entertainment in those days before cinema, radio and television.

Sometime in 1899, Louise took on a 'toy boy', nineteen-year-old Eudore Lucas, as her lover. Eudore was a young French bank clerk who lived nextdoor to her and was in Britain training in finance. He was paid about £3 a week, which both agreed made marriage out of the question. Eudore was aware that Louise had a son, although what his attitude was to Manfred is unclear.

On 16 October 1899, Mrs Gentle received a letter from Louise telling her Manfred's father was going to have the boy to live with him in France and that Louise would collect him on Friday, 27 October to take him to France. However, Louise had also made another arrangement; she was going to Brighton with Eudore for what could be described as a 'dirty weekend' and they had booked two adjoining rooms in a cheap hotel there.

On the Friday, Louise put a clinker brick from her garden into her Gladstone bag before going to meet Helen Gentle at Stamford Hill. After tearful farewells, she led Manfred away with a parcel of his clothes that Mrs Gentle had packed for the journey and went to London Bridge railway station.

Manfred was dressed in a blue 'frock' and had a sailor's hat on. Frocks were quite popular for small boys in those days. Mother and son were next seen at London Bridge station's First Class waiting room at 1.45 p.m. on the Friday. Around 3 p.m. Mrs Ellen Rees, the attendant in the waiting room, noted the little boy seemed distressed and suggested to Louise that perhaps he was hungry. Louise and Manfred then left rather hurriedly, Louise saying she was going to buy Manfred a cake. She returned without him about three hours later to catch a train for Brighton for her rendezvous with Eudore on the Saturday.

At Dalston Junction station, an unsuspecting lady had a horrible shock when she went to the ladies toilets at about 6.20 p.m. and discovered the body of a child. It was a male child and was naked except for a black shawl. The face and head had been battered and there were two pieces of a broken clinker brick lying by the body. These were found to be of the same type as in Louise's garden. Manfred had been beaten unconscious and then suffocated, perhaps using a hand over his mouth and nose according to Dr J.P. Fennell, the doctor who examined the still warm body. Louise was familiar with this station as she went there regularly on her journey to one of her piano pupils.

Saturday's newspapers were full of the story of Manfred's discovery, as the Victorian's were very fond of a 'good murder' and every detail was reported.

Louise had sent Helen Gentle a letter which arrived on Monday the 30th saying that Manfred was missing her, and that he had been sick crossing the Channel on the ferry but that all was well now. However, Helen Gentle was suspicious of the letter, having read about the discovery of the body of a child of Manfred's age, and informed the police of her suspicions. She later identified the body as Manfred and was also able to identify the parcel of clothes which she had made up for him and which were found in the left luggage office at Brighton station together with the frock and sailor's hat.

Back in Stoke Newington, the black shawl found on Manfred was identified by a shop assistant as having come from his establishment and being sold by him on 24 October to Louise who, being half-French, had a distinctive accent.

She was also identified by witnesses on London Bridge station as having been with the child earlier in the day.

Louise had read about the discovery of Manfred's body and when she visited her sister later was clearly in a distressed state. She is reported to have said, 'I'm hunted for murder, but I didn't do it' and implicated Eudore in the crime.

She was soon arrested at her other sister's home. She was picked out in an identity parade by Mrs Rees, the waiting room attendant, and was duly charged with murder, being committed for trial at the Old Bailey in December 1899.

Louise was tried before Mr Justice Bruce between 13 and 18 December 1899. Her defence, led by Lord Coleridge, claimed that Louise had entered into an agreement with two women, called Browning who on payment of £18 a year, were going to look after Manfred for the foreseeable future and that it must have been them who murdered him. She claimed to have given them a £12 deposit before handing Manfred over to them. This may sound far fetched now but would have had a lot more credibility at the time when 'baby farming' murder cases were common.

However, as the two Mrs Brownings could not be found and a receipt for the £12 could not be produced, Louise's story was not believed by the jury. The evidence against her seemed conclusive and she was inevitably found guilty. She collapsed in the dock on hearing the verdict and had to be revived to hear her sentence

She was taken from the court into the adjoining Newgate Prison where she spent Christmas and New Year 1900. She is said to have confessed to the murder in the condemned cell.

A petition got up by other French women working in London was sent to Queen Victoria but was ignored.

There was to be no reprieve and at 9 a.m. on the morning of 9 January, she faced her appointment with James Billington from Bolton. She wore a long dress, as was customary, and was attended by the chaplain, two male warders and the assistant executioner.

Billington placed a body belt round her waist to which her wrists were strapped and then led her across the yard to the execution shed and onto the trap. Once there, her legs were pinioned by a leather strap outside her skirt and the noose placed around her neck. When all was ready, he put the white hood over her head and operated the lever plummeting her through the trap doors. Her broken body dangled still in the pit and was examined by the prison doctor to ensure that life was extinct. After hanging for the regulation hour, her body was removed from the rope and taken for inquest. She was buried in an unmarked grave within the prison later in the day.

By the standards of the day, Louise was seen as an immoral woman. The case against her was strong and there was no doubt of her guilt or the justice of her sentence for a crime that was clearly premeditated and violent. To many people, the killing of a child by its mother is particularly shocking. But her case is a good example of how social values have changed in the last 100 years.

In Victorian England, having an illegitimate child had a serious stigma and it was no doubt considered equally scandalous behaviour to have a relationship with a much younger man.

There was no effective contraception in the 1890s – a silk handkerchief being about all that was available – and so unwanted pregnancies were commonplace, as were 'back street' abortions and the practice of giving unwanted children to people who purported that they were going to look after them, the so-called 'baby farmers'.

Bringing up a small child at that time also meant that it was virtually impossible for the mother to find work in order to support herself. There was neither Social Security nor any day nurseries in the modern sense. Helen Gentle's charges were by no means cheap when one considers what people earned at that time so, no doubt, Manfred was a financial burden on Louise as well as an emotional one in that he was an encumbrance to her relationship with Eudore. One wonders if she had ever really bonded with Manfred and whether she actually loved the child or found him an embarrassment in Victorian society.

7

NEVER TOO YOUNG TO DIE: TEENAGE EXECUTIONS

This chapter is specifically about those girls who would legally be considered juveniles today, i.e. under eighteen years old at the time of their offence and who now would be prohibited from execution by international human rights treaties, not to mention public opinion.

The law of the eighteenth and early nineteenth centuries did not accept the concept that teenagers did not know the difference between right and wrong and punished teenage girls just as severely for the most serious crimes as their adult counterparts. There was a strong presumption against those who committed murder for gain, murder by poisoning or brutal murders, especially of their superiors. Court records often did not give the age of defendants sentenced to death and in some cases executions were not reported in the newspapers of the day so it is not easy to trace all of the executions of children in the eighteenth century.

With the small amount of detail that remains, let us examine the six confirmed cases of girls who were executed between 1735 and 1799.

On Saturday, 18 March 1738 sixteen-year-old Mary Grote (or Groke) was tied to a hurdle and drawn along in a procession behind a cart containing two men, John Boyd and James Warwick, to Gallows Hill on the outskirts of Winchester in Hampshire. Here she was held until the two men had been hanged before being led to a large wooden stake nearby. She was chained to this and bundles of faggots placed round her. The executioner would have endeavoured to strangle her with a rope noose before igniting the fire and reducing the hopefully unconscious girl to ashes. Mary had been convicted of petty treason murder, by poisoning, of her mistress Justine Turner.

Seventeen-year-old Catherine Connor went to the gallows at London's Tyburn on Monday, 31 December 1750 for publishing a false, forged and counterfeit Will, purporting to be the Will of Michael Canty, a sailor in the Navy, on 29 October of that year. She told the court that she could neither read nor write and that the forgery was made by a Mr Dunn, although she was present at the time. Catherine was one of fifteen prisoners to hang that day.

Elizabeth Morton, aged fifteen, was hanged at Gallows Hill, Nottingham on 8 April 1763 for the murder of the two-year-old child of her master John Oliver, for whom she worked.

On Saturday, 16 September 1786 seventeen-year-old Susannah Minton suffered for arson at Hereford before a large number of onlookers. She had been convicted of 'voluntarily and maliciously setting fire to and burning a barn, the property of Paul Gwatkin, in the parish of Kilpeck on the 11th of November 1785.' She had been tried at the Lent Assizes but was respited to the Summer Assizes, possibly because she had claimed that she was pregnant.

Sarah Shenston, an eighteen-year-old, was hanged at Moor Heath on the outskirts of Shrewsbury in Shropshire on Thursday, 22 March 1792. She suffered for the murder of her illegitimate male child whose throat she cut immediately after birth, in the parish of Albrighton, on 30 September 1791.

At the Dorset Lent Assizes in Dorchester in March 1794, fifteen-year-old Elizabeth Marsh was convicted of the murder of her grandfather, John Nevil. In accordance with the provisions of the Murder Act of July 1752 she was required to be hanged in public two days later, which would have been a Sunday, a day on which executions were not permitted. As was normal the judge in her case delayed sentencing her to the end of the Assize thus giving her an extra day of life. Elizabeth would have been kept in chains and only allowed bread and water between sentence and execution. She was hanged on Monday, 17 March and was the first person to be executed outside the new County Gaol in Dorchester. Her body was afterwards given to local surgeons for dissection.

THE NINETEENTH CENTURY

Six girls aged eighteen or under were publicly hanged in the first half of the nineteenth century. Children, like adults, continued to be sentenced to death for a very large number of felonies up to 1836 although it was normal for younger children to have their sentences commuted for the less serious crimes as there was growing public disquiet about hanging children for minor crimes. There is little actual evidence of anyone under fourteen years old being hanged in the nineteenth century, despite what you might read in some books to the contrary. Executions were decreasing rapidly, both for adults and young offenders after 1836, as the number of capital crimes reduced and public attitudes began to change.

Ann Mead
A Hertfordshire Poisoning

Ann, aged sixteen was found guilty of the murder of Charles Proctor, aged sixteen months, by feeding him a spoonful of arsenic at Royston in Hertfordshire. She expiated her crime on the New Drop gallows outside Hertford prison on Thursday, 31 July 1800, watched by a large crowd.

Mary Voce
A Nottinghamshire Poisoning

Mary Voce was hanged at Gallows Hill, Nottingham on Tuesday, 16 March 1802 for poisoning her child. In some reports she is said to have been born in 1788, which would make her only fourteen. It is interesting that the newspapers of the day found little noteworthy in the execution of a teenage girl and gave her story very little coverage.

Mary Morgan
The Last Woman Hanged in Presteigne

Mary was a sixteen-year-old kitchen maid at the imposing Maesllwch Castle near Glasbury, the home of Walter Wilkins Esq., the Member of Parliament for the county of Radnorshire (now part of Powys in Wales). She had become pregnant but had tried to conceal the pregnancy to be allowed to stay on in the servant's quarters in the castle. On a Sunday in September 1804 she complained of feeling unwell and went up to bed. She was visited in the evening by the cook who accused Mary of having given birth to a baby. Mary initially denied this but later admitted that he she had indeed given birth and that she had killed it immediately, severing its head with a penknife. The baby was found under the pillows in Mary's bed. An inquest was held two days later and the jury returned a verdict of murder against Mary, declaring that:

> Mary Morgan, late of the Parish of Glazebury, a single woman on the 23rd day of September being big with child, afterward alone and secretly from her body did bring forth alive a female child, which by the laws and customs of this Kingdom was a bastard. Mary Morgan moved and seduced by the instigation of the devil afterwards on the same day, feloniously, willfully and of her malice aforethought did make an assault with a certain penknife made of iron and steel of the value of sixpence, and gave the child one mortal wound of the length of three inches and the depth of one inch. The child instantly died.

Mary was arrested but was not well enough to be taken to Presteigne for trial until 6 October. She thus remained in prison until the following April when she was arraigned at the Great Sessions for Radnorshire before Judge Hardinge. After a brief trial on 11 April 1805 she was convicted and received the death sentence. She was returned to Presteigne Gaol to await her appointment with the hangman two days later.

It was quite normal at this time for executions to take place at a later time of the day then became the custom later, so as to give local people the opportunity to get to the execution site. Mary was hanged at Gallows Lane in Presteigne on Saturday, 13 April at around midday, having been conveyed from the gaol in a horse-drawn cart seated on her coffin. The terrified girl was barely conscious when she arrived at the gallows and had to be supported during the preparations. It is probable that she was hanged from the back of the cart rather than on the New Drop style of gallows which was slowly coming into vogue at

this time. Her body was buried in unconsecrated ground near
the church later that afternoon and was for whatever reason not
sent for dissection.

Mary's case was one that attracted the conspiracy theorists
of the day. It has been claimed that a gentleman who attended
Mary's trial immediately set off to London to seek a reprieve
for her, but failed to get back in time to save her. This is at
least highly unlikely; one could not ride to London and back
on a single horse in two days in 1805. It is still quite a long
journey now.

It has also been claimed that the father of Mary's daughter
was Walter Wilkins the Younger – the son of her employer – or
alternatively one of the men on the jury that convicted her.
However there is little evidence to support either theory and
the father was more probably one of her fellow servants.

Two grave stones were erected in Mary's memory in
St Andrew's parish churchyard in Presteigne: one by a friend
of Judge Hardinge, and another by an anonymous donor.

Although to kill her baby in the way she did may strike
most of us horrible it is difficult to understand both the social
and economic pressures that Mary faced at the time. Had the
pregnancy been discovered she would have almost certainly
lost her job and with it her place to live and meagre income.
There was no social security then and she could only hope
for handouts to live on until she could find some alternative
employment. Not easy with a baby to bring up and with the
social stigma of being an unmarried mother which was a very
real one 200 years ago.

Hannah Bocking
Murder in the Shadow of the Gibbet

On Monday, 22 March 1819, sixteen-year-old Hannah
Bocking became probably the youngest girl to be executed

in the nineteenth century when she was publicly hanged at Derby for the murder, by poisoning, of Jane Grant.

Hannah came from Litton in Derbyshire and in the summer of 1818 had applied for a job as a servant but had been unsuccessful due to 'her unamiable temper and disposition'. The job went to another local girl, Jane Grant, instead. Hannah knew Jane but hid her jealousy from her and pretended to be friends with her.

Hannah and Jane went together to get some cattle from a field at Wardlow Mires. Dangling from a gibbet nearby was the rotting corpse of Anthony Lingard who had been hanged and gibbeted in 1815 for the murder of Hannah Oliver. Here Hannah offered Jane a cake which she had previously laced with poison. Jane died in agony a little while later. It seems a strange location to commit a murder and clearly Hannah was not deterred by the possibility of her own execution.

Hannah was soon arrested and charged with killing Jane. She was committed to Friar Gate Gaol in Derby to await the next assizes the following year. She duly came to trial at the Derbyshire Lent Assizes nearly six months later. Initially she first tried to implicate members of her family in the crime but finally confessed that she had bought the poison some ten weeks before the murder. She was convicted of the crime and on Friday, 19 March sentenced to be hanged and anatomised the following Monday. She was sent back to Friar Gate Gaol and placed in the condemned cell which is a small dank room in the basement with little natural light that can still be visited today.

On the Monday morning, she was led back up the stone steps from the prison basement, through the main gate and out onto the pavement where in front of a large number of eager spectators, she ascended the steps of the New Drop gallows erected in front of the gaol. After the usual preparations and time for prayer a white night cap was drawn down over her face and the trapdoor released. It was not reported whether she died easily or not but 'at the moment, when she was launched into eternity, an involuntary shuddering pervaded the assembled crowd, and although she excited little sympathy, a general feeling of horror was expressed that one so young should have been so guilty, and so insensible.' Her body was dissected after death as required by law.

Catherine Foster
A Teenage Poisoner

Catherine was one of two teenage girls publicly hanged in the period from 1840 to 1868. She was just seventeen years old when she poisoned her husband John, to whom she had been married for only three weeks at Acton near Sudbury in Suffolk.

John and Catherine had known each other since she was at the village school and had been having a relationship for two years or so, after Catherine had left school and gone into service. John was seven years Catherine's senior and it is probable that he was rather keener on her than she was on him. He also wanted to move out of his mother's home as his sisters both had small children who got on his nerves. The relationship with Catherine continued and he persuaded her to marry him, which she did on Wednesday, 28 October 1846 at Acton church. The newlyweds went to live with Catherine's mother, Maria Morley, at her cottage in the village. Catherine stayed with John until the Saturday when she left to visit her aunt in the village of Pakenham for the next ten days.

On Tuesday, 17 November Catherine decided to cook dumplings for dinner. That afternoon, her mother and John were out at work so only Catherine and her younger brother, eight-year-old Thomas, were in the house. John was a healthy young farm labourer who had previously enjoyed good health. He came home from work some time after 6 p.m. and went into the yard to wash his hands before eating. Catherine and Thomas were eating when he came back in and she took his dumpling, wrapped in a cloth, from the stove and gave it to him. He began to eat it but almost immediately became ill and had to go back into the yard where he threw up. Catherine took the remains of John's dumpling out into the yard and broke it up for the chickens. By 7 p.m. when Mrs Morley returned John had gone up to bed, retching and experiencing severe stomach cramps. This continued through the night and in the morning Catherine went to the nearby village of Melford to fetch the doctor, Mr Robert Jones. She told the doctor that John had a stomach complaint but omitted to mention the vomiting, so he suspected a case of English cholera, especially as it had recently been rife. He prescribed some medicine which she took home with her and said he would call on John later. Her mother returned home about 3 p.m. and John died an hour later. Mr Jones arrived at about 5 p.m. and was very surprised to find John dead. He reported the death to the coroner who ordered an inquest and a post-mortem.

Mr Jones and another local surgeon carried out the autopsy and removed John's stomach for analysis which was sent to Mr E. W. Image in Bury St Edmunds. He detected a large amount of arsenic in it and confirmed that this was the cause of death. John was not the only victim, the chickens – who had eaten bits of the dumpling and John's vomit which Mrs Morley had thrown into the adjoining ditch – had also died. Their crops were found to contain arsenic and suet, an ingredient of dumplings. The coroner's jury returned a verdict of murder and charged Catherine with the crime. She was therefore arrested and committed to Bury St Edmunds Gaol, charged with poisoning John.

Catherine was examined by the magistrates whilst in prison in the presence of the gaoler's wife, Mrs James. Her mother was present and took young Thomas with her. Catherine is alleged to have said to him 'You good for nothing little boy, why did you tell such stories' and refused a cake he had brought her.

The police made a search of Mrs Morley's house on Monday, 24 November. The constable of Melford, George Green and Sergeant Rogers took samples of flour and also the muslin cloths that were used for cooking dumplings in and sent them to Mr Image for analysis. The flour did not contain any poison but one of the muslin clothes tested positive for it.

Catherine was tried at the Suffolk Lent Assizes on 27 March 1847 on the charge of the wilful murder of John Foster. She appeared calm in court and pleaded not guilty. The prosecution was led by Mr Gurdon and he called a number of witnesses to give the background to the case, John's previous robust health, the administration of the arsenic and the forensic evidence from Mr Image who had carried out Reinsch's test and Marsh's test to be certain that what had been found in John's stomach was indeed arsenic. Perhaps the most damning evidence against Catherine came from her brother Thomas. On the day that Catherine made the dumplings Thomas had got home from school at 3 p.m. He told the court he saw his sister empty the contents of a small paper packet into the mixture and then throw the paper onto the fire. Elizabeth Foster, John's mother, told the court that she had heard that her son was ill but by the time she got to Mrs Morley's house he had died. When she arrived she found Catherine and Mrs Morley there and asked Catherine why she had not been sent for earlier. Catherine told her that John had been too ill to leave and that she had nobody to go and fetch Elizabeth.

Catherine's defence was presented by Mr Power who opened by saying that in view of the handbills that had been circulated around Suffolk proclaiming his client a murderess before she was even tried it made a fair trial very difficult. He endeavoured to destroy the alleged motive for the murder by showing that Catherine and John had actually been in love using the letters that she had written him before their marriage, which were found in his effects after he had died. He also told the jury that, when Catherine had suggested visiting her aunt, John had told her to take a month but she returned after just ten days. None of this succeeded and the jury found Catherine guilty after fifteen minutes of discussion. As it was nearly 7 p.m. sentencing was postponed until 9 a.m. the next morning. Catherine displayed no emotion at the verdict and very little when she was sentenced to hang the following day.

Little is reported of her time in the condemned cell where she received the ministrations of the chaplain and the Rev. Otley, her parish priest. She made a confession which did not give any reason for the killing. She wrote a letter to her mother in which she said that she was not sorry that she would die because she would go to a better place where she would be reunited with John. She appears to not to have been hysterical as some women were in this position and to have remained composed.

The hanging was carried out on Saturday, 17 April 1847 by William Calcraft on the New Drop gallows, erected in the meadow outside Bury St Edmunds Gaol. A crowd of some 10,000 people had turned up to see it and Catherine made a speech from the platform imploring other girls not to follow her example and to stick to her marriage vows.

It is not recorded that she 'died hard' as was then the expression so it is probable that she struggled very little. The execution was described as a deeply moving spectacle by witnesses. Catherine's body was afterwards buried within the prison as was now the legal requirement and quicklime was added to the coffin, as it was thought to speed decomposition. She was the last female to be hanged in public at Bury St Edmunds. A broadside was printed of her crime and execution.

Future executions at this prison took place on the flat roof between the infirmary and the entrance to the porter's lodge as it was felt that the crowd had been able to get too close to the gallows and its teenage prisoner.

What made a seventeen-year-old girl poison her husband of three weeks? We cannot know whether she was in love with him or not but there appears no reason for her to hate him or want him dead. It has been suggested that she was pushed into marriage by her mother but this was not what Maria Morley told the court. In fact almost the opposite, she seemed concerned that Catherine was too young at seventeen. Was there someone else in Catherine's life? Again there is no evidence of this. There has never been any suggestion that she stood to benefit financially from the murder. Perhaps she felt trapped in a situation that she did not want and saw killing John as the easiest way out. It has been suggested that Catherine's father also committed a murder in July 1838. If so, he was not hanged for it.

Sarah Harriet Thomas
Bristol's Last Public Hanging

Sarah's was to be Bristol's final public hanging on the flat roof of the gatehouse of New Gaol in Cumberland Road. She was a house maid to sixty-one-year-old Miss Elizabeth Jefferies who, according to Sarah, did not treat her well and had locked in the kitchen all night among other perceived abuses. There was almost certain to be conflict between a cranky, elderly spinster and a rebellious young girl and this culminated in Sarah bludgeoning Miss Jefferies to death with a large stone as she slept, on the night of Sunday, 4 March. Sarah also killed Miss Jefferies' dog and threw its body into the lavatory. She left the house, but not without helping herself to some of her mistress' jewellery. Miss Jefferies' brother was alerted to a possible problem by a neighbour who noticed that the window shutters were still closed and called the local constable to help him investigate.

When they forced entry they made the gruesome discoveries. Suspicion immediately fell upon Sarah and she was arrested the next day at her mother's house in Pensford. Initially she told the police that another girl had committed the killings and that she had only been involved with ransacking the house.

She was tried at Gloucester on 3 April, the public gallery being particularly crowded to hear every gruesome detail. Sarah seemed not to treat the court proceedings seriously until she was convicted and the judge donned the black cap and sentenced her to be hanged by the neck until she was dead. On hearing these words of doom she collapsed and had to be carried from the dock by two warders. A petition was got up to save her but this was to no avail. Sarah made a confession seventeen days before her execution and it was read to her every day in case she wanted to correct it. In the confession she told of the ill treatment that she had endured from Miss Jefferies and spoke of her regret in having committed the killings.

On Thursday, 19 April the gallows was erected and William Calcraft, the hangman, arrived from London. The following morning a huge number of people had assembled in front of the prison to watch Sarah die.

She was dragged up two flights of stairs by six warders onto the gatehouse roof and then up a few more steps onto the platform. She was held on the trap by two warders whilst Calcraft strapped her legs, placed the white hood over her head and tightened the halter style noose around her neck. As the preparations continued Sarah cried out 'I wont be hanged; take me home!' Calcraft quickly operated the trap and Sarah's body dropped about 18in through it, quivering for a few moments before becoming still. Everybody present on the gatehouse roof was upset by the distressing scene they had witnessed and the governor of the prison fainted. Sarah's body was buried in private in an unmarked grave within the prison later in the day.

Even the by now veteran hangman, Calcraft, was greatly affected by this job and said later that Sarah Thomas was 'in my opinion, one of the prettiest and most intellectual girls I have met with.'

A crime reporter, one Mr E. Austin, who attended the execution reported: 'Ribald jests were bandied about and after waiting to see the corpse cut down, the crowd dispersed, and the harvest of the taverns in the neighbourhood commenced.' However, some in the crowd felt repulsed by what they had seen and felt pity for the poor girl. Sadly for the majority it was probably seen much more as a free pornographic show put on by the authorities for their voyeuristic pleasure.

Sarah was the last of nine teenage girls hanged between 1800 and 1849. One hundred years earlier she would have suffered a far worse fate as her crime would have been deemed to be petty treason and she would have been burnt at the stake for it.

Constance Kent, who confessed to murdering her brother when she was sixteen, had her death sentence commuted to life in prison in 1865 due to her age at the time of her crime and changing attitudes towards the death penalty, particularly for women. She served twenty years in prison.

A further six nineteen-year-old girls were hanged in the nineteenth century. They were Sarah Lloyd for stealing in a dwelling house, Martha Chapple for the murder of her bastard, Mary Chandler for stealing in a dwelling house, Sarah Fletcher for the murder of a child, Catherine Kinrade for being an accessory to murder and Mary Ann Higgins for the murder of her uncle.

8

THE CARNIVAL IS OVER: NINETEENTH-CENTURY EXECUTIONS 'WITHIN THE WALLS'

The 1864 Royal Commission on Capital Punishment which sat for two years concluded that there was no case for abolition of the death penalty but did recommend ending public executions and this was given the force of law by the passing of the Capital Punishment (Amendment) Act 1868 on 29 May that year.

It was argued that the fact that executions were public events with all the lewd behaviour that generally accompanied them was one of the reasons why so many women were being reprieved in the 1850s.

The new Act did allow the sheriff of the county in which the execution took place the discretion to admit newspaper reporters and other witnesses, including the victim's relatives, to the hanging. The first nominally private hanging was carried out on Thursday, 13 August 1868, when eighteen-year-old Thomas Wells was executed at Maidstone.

Twenty-two women kept their date with the hangman between December 1868 and December 1899. Initially a select few still got to see the execution but they soon became totally private affairs with the press usually being excluded as well when the criminal was female. The first four women to die in this period suffered short-drop hanging; they were Priscilla Biggadyke, Margaret Waters, Mary Ann Cotton and Mary Ann Barry. All subsequent prisoners were given a much easier death by the long-drop method, introduced by William Marwood in 1872, which was adopted for all future British hangings from late 1874. Francis Stewart became the first woman to suffer it. In just seven years executions had gone from being a huge public spectacle with the prisoner often slowly strangling to death to a solemn but dignified procedure that brought about a quick and hopefully pain-free death.

Priscilla Biggadyke
The 'Stickney Murderess'

Priscilla Biggadyke was the first woman to be executed within the walls of the prison in which she was last confined when she was hanged at Lincoln Castle on 29 December 1868. Hers was to be the third and last 'private' execution of 1868 under the provisions of the new Act.

Priscilla Whiley was born in the village of Gedney, Lincolnshire, in 1833 and married Richard Biggadyke in 1855. They lived in a tiny two-room cottage in the village of Stickney, a few miles north of Boston in Lincolnshire, with three children and two male lodgers, thirty-year-old Thomas Proctor and twenty-one-year-old fisherman George Ironmonger. All seven slept in one room of the cottage in two beds close together. As one can well imagine, this caused friction in the marriage which was not going too well by the mid-1860s. It was rumoured that there was a relationship between Priscilla and Thomas Proctor and it has been said that Richard suspected that Priscilla's last baby was Thomas' not his.

Priscilla had made some cakes on Wednesday, 30 September
1868 and she, Thomas and George ate tea together at 5 p.m.
The two lodgers had a cake each and saved one for Richard
when he got home from work a little later. Richard ate his
and quickly became ill, with violent stomach cramps and
vomiting. A Dr Maxwell was sent for but Richard's condition quickly deteriorated and he died at 6 a.m. the following
morning. Dr Maxwell carried out a post-mortem examination and noted that Richard's stomach lining was inflamed.
As a result an inquest was held before the coroner, Mr Walter
Clegg, on the following Saturday and Dr Maxwell suggested
that Richard had been poisoned. It was therefore decided to
send the stomach and its contents for analysis to Professor A.S.
Taylor at Guys Hospital. The inquest was adjourned pending his findings and re-opened a week later. Professor Taylor
was able to confirm that Richard Biggadyke had died from
arsenic poisoning.

Priscilla and Thomas Proctor were arrested by Superintendent Wright of Spilsby on Saturday 3 October and
charged with Richard's murder. He cautioned Priscilla not to
say anything to incriminate herself and she told him that she
had found a suicide note in Richard's pocket giving mounting
debt as the reason for killing himself. Wright asked her what
she had done with the piece of paper and she told him she had
burned it. He pointed out to her that Richard was illiterate
and she suggested that somebody else had written the note
for him.

Priscilla and Thomas appeared before magistrates at Spilsby,
their nearest market town, on Monday, 19 October, charged
with the wilful murder of Richard Biggadyke and were
remanded in custody. On 15 October, Priscilla had made a
statement under caution to Mr John Yarr Phillips, the governor of the Spilsby House of Correction, to which she had
been remanded. She told Mr Phillips that she had administered the poison but also implicated Thomas Proctor in the

crime. She suggested that she had seen him pour some white powder into her husband's tea and afterwards place some more into a medicine bottle, some of whose contents she later gave to Richard. Thomas declined to make a statement and told the police he would wait for his trial to speak. Both prisoners were committed for trial at the Lincolnshire Winter Assizes. It was later directed by the judge that the trial of Thomas should not proceed as there was insufficient evidence. So Priscilla was to stand alone in the dock to face the murder charge.

The trial took place on Friday 11 December 1868, before Mr Justice Byles, with a Mr Bristowe leading for the prosecution and a Mr Lawrence for the defence. The proceedings lasted just seven hours. Mr Bristowe told the jury of the living conditions of the family and of the endless rows between Priscilla and Richard, citing these as the motive for the murder.

Testimony was heard from Eliza and Edwin Fenwick who knew the Biggadykes and the state of their marriage. Eliza told the court of the suggestion by Priscilla to Eliza that she might use 'white mercury', as arsenic was known locally, to deal with the mice in her house. Professor Taylor gave his forensic evidence to the court as to the cause of Richard's death. Superintendent Wright told of the arrest and the statements made to him by Priscilla under caution, while Mr Phillips told the court of Priscilla's 'confession', which he had taken down and she had signed with her mark as she could neither read nor write. Other witnesses who had appeared at the inquest also added their testimony. Her defence must have been a struggle for Mr Lawrence but he addressed the jury for some forty-five minutes on her behalf. Mr Justice Byles then summed up the evidence for the jurors and pointed to the conflicting stories that Priscilla had told Mr Phillips, the coroner, and Superintendent Wright. He told the jury that although there was no question that Richard died of arsenic poisoning, having previously been in excellent health, they had to decide whether it was Pricilla who had administered it.

The jury did not retire and after a few minutes' discussion found Priscilla guilty with a recommendation to mercy. On being asked why by the judge they said it was because the evidence against her was entirely circumstantial. Mr Justice Byles was not impressed with this and clearly did not make the same recommendation to the Home Secretary in his report.

The Clerk of the Court asked Priscilla why sentence of death should not be passed upon her to which she made no reply, but for the first time during the trial she exhibited some emotion, shedding a few tears. Priscilla was then condemned to death in the usual form and reportedly walked firmly from the dock.

Only two and a half weeks were to elapse between trial and execution which was set for Monday, 28 December. Priscilla was housed in the one condemned cell of the female section of the prison. There were two condemned cells in the male section. Here she was guarded round the clock and visited daily by the chaplain, the Rev. H. W. Richter. She was also visited by her brother and three sisters who advised her to make a confession which she absolutely refused to do.

It was reported that she had considered both suicide and escape and had asked one of her warders to change clothes with her so that she could walk out. Whether this is really true or a flight of fantasy on the part of either Priscilla or a newspaper reporter we will never know.

On Sunday the 27th she ate well and attended service in the prison chapel. It was recorded that she slept well on Sunday night and on Monday morning was visited at 7 a.m. by the chaplain who again did all he could to drag a confession out of her. She still adamantly refused to give this and he persisted with his exhortations to the steps of the gallows.

The preparations for the execution had been started the previous day with the gallows being set up close to the court on the Castle Green. Thomas Askern from York had been commissioned by the under sheriff of Lincolnshire to carry out the hanging. Askern went for Priscilla at around 8.45 a.m. and pinioned her in the condemned cell. At 8.50 a.m. she was led out supported by two warders in a procession consisting of the governor, the chaplain reading the service for the dying, the under sheriff and Askern, to make the 200yd walk to the gallows. She is said to have told the warders 'I hope my troubles are ended.' She then asked one of the warders 'shall we be much longer?' to which he replied, 'No, not much.' When the place of execution was reached Priscilla was given a chair to sit on whilst the Rev. H.W. Richter made one final attempt to get his confession. Again Priscilla refused to confess and told him that she had nothing to do with the crime. She was now helped up the steps onto the platform and was able to stand unaided whilst Askern completed the preparations. As he hooded her she said 'All my troubles are over; shame, you're not going to hang me. Surely my troubles are over.' As the cathedral clock was striking nine Askern released the trap and her body dropped a short distance, struggling on the rope for some three minutes before becoming still.

Outside the castle a small crowd of people had assembled to see the black flag raised over the keep tower.

In accordance with the new Act not only was the execution to be carried out within the prison but there had to be a formal inquest afterwards. After Priscilla had been hanging for an hour her body was taken down and taken back to a cell where it was viewed by the coroner's jury. It was reported that her face was white but showed no distortion. The prison doctor, Mr Broadbent, gave his opinion that the execution had been carried out to the normal standards of the time but commented that he had not seen the noose positioned in this way previously. Thomas Askern had placed the eyelet of the rope under Priscilla's chin thus throwing the head back which he claimed destroyed all sensation but did not prevent breathing. There seemed to be no attention paid to Priscilla's lengthy and visible struggling however. The jury accepted what they were told and returned a verdict that they were satisfied that the execution had been carried out properly. Priscilla's body was buried within the Lucy Tower in the castle, alongside those of the others executed there after 1834, under a simple headstone bearing her initials and the date.

All the proceedings in this case were reported in the local press, including the execution which they were able to witness.

It has been claimed that on his deathbed in March 1882, Thomas Proctor confessed that it was he rather than Priscilla that administered the poison to Richard Biggadyke. It is thought that Priscilla received a posthumous pardon as a result.

Priscilla became the last person to be hanged at Lincoln Castle. A new County Gaol opened in Greetwell Road in Lincoln two years later.

Mary Ann Cotton
Britain's First Serial Killer

Mary Ann Cotton was until recently Britain's most prolific serial killer. It is estimated that she murdered between fifteen and twenty-one victims.

Mary Ann was born in 1833 to Michael and Margaret Robson and had a brother Robert in the mining town of East Rainton between Durham and Sunderland. Her coal miner father died as the result of an accident when she was nine in the spring of 1842 and her mother subsequently remarried, to another miner, one Mr George Stott.

At the age of sixteen Mary Ann went into service as a domestic servant, as did most of her contemporaries. She married for the first time on 18 July 1852 at the age of twenty to a coal miner named William Mowbray by whom she had four children over the ensuing five years. They decided to move from the North East to the West Country soon afterwards, where William worked on railway construction. Here their first daughter, also called Mary Ann, was born, dying of 'gastric fever' on 24 June 1860. They lived in Devon and Cornwall for about four years before moving back to the mining village of Murton a few miles from East Rainton. On 5 April 1857 another daughter, Margaret Jane, was born at Murton but died soon after. In September 1857 Mary Ann gave birth to another girl whom they christened Isabella. On 1 October 1861 she had yet another girl which was also named Margaret and finally in November 1863 a son was born, John Robert, who died within a year.

William Mowbray gave up coal mining to become a sailor and insured his life and that of his children with the British and Prudential Insurance Company. During a period of shore leave he became ill and died of 'gastric fever' and diarrhoea as each of his children had done or were soon to do. On each death Mary Ann collected a small amount of insurance money.

In May 1865 Margaret Jane Mowbray died at the age of three and Isabella was sent to live with Mary Ann's mother, Margaret Stott to enable Mary Ann to take a nursing job at Sunderland Infirmary Hospital. Working on the wards she met thirty-three-year-old George Ward who was recovering from a fever and when he was discharged the couple got married on 28 August 1865. This marriage was to last just over a year, George dying on 21 October 1866 of gastric fever. It is unclear whether this death was from natural causes or whether he was another of Mary Ann's victims.

As she was now on her own again she looked around for suitable employment and spotted a vacancy for a housemaid at the home of shipyard foreman Mr James Robinson in Pallion where she was to look after his four children after the death of his wife. Unsurprisingly the children, two boys and two girls, soon succumbed to Mary Ann's attentions, all dying of 'gastric fever'. Ten-month-old John Robinson was the first victim, dying on 23 December 1866, just a week after Mary Ann had joined the household. Mary Ann had soon begun an affair with James and became pregnant by him.

Her mother, Mrs Stott, became ill and Mary Ann went to look after her, so well that Margaret Stott survived for just nine days, dying in March 1867 apparently from pneumonia. As a result of her death Mary Ann had to take her daughter Isabella back. Once back in the Robinson household the death rate accelerated rapidly with three more deaths in just ten days. On 21 April six-year-old James Robinson junior succumbed, followed by eight-year-old Elizabeth Robinson on 26 April and finally Isabella on 2 May. James Robinson's sisters became very suspicious of Mary Ann, who also became ill for a short time before recovering. James married the now five months pregnant Mary Ann on 11 August 1867. Mary Isabella was born on 29 November 1867 and lived for just a month before dying of the usual cause. James and Mary Ann split up soon after; it is thought due to disagreements over money and James' reluctance to allow Mary Ann to take out a life insurance policy on him. Unwittingly, perhaps, he had saved his own life.

Once more unemployed she took a job as a matron in a women's prison in Sunderland until she found a position more to her liking. This was with a ship's captain working as housekeeper. She waited until the captain's next voyage to rob him of a considerable amount of his possessions before moving to Spennymoor where she took up a job with a Dr Hefferman. She was soon dismissed for stealing money from the practice.

Her next move was to the mining town of Walbottle in Northumberland where she was to meet a newly widowed coal miner, Frederick Cotton, who was struggling to bring up two young sons after his wife Adelaide had died. Mary Ann and Frederick were married on 17 September 1870 at St Andrews church in Newcastle upon Tyne, despite Mary Ann still being married to James Robinson. They moved to Newcastle upon Tyne and here Mary Ann gave birth to their first child, christened Robert Robson Cotton. They later moved to

20 Johnson Terrace, West Auckland, and here Mary Ann took out life insurance on her new family. Soon afterwards thirty-nine-year-old Frederick became ill with the usual symptoms of 'gastric fever' and died within hours on 19 September 1871, after being married for just a year and two days.

Joseph Nattrass came into Mary Ann's life about three months after Frederick's death and went to live with her at Johnson Terrace. Joseph made the fatal mistake of making Mary Ann the sole beneficiary of his will. Mary Ann took up employment as a nursemaid to Mr Quick-Manning at Brookfield Cottage West Auckland. Mr Quick-Manning was an excise officer at the West Auckland Brewery. As usual with Mary Ann the men she met seemed to fall for her very quickly and Mr Quick-Manning was no exception. Joseph now had to be eliminated and died of 'gastric fever'. In fact in the space of three weeks, between 10 March and 1 April 1872, there were to be three deaths in Mary Ann's extended family. These were Frederick Cotton's ten-year-old son, also named Frederick, fourteen-month-old Robert Robson Cotton and Joseph.

One child had survived from her former relationships; this was Frederick's son Charles Edward Cotton, who died on 12 July 1872 from the usual cause. For once though, Mary Ann had made an error of judgement that was to prove fatal. She had sought the help of Thomas Riley, an overseer of the poor at West Auckland, to get Charles Edward into the workhouse there so that she would once again be able to earn a living. He told Mary Ann that she would have to go into the workhouse too, to which she replied: 'I'll not be troubled long. He'll go like the rest of the Cotton family'. Mr Riley had seen that Charles Edward was in reasonable health just a week before his death and became suspicious when he died so soon after. He reported his suspicion to Sergeant Tom Hutchinson of West Auckland police. The death was therefore reported to the coroner and an inquest was held at the Rose and Crown public house next door to Mary Ann's home by Dr Kilburn.

He had very limited time in which to carry out a post-mortem and his initial findings were that Charles Edward had died of natural causes the usual 'gastric fever'. However Dr Kilburn was not satisfied with the post-mortem and had taken the precaution of retaining some of the child's organs so that he could carry out a proper analysis. The analysis revealed the presence of two and a half grains of arsenic and was confirmed by further tests carried out by a Dr Scattergood from Leeds. As a result Mary Ann was arrested by Superintendent Henderson on the suspicion of poisoning Charles Edward Cotton on Thursday 18 July 1872. It was found that she stood to gain £4 10s from Charles Edward's death from the Prudential Insurance Company, who had refused to pay out because she did not have a death certificate.

She was committed for trial at Durham Assizes and whilst she was on remand moves were made to exhume some of the bodies of the other people in her family that had died at West Auckland. All the bodies were found to contain arsenic. Frederick Cotton junior had over two grains of arsenic in him, whilst Joseph Nattrass had nearly eighteen grains and Robert Robson Cotton sufficient to cause the death of an infant. She was now charged with the murder of four people: her stepson Charles Edward, Joseph Nattrass, Frederick Cotton and Robert Robson Cotton.

Mary Ann was pregnant at the time of her arrest and gave birth to a daughter named Mary Edith Quick-Manning Cotton in Durham Prison in January 1873.

She came to trial at Durham Assizes on the charge of murdering Charles Edward Cotton on Thursday 5 March 1873, the proceedings lasting three days. The trial judge was Mr Justice Archibald, with Sir Charles Russell leading for the prosecution and Thomas Campbell Foster conducting Mary Ann's defence.

The jury heard the evidence outlined above and were told that some six weeks before Charles Edward's death she had sent him to buy soft soap and arsenic from the local chemist which was used to kill bed bugs. The chemist refused to serve the child and so Mary Ann persuaded one of her neighbours, Mary Dodds, to get it for her. The mixture contained 240 grains of arsenic, enough to poison eighty people.

Thomas Campbell Foster presented an ingenious defence on Mary's behalf. He told the court that the Cotton family had all died in the same room, which had green floral wallpaper which contained arsenic. When the wallpaper was washed with soap, a poisonous dust was created in the room which was inhaled by the family and led to their deaths and the arsenic found in their organs. The prosecution countered this argument by pointing out that many of the other people who had been close to Mary Ann and who had died had never entered the room. The jury found her guilty and Mr Justice Archibald passed sentence of death upon her.

The *Newcastle Journal* ran the headline 'Mary Ann Cotton Wholesale Poisoner.'

In the condemned cell at Durham prison Mary Ann was allowed to keep her newborn baby with her until a week before her execution. The baby was adopted by William and Sarah Edwards, a childless couple from Johnson Terrace.

Amazingly there was a petition got up to save the by now forty-one-year-old murderess, possibly out of sympathy for her newborn child, but this was rejected. It would be hard to think of a less deserving case for mercy.

On the Saturday before the execution the simple gallows, comprising two uprights and a crossbeam and double leaf trap, was erected over a brick-lined pit in the condemned prisoner's exercise yard where it would be hidden from view until Mary Ann and her escorts rounded a corner.

Although executions were no longer in public little else had changed and the press were still admitted to witness the proceedings and their accounts still remain. William Calcraft, probably assisted by Robert Anderson, had been hired by the under sheriff of Durham to carry out the execution.

There had been some discussion in view of her emotional state as to whether Mary should be hanged strapped to a chair. The pit beneath the trapdoors was apparently widened to accommodate this, although in the event the chair was not needed.

The execution was set for 8 a.m. on Monday 24 March 1873 and Mary breakfasted on just a few sips of tea. Throughout her time in prison she had refused to confess or accept religious counsel but during her last few hours, became most devout and contrite. She prayed with the three matrons who guarded her and, recalling her childhood Sunday school lessons, declared her favourite hymn to be *Rock of Ages*.

It is said that Mary made the warders wait to escort her to the gallows while she brushed her long black hair. When she was ready, she let Calcraft pinion her wrists in front of her with a leather strap and place a further leather strap around her elbows and upper body. Wearing a black and white checked shawl, Mary walked resignedly to the gallows. Once on the trapdoors, her legs were strapped and the white hood placed over her head, followed by the simple halter noose. Two warders supported her during this preparation. The trap was released from under her and she dropped about 18in. For a moment she hung still, presumably stunned by the impact of the rope, but then she began to struggle violently, her agonies lasting some three minutes before she dangled lifeless in the pit.

Following the formal inquest, a plaster cast was taken of her face and she was buried in the western part of Durham Prison at 2 p.m. A broadside was printed and the *Newcastle Daily Journal* published a special edition on the day of execution. Madame Tussaud's waxworks made a model of her for their Chamber of Horrors. She is said to still haunt her old home in Newcastle upon Tyne.

Mary Ann seemed to have become addicted to murder by arsenic poisoning when she found how easy it was to do, how she could get away with it, and how each killing could earn her a small amount of life insurance or remove some inconvenient person in her life or both.

Today it would be impossible to get away with so many murders of this sort but in those days in poor areas like the Durham coal fields, public hygiene standards were low and child and adult mortality rates very high. By moving around, she was able to get different doctors to sign death certificates so that she was not immediately suspected. Communications were very limited; there were no telephones in 1873, so the doctors were unlikely to talk to each other and post-mortems were rarely carried out on deaths that appeared natural. Gastric fever was a common cause of natural death at this time.

Mary Ann could potentially have killed up to twelve children and stepchildren, a friend, a lodger, three husbands and her mother in twelve years. It is impossible to be sure of the cause of death of the earlier victims as they were too decomposed to test. She never confessed to a single killing. Mary Ann seemed to have a magnetic attraction for men – she was never without one for long.

Kate Webster
Gruesome Murder at Richmond

Kate was a rather incompetent career criminal who had served several prison terms for various thefts and offences of dishonesty, both in her native Ireland and in England. These included a period of twelve months in 1877 in London's Wandsworth Prison, where she would ultimately die.

She was born Catherine Lawler in 1849 in Killann, Co. Wexford, in what is now the Irish Republic and started her criminal career at an early age. She claimed to have a married a sea captain called Webster by whom, according to her, she had had four children. Whether this is true is doubtful however. She moved to Liverpool stealing money for the ferry fare and continued stealing once she arrived there. This was to earn her a four-year prison sentence at the age of eighteen. On release, she went to London and took work as a cleaner, often 'cleaning out' her employer's possessions before moving on. In 1873 she settled at Rose Gardens in London's Hammersmith area. Her next-door neighbours were Henry and Ann Porter whom she got on well with and who feature later in the story. She moved to Notting Hill to a new job as a cook/house-keeper to Captain Woolbest and whilst in his employ met a man named Strong with whom she went to live and became pregnant by. She duly gave birth to a son on 19 April 1874 and was promptly abandoned by Strong. Without any means of support (there was no Social Security then), Kate resorted to her usual dishonest practices and served several prison sentences as a result.

On release from Wandsworth in 1877 she again sought domestic work, firstly with the Mitchell family in Teddington, of whom she was to say that they didn't have anything worth stealing. She was constantly on the move and used several aliases including Webster and Lawler.

Sarah Crease, another domestic servant, became friends with Kate somewhere around this period and found herself looking after Kate's son during his mother's spells in prison.

On 13 January 1879 Kate entered the service of Mrs Julia Martha Thomas at No.2 Vine Cottages, Park Road, Richmond. To begin with, the two women got on well and Kate recorded that she felt she could be happy working for Mrs Thomas, who was comfortably off, although a rather eccentric woman in her mid-fifties. Soon, however, the poor quality of Kate's work and her frequent visits to local pubs began to irritate Mrs Thomas and after various reprimands, she gave Kate notice with her dismissal to take effect on Friday, 28 February. This period of notice was a fatal mistake on the part of Mrs Thomas and she became increasingly frightened of her employee during this period, so much so that she asked friends from her church and relatives to stay in the house with her. Friday the 28th arrived and as Kate had not managed to find a new job or any accommodation, she pleaded with Mrs Thomas to be allowed to remain in her house over the weekend. Sadly, Mrs Thomas agreed to this, a decision that was to cost both women their lives.

On the Sunday morning, 2 March 1879, Mrs Thomas went off to church as usual. Kate was allowed Sunday afternoons off work but had to be back in time for Mrs Thomas to go to the evening service. This Sunday afternoon Kate went to visit her son, who was in the care of Sarah Crease, and then went to a pub on the way back to Vine Cottages. Thus she got back late which inconvenienced Mrs Thomas, who again reprimanded her before rushing off for the church service. Fellow members of the congregation noticed that she seemed agitated; whether this was because she suspected Kate's dishonesty and feared her home was being robbed we do not know. Whatever the reason, Mrs Thomas left church before the end of the service and went home, sadly without asking anyone to accompany her. Precisely what happened next is unclear. In her confession prior to her execution, Kate described the events as follows:

> We had an argument which ripened into a quarrel, and in the height of my anger and rage I threw her from the top of the stairs to the ground floor. She had a heavy fall. I felt that she was seriously injured and I became agitated at what had happened, lost all control of myself and to prevent her screaming or getting me into trouble, I caught her by the throat and in the struggle choked her.

At her trial, the prosecution painted a rather different picture. Mrs Thomas' next door neighbour, Mrs Ives, heard the noise of the fall followed by silence and at the time thought no more of it. Little was she to suspect what was to happen next.

Kate, of course, had the problem of what to do with the body but instead of just leaving it and escaping, she decided to dismember it and then dispose of the parts in the river. She set about this grim task with a will, firstly cutting off the dead woman's head with a razor and meat saw and then hacking off her limbs. She par-boiled the limbs and torso in a copper on the stove and burned Mrs Thomas' organs and intestines. Even Kate was revolted by all this and the enormous amount of blood everywhere. But she stuck to the job and systematically burnt or boiled all of the body parts and then packed the remains into a wooden box, except for the head and one foot for which she could not find room. It has been said that Kate even tried to sell the fatty remains from boiling the body as dripping. Mrs Ives was later to report a strange smell from next door caused by the burning. Kate disposed of the spare foot on a manure heap but was left with the problem of the head, which she decided to place into a black bag. She continued to clean up the cottage on the Monday and Tuesday and then 'borrowing' one of Mrs Thomas' silk dresses went to visit the Porter family on the Tuesday afternoon, taking the black bag containing the head with her. She told the Porters that she had benefited under the will of an aunt who had left her a house in Richmond which she wanted to dispose of, together with its contents, as she had decided to return to Ireland. She asked Henry Porter if he knew a property broker (estate agent) who might be able to assist her. Later in the evening Kate excused herself and went off, ostensibly to visit another friend, returning later without the black bag which was never found. Both Henry Porter and his son Robert had carried the bag for Kate at various stages of their walk to the railway station and two pubs along the way and both noticed how heavy it was. This left Kate with the rest of the human remains in the box to dispose of and she sought the services of young Robert Porter to help her in this, taking the lad back home with her for the purpose. She and Robert carried the box between them to Richmond Bridge, where Kate said she was meeting someone who was taking the box and told Robert to go on without her. Robert was to hear a splash of something heavy hitting the water below a few moments before Kate caught up with him again.

The box was discovered the next morning by a coal man who must have had a horrible shock when he opened it. He reported his discovery to Inspector Harber at Barnes police station and the police had the various body parts examined by a local doctor who declared that they were from a human female and noticed that the skin showed signs of having been boiled. Without the head, however, it was not possible to identify the body.

Kate meanwhile was calling herself Mrs Thomas and wearing the dead woman's clothes and jewellery. She kept up pressure on Henry Porter to help her dispose of the property and he introduced her to a Mr John Church (a publican and general dealer), who she persuaded to buy the contents of the house. Kate and Church seemed to become friends quickly and went drinking together several times. The real Mrs Thomas had not been reported missing at this stage and the papers referred to the human remains in the box as 'the Barnes Mystery', a fact known to Kate as she could read, as could the Porter family. Robert told his father about the box he had helped Kate carry which was like the one described in the papers.

Kate agreed a price for the furniture and some of Mrs Thomas' clothes with John Church and he arranged for their removal. Unsurprisingly, this was to arouse the suspicion of Mrs Ives next door who questioned Kate as to what was going on. Mrs Church was later to find a purse and diary belonging to Mrs Thomas in one of the dresses. There was also a letter from a Mr Menhennick to whom Henry Porter and John Church paid a visit. Menhennick knew the real Mrs Thomas and it became clear from the discussion that it could well be her body in the box. The three men, together with Menhennick's solicitor, went to Richmond police station and reported their suspicions. The next day a search was made of No.2 Vine Cottages and an axe, razor and some charred bones were recovered, together with the missing handle from the box found in the river. Thus on 23 March, a full description of Kate Webster was circulated by the police in connection with the murder of Mrs Thomas and the theft of her effects.

Kate had decided to flee to Ireland taking her son with her. She was arrested on 28 March and kept in custody awaiting collection by two detectives from Scotland Yard. She was brought back to England and taken to Richmond police station where she made a statement on 30 March and was formally charged with the murder. The statement accused John Church of being responsible for Mrs Thomas' death and he was subsequently arrested and charged with the murder too. Fortunately, he had a strong alibi and had also assisted the police in discovering the crimes. At the committal hearing, the charges against him were dropped while Kate was remanded in custody. She was transferred to Newgate prison to save the long journey by horse drawn prison van across London each day to the Old Bailey.

Her trial opened on 2 July 1879 before Mr Justice Denman at the Central Criminal Court next door to Newgate. In view of the seriousness of the crime, the Crown was led by the Solicitor General, Sir Hardinge Gifford, and Kate was defended by Mr Warner Sleigh.

A hat maker named Mary Durden gave evidence for the prosecution telling the court that on 25 February, Kate had told her she was going to Birmingham to take control of the property, jewellery, etc. that had been left her by a recently deceased aunt. This, the prosecution claimed, was clear evidence of premeditation, as the conversation had occurred six days before the murder. One of the problems of the prosecution case, however, was proving that the human remains the police had found were actually those of Mrs Thomas. It was a weakness that her defence sought to capitalise on, especially as without the head there was no means of positively identifying them at that time. Medical evidence was given to show that all the body parts had belonged to the same person and that they were from a woman in her fifties. The defence tried to suggest that Mrs Thomas could have died of natural causes, in view of her agitated state, when she was last seen alive leaving church on the Sunday afternoon. Both Henry Porter and John Church gave evidence against Kate describing the events of which they had been involved, and her defence again tried to point the finger of suspicion at them. In his summing up, the judge, however, pointed to the actions and previously known good characters of both men. Two of Kate's friends, Sarah Crease and Lucy Loder, gave evidence of her good nature.

Late on the afternoon of Tuesday, 8 July, the jury retired to consider their verdict, returning just over an hour later to pronounce her guilty. Before she was sentenced, Kate yet again made a complete denial of the charge but cleared Church and Porter of any involvement in the crime. As was normal, she was asked if she had anything to say before she was sentenced and she claimed to be pregnant. She was examined by some of the women present in the court and this claim was dismissed as just another of her lies. She went back to Newgate and was transferred the next day to Wandsworth Prison to await execution, guarded round the clock by teams of female prison officers.

Kate was to make two further 'confessions' in Wandsworth, the first implicating Strong, who was the father of her child. These allegations were also found to be baseless.

Kate was informed by her solicitor that no reprieve was to be granted to her, despite a small amount of public agitation for commutation. So on the eve of her hanging, Kate made another confession to the solicitor in the presence of the Catholic priest attending her, Father McEnrey, which seemed somewhat nearer the truth. She stated that she was resigned to her fate and that she would almost rather be executed than return to a life of misery and deception.

The execution was to take place three clear Sundays after sentence and was set for the morning of Tuesday, 29 July at Wandsworth. Wandsworth was originally the Surrey House of Correction and had been built in 1851. It took over the responsibility for housing Surrey's condemned prisoners on the closure of Horsemonger Lane Gaol in 1878. Kate was to be only the second person and the sole woman to be hanged there.

At 8.45 a.m., the prison bell started to toll and a few minutes before 9 a.m. the under sheriff, the prison governor, Captain Colville, the prison doctor, two male warders and William Marwood formed up outside her cell. Inside, Kate was being ministered to by Father McEnrey and attended by two wardresses. She would have typically been offered a stiff tot of brandy before the execution commenced. The governor entered her cell and told her that it was time and she was led out between the two male warders, accompanied by Father McEnrey, across the yard to the purpose built execution shed which was nicknamed the 'Cold Meat Shed.' Having the gallows in a separate building spared the other prisoners from the sound of the trap falling, and made it easier too for the staff to deal with the execution and removal of the body afterwards. As Kate entered the shed, she would have seen the large white painted gallows with the rope dangling in front of her with its simple noose lying on the trapdoors. The idea of coiling up the rope to bring the noose to chest level came later, as did the brass eyelet in the noose. Marwood stopped her on the chalk mark on the double trapdoors and placed a leather body belt round her waist to which he secured her wrists, while his assistant (probably one of the warders), strapped her ankles with a leather strap. She was not pinioned in her cell, as became the normal practice later. She was supported on the trap by the two warders standing on planks, set across it. This had been the normal practice for some years in case the prisoner fainted or struggled at the last moment. Marwood placed the white hood over her head and adjusted the noose, leaving the free rope running down her back. Her last words were, 'Lord, have mercy upon me.' He quickly stepped to the side and pulled the lever, Kate plummeting down some 8ft into the brick-lined pit below. Marwood used significantly longer drops than were later found to be necessary. The whole process would have taken around three minutes in those days and was considered vastly more humane than Calcraft's executions.

The black flag was hoisted on the flag pole above the main gate, where a small crowd of people had gathered. They would have seen and heard nothing and yet these rather pointless gatherings continued outside prisons until abolition.

Later in the day, Kate's body was buried in an unmarked grave in one of the exercise yards at Wandsworth. Nobody else was to be buried in this grave although after the nine-tieth execution, the authorities started to re-use male graves, but not hers. She is listed in the handwritten prison records as Catherine Webster, interred 29/07/1879. Although she was the second person to be executed at Wandsworth, she was buried in grave no.3 as the graves were numbered 1, 3, 5, etc. on one side of the path, while on the other side they were numbered 2, 4, 6, etc. and it was decided to use those on one side first. A flowerbed covers these graves nowadays.

If the events of that Sunday evening were exactly as Kate described them, it is strange that Mrs Ives did not hear the quarrel or any other noises from next door. Again why were there bloodstains at the top of the stairs if Mrs Thomas' injuries had occurred at the bottom? It is generally held that Kate lay in wait for Mrs Thomas and hit her on the head with an axe causing her to fall down the stairs, where she then strangled her to prevent any further noise. This would, of course, make the crime one of premeditated murder and is much more in line with the forensic evidence. Whether Kate decided to kill Mrs Thomas in revenge for her earlier telling off or whether it was because she saw a great opportunity to steal from Vine Cottage, or both, is unknown. It is not unknown for previously non-violent criminals to turn to violent murder. But what turned Kate to such appalling violence? Did she just snap or had she spent two hours or so thinking about it?

Postscript

It was reported in October 2010 that Julia Martha Thomas' skull had finally been discovered in the grounds of Sir David Attenborough's property in Park Road, Richmond, by workmen excavating for an extension. He had purchased a former pub called 'The Hole in the Wall' which was adjacent to his property and had demolished the rear of the pub. It is highly likely that Kate Webster frequented this pub. The coroner's report stated that the skull had fractures consistent with falling down stairs and also had depleted collagen, which suggested it had been boiled.

Mary Eleanor Wheeler (Pearcey) 'The Hamstead Tragedy'

Mary Eleanor Wheeler was born in Kent on 26 March 1866 to James and Charlotte Wheeler, but little detail is known of her childhood. At the time of her arrest, she was 24 and was described as being 5ft 6in tall with 'lovely russet hair and fine blue eyes'. She was of normal build and had nice, shapely hands. Her face was not overly pretty but she seemed to have no difficulty in attracting men. In her late teens, she had a relationship with a carpenter named John Charles Pearcey and, although they never married, Mary took his name and continued to use it after they split up. She was arrested, charged and tried under this name.

Mary associated with better-off men and had never worked or ever needed to. One of her several admirers, Charles Creighton, had rented rooms for her at 2 Priory Street,

Kentish Town, in North London, around 1888, when she met Frank Samuel Hogg. She was known to suffer from depression and had only her aged mother and a sister as relatives. She also drank quite heavily. In addition to Mr Creighton, who visited her once a week, she also fell for Mr Hogg, who was a furniture remover and impressed Mary by having printed business cards. Mary used to put a light in her window to let Frank know that she was free and he had a key to the house. There was, however, one serious snag to Mary's happiness. Frank was married and had a daughter, both his wife and the little girl being called Phoebe.

Phoebe Hogg was 32 at the time of her death and had been quite ill in February 1890. She had married Frank Hogg in November 1888, when she was three months pregnant by him, and had given birth to their daughter, Phoebe Hanslope Hogg, in the summer of 1889. Frank's affair with Mary had been going on both before and during the marriage.

On the morning of 24 October 1890, Mary, it is alleged, asked a young lad to run an errand for her. She gave Willie Holmes a penny for delivering a note to Phoebe Hogg, inviting her to tea that afternoon. Around 4 p.m., Charlotte Priddington, Mary's neighbour, heard the sound of breaking glass coming from Mary's house and called over the fence to check that she was okay but received no reply. At 7 p.m., a woman's body was discovered lying on a pavement in Crossfield Road by a man returning from work, and he promptly reported it to a policeman. The woman's head was wrapped in a cardigan which he removed to yield the blood-stained face of Phoebe Hogg with a huge gash in her throat.

The body was removed and taken first to Hampstead Police Station and then to the morgue. It was found that the deceased had a fractured skull and that the throat had been cut so violently as to nearly sever the head. There were also bruises on the head and arms, consistent with her having tried to defend herself. The murder weapons were a fire poker and a knife.

Examination of the place where the body was found indicated that the murder had taken place elsewhere. At this time, the police did not have an identity for the corpse.

Later that evening, a constable on the beat discovered a heavily bloodstained pram in Hamilton Terrace about a mile from where the woman's body was found. The following morning the body of a small child was discovered. She was found to have died from suffocation and was otherwise unmarked except for a few scratches. It was possible that little Phoebe had either been suffocated during or after the murder of her mother or, alternatively, had been placed in the pram alive with her mother's body on top of her, and that it was the weight of her mother's body that suffocated her.

Frank Hogg and his sister Clara reported Phoebe missing after reading about the discovery of the woman's body in the Saturday evening paper. Frank sent Clara round to Mary's to ask if she had seen Phoebe, which Mary denied, but she agreed to accompany Clara to the morgue to see if was indeed Phoebe's body. Mary's behaviour there was very strange. Having consented to go with Clara when first shown the body, Mary reportedly said, 'That's not her', although Clara identified Phoebe's clothes. She did her best to try to prevent Clara identifying the body and became almost hysterical when the full extent of Phoebe's injuries became apparent.

The police asked Mary and Clara to view the pram, which Clara identified as belonging to Phoebe. A neighbour of Mary's stated that she had seen Mary pushing the pram with a large object in it on the evening of the murder.

Frank Hogg was informed of the positive identification of his wife and, as a possible suspect himself, was searched by the police. He confessed to having the affair with Mary when the key to her house was found. The police decided to interview Mary next as they were already suspicious of her behaviour in the mortuary and so went round to Priory Street and carried out a thorough search of her home. They found substantial bloodstains and spatters in the kitchen, together with a blood-stained carving knife and fire poker. There were also clear signs of a struggle – with two broken windows in the kitchen. A rug showing bloodstains smelt strongly of paraffin where an attempt had been made to clean it. Mary's behaviour became more bizarre during the police search. She sat at her piano, singing and whistling loudly, and attempted to explain away the bloodstains by saying that she had been 'killing mice, killing mice' – a hardly credible excuse.

Detective Inspector Banister decided to arrest Mary at this point and charge her with the murders of both mother and child. When Mary was searched, bloodstains were found on her clothes, scratches on her hands, and two wedding rings were on her fingers, one of which was later identified as Phoebe Hogg's. Mary was kept in custody in Holloway prison and appeared at a committal hearing at Marylebone police court on 28 October, for a magistrate to hear the *prima facia* evidence against her and commit her for trial.

While in the police court awaiting the committal hearing, she told Sarah Sawhill, the woman looking after her, that Mrs Hogg had indeed come to tea that afternoon and that, as they were having tea, Mrs Hogg had made a remark that offended Mary and an argument developed. Mary realised that she was incriminating herself and declined to say any more.

Mary was tried, under the name of Pearcey, at the Central Criminal Court of the Old Bailey before Mr Justice Denman, who had tried Kate Webster eleven years earlier. Her three-day trial opened on 1 December 1890. The prosecution was led by Mr Forrest Fulton, assisted by Mr C.F. Gill, and her defence by Mr Arthur Hutton. Mary entered a formal plea of not guilty and then the prosecution began to outline its case against her. They read out various letters that Mary had written to Frank Hogg, which were claimed to show the depth of her passion for him prior to his forced marriage to Phoebe, consequent upon her pregnancy. Mary had told Frank that even if he had to marry Phoebe, she did not want him to leave her and that she should treat Phoebe as a friend (which for a time, at least, it appears she did). The suggested motive for the murder was jealousy of Phoebe, now that Mary had to share Frank with her. Evidence was also given regarding the place of the crime and the nature and method of infliction of Phoebe's injuries. John Pearcey identified the cardigan found round Phoebe's head as one he had given to Mary, and evidence was given of the blinds being drawn in Mary's house on the afternoon of the murder. Arthur Hutton questioned the circumstantial evidence against her and also whether a woman of her size and build would be capable of inflicting such dreadful injuries on the deceased. Mary gave no evidence at the trial and remained impassive throughout. She was found guilty after just fifty-two minutes on the lunchtime of the third day. In accordance with normal practice Mary was asked 'if she had anything to say why the Court should not give her judgement of death in accordance with the law', to which she replied, 'I say I am innocent of this charge'. Mr Justice Denman then donned the black cap and sentenced her to hang.

There was no appeal in those days – it was to be 1907 before the Court of Criminal Appeal was set up. However, her solicitor made considerable effort to save her, alleging that she was not in control of herself at the time of the killing and that this was due to the epileptic fits that she had suffered from since birth. On 16 December, the Home Office wrote to Mr Freke Palmer, informing him that a medical inquiry under the Criminal Lunatics Act of 1884 had been granted. This was to be carried out on the Friday by three doctors, Bennett, Gilbert and Savage, whose hour-long interview with Mary did not find evidence of legal insanity and, after due consideration of their report, her case papers were marked with the fatal words 'the law must take its course'. This decision was communicated to her solicitor on Saturday, 19 December.

At Mary's request, Frank Hogg was given permission to visit her on the Monday afternoon in Newgate but he did not show up, which greatly upset Mary, who wept inconsolably on her bed when she realised he was not going to come. Other than that, she remained very composed through her last day and night. On her final afternoon, Mary was visited by Freke Palmer, her solicitor, whom she asked to deal with certain bequests and also to place a personal advert for her in the Madrid newspapers which was to read: 'MECP Last wish of MEW. Have not betrayed. MEW' (Mary Eleanor Wheeler). Mary refused to elaborate on the meaning of this message, except for saying that it had nothing to do with the murder, but was to do with her erstwhile short-lived marriage to a man whom she refused to name. She also refused point blank to confess to Palmer, despite persistent questioning, with the promise that he would put any relevant facts before the Home Secretary in a last-ditch attempt to get a reprieve. Her mother and older sister visited her for the final time on the Monday and Mary told them that she did not want to be reprieved because she would have to spend years in prison surrounded by criminals.

Mary was to be hanged by James Berry two days before Christmas 1890 (three clear Sundays after sentence) at London's Newgate prison. On arrival back at Newgate from the Old Bailey, she would have been made to take a bath and been given a prison uniform – a plain, grey shift dress – before being taken to the infirmary where she was confined until the evening of 21 December, when she was moved to the condemned cell. She was guarded round the clock by teams of three matrons (wardresses). The Rev. H. Duffield ministered to her spiritual needs and remained with her until just before 8 a.m. on the Tuesday morning.

The Sheriff of London, Sir James Whitehead, had decided to exclude newspaper reporters from her hanging, presumably out of deference to her sex and age. The execution was

scheduled for Tuesday, 22 December, and Berry arrived at
the prison on the Saturday. Mary noticed him looking at her
through the Judas (peep) hole in her cell door and remarked
to the women guarding her, 'Oh, was that the executioner?
He's in good time, isn't he? Is it usual for him to arrive on the
Saturday for the Monday?' (Home Office regulations required
the hangman to be at the prison by 4 p.m. on the afternoon
prior to the hanging.) The matrons reported that, on the night
before her execution, 'her fortitude was remarkable'. She
dressed herself in the clothes she had worn for her trial. She
only drank a little tea and was not able to eat any breakfast.

Berry entered the condemned cell a few moments before
8 a.m. 'This is Berry,' whispered one of the matrons. 'I know,'
she replied. Berry said, 'Good morning, madam' to Mary
and shook hands with her. He then went on, 'If you're ready
madam I will get these straps round you', to which Mary
replied that she was quite ready. So Berry placed the leather
body belt around her waist and secured her wrists to it in
front of her. According to James Berry, the Sheriff of London,
Sir James Whitehead, asked if she had any final statement, to
which she replied, 'My sentence is a just one and much of the
evidence against me false.'

Two of the wardresses guarding her now took up position,
one on each side of her; Mary told them she didn't need assistance and would be able to walk by herself, but this of course
had to be ignored as it was a Home Office requirement that
she be escorted. One of the women said she would accompany
Mary, who said, 'Oh well, if you don't mind going with me, I
am pleased', and then kissed all three women affectionately
before the procession started out from the cell along the cor-
ridor and across the yard to the execution shed. It consisted of
the Sheriff; the under sheriff, Mr Metcalfe; the Chaplain, the
Rev. Duffield; the Governor of Newgate, Colonel Milman;
the prison doctor, Dr P.F. Gilbert; and at least three male warders. Berry reportedly drew the white hood over Mary's head

as she emerged into the yard to prevent her from having to see the instrument of her doom.

The gallows at Newgate was a large structure, constructed in 1881, and capable of taking up to four prisoners side by side, although on this occasion only a single noose dangled from the six links of iron chain attached to the metal bracket in the centre of the beam. Mary weighed 126lbs and stood at 5ft 6in tall, so Berry set a drop of 6ft for her. Once on the drop, she was supported by two male warders while her legs were pinioned and the brass eyelet of the noose was positioned under the angle of her left jaw and the rope drawn tight. Berry checked that the scaffold was clear and quickly pulled the lever. The 'ponderous' trapdoors crashed down and Mary disappeared from view, leaving just the taut rope in sight. She died without a struggle – her neck broken instantly by the length of the drop and the position of the eyelet. Dr Gilbert felt for a pulse and, finding none, was able to declare life was extinct.

Outside the prison on that bitterly cold December morning, some 300 people, including many women, had gathered to witness the sounds of St Sepulchre's church bell tolling and the black flag flying above the prison to denote that the execution had been carried out. Mary apparently evoked little public sympathy, perhaps due to murdering the child, and there was a cheer from the crowd as the flag was hoisted.

Her body was left dangling on the rope for the customary hour in the brick-lined pit beneath the trap and then removed and placed in a coffin atop of the now-closed trapdoors for viewing by the coroner's jury. The inquest was held at noon before Mr Langham, the coroner for the City of London. She was buried later in the day in an unmarked grave within Bird Cage Walk in Newgate. Quicklime was added to the plain deal coffin and holes bored into it to hasten decay, as it was thought to do at the time.

Madame Tussauds made a wax model of her for the Chamber of Horrors, as was normal in celebrated cases, and bought the pram from Frank Hogg together with some of the other effects. There was a broadside on the case and pictures in *The Illustrated Police News*.

There was reliable evidence that Mary had been an epileptic since childhood and her solicitor, Freke Palmer, unearthed a considerable volume of evidence on her epilepsy and two suicide attempts, which he suggested indicated that Mary was less than sane. It should be noted, however, that epilepsy is not, nowadays, considered a form of mental illness. To have epilepsy is to have recurrent seizures. A seizure is a temporary state of abnormal electrical activity within the brain. The word 'temporary' is important, and these occasional seizures do not in themselves amount to mental illness. Epileptic automatism has been successfully used as a defence in murder trials because it proves that the person could not have formed the intent to kill while they were having the seizure.

However, in Mary's case, none of this added up to a legal defence of insanity, which was governed by the M'Naughten Rules. This had arisen from the case of Daniel M'Naughten, who in 1843 tried to kill the Prime Minister, Sir Robert Peel, against whom he had an imaginary grudge, but instead shot his secretary, Mr Drummond. The court found him not guilty of the crime by reason of insanity because, at the time it occurred, he either did not know what he was doing or, if he did, he did not know that it was wrong. In M'Naughten's case, it was found that he didn't know what he was doing at the time of the shooting. M'Naughten Rules were interpreted very strictly in Mary's days (it was to be widened later) and there was little scope for this defence to succeed. Palmer publicly expressed his disappointment with the Home Secretary, saying that it seemed that the whole world was against her. There is a distinct element of truth in this, probably caused as much as anything by the murder of the baby and by her promiscuous behaviour, as it would have been seen through Victorian eyes.

If Mary wasn't insane (at least according to the legal definition at the time), was she suffering from a personality disorder?
As stated earlier, she had twice tried to commit suicide in the
previous ten years.

Like many murderers, Mary was a first-time offender –
there is no evidence of previous convictions for any offence
nor any use of violence. Evidence of pre-meditation was put
forward at her trial and yet there is very little evidence that
Mary tried to cover her tracks or to clean up the house afterwards, which one might have expected her to have done. Was
she in an epileptic state at the time of the crime or had she
perhaps been drinking prior to it to give herself courage for
the grim task ahead? One of her neighbours said in evidence
that she appeared 'boozed' when she saw her after the murder,
and this symptom can be found in people recovering from an
epileptic fit and can be seen in the eyes.

Mary was described by James Berry as the calmest person
present at her execution. Was she, like so many other murderers, resigned to her fate and keen to rid herself of the burden
of guilt and of the secrets she carried?

It was reported in the press and Berry repeats it in his mem-
oirs that Mary confessed the justice of her sentence just before
she was led to the gallows, but one wonders whether this is
what they would have liked her to have said rather than what
she actually said. Did she perhaps say, 'My sentence is an unjust
one and much of the evidence against me false'? She had
refused absolutely to confess to her mother or her solicitor
prior to the execution, both of whom questioned her closely.
She was aware of her imminent death, as she told her mother,
but would not budge on her story of knowing nothing at all
about the killing. Palmer pressed Mary repeatedly on whether
she had any recollection at all of the events, but Mary declined
to admit any and brought the meeting to a very definite close,
having asked him again to place the advert for her in the
Spanish papers. It may be that she had come to believe that

she must have killed Phoebe and the baby, as everyone said she had done, and, therefore, accepted responsibility for the crime without actually being able to remember it.

I believe that she did actually kill Phoebe and the baby – the evidence for her being the killer is very strong – but feel that it was more likely to be because of an argument and fight that developed between the two women rather than it being a premeditated crime. She may well be found to have 'diminished responsibility' nowadays, although, of course, the concept wasn't recognised then.

It is, however, quite possible that she was either still in denial of the crimes, which had, after all, only taken place two months earlier, or genuinely could not remember anything, if, as Palmer suggests, she was in an epileptic state at the time. It is not unusual for people to block out the memories of particularly horrible events from their minds, and the murder of Phoebe Hogg was certainly a horrific one. Mary's behaviour in the mortuary is odd, to say the least – while one can accept that the sight of Phoebe's corpse would be upsetting for anyone, at that stage only Mary and Clara knew who it was on the slab. Her behaviour when the police were searching her house is even more bizarre. Is this strange behaviour evidence of Mary being in denial or revolted by what she had done?

The defence questioned whether a woman of Mary's size and build would have the physical strength to inflict the appalling injuries on Phoebe Hogg, and it does seem a fair question, although there is no evidence that anyone else was involved. Phoebe was said to be 5ft 6in tall and seemed to have put up quite a fight, as witnessed by the broken windows, etc., in the house when the police examined it later.

Evidence of premeditation was given to the court – the written invite to Mrs Hogg to come to tea and the alleged pulling down of the blinds to provide privacy during the attack. But what was it that made Mary lash out with such violence against Phoebe Hogg on that particular occasion?

Did they quarrel over Frank or was it something one of them said that started an argument, as suggested by Mary in the conversation with Sarah Sawhill? Was it, as the prosecution alleged, a premeditated plan hatched by Mary out of jealousy to eliminate her rival? She seemed to be aware of the punishment for murder but made virtually no effort to destroy the evidence of the crime nor did she take a lot of trouble in the disposal of the bodies, which seems strange if she had planned the murder and had hoped to escape the consequences. Sadly, we will never know the answers to these questions.

Mary Ann Ansell
The Poisoned Cake

In Victorian times attitudes to mental illness were very different to those of today, the policy being to confine patients diagnosed with such illnesses to large asylums which were being built all over the country. One such facility was Leavesden Mental Asylum which had been built at Abbots Langley in Buckinghamshire by the Metropolitan Asylums Board to serve North London. It was opened in 1870 to house 'quiet and harmless imbeciles' and soon had over 1,500 patients, of which some 900 were women. One of these was nineteen-year-old Caroline Ansell, who had come from a family with a background of mental health problems.

Caroline's older sister, Mary Ann, aged twenty-two, worked as a maid to a wealthy household in Coram Street in the Bloomsbury area of London and was engaged to a young man. Neither Mary Ann nor her fiancé had any money and had had to postpone their wedding because they could not afford the cost of a marriage licence which was 7s 6d. This situation did not suit Mary Ann who devised a plot to insure her sister's life and then kill her to obtain the pay out. For a premium of three old pence a week she would get £11 on the death of her sister.

This was to be accomplished using a phosphorous based rat poison which she bought from a local shop near where she worked. She stirred the poison into a cake mix, baked the cake and sent it through the post to her sister on Ward 7 at Leavesden on 9 March 1899. Caroline decided to share the cake with some of her friends and all became ill. However Caroline ate considerably more of the cake than the rest had and therefore had far more severe symptoms. The staff were at full stretch at the time, dealing with an outbreak of typhoid amongst the inmates and it was some time before Caroline was seen by a doctor. He immediately admitted her to the infirmary but it was too late to save the poor girl. An autopsy was carried out by Dr Blair who declared the cause of death to be phosphorous poisoning. This was traced back to the remains of the cake and via the postmark on the wrapping paper it came in, back to Mary Ann. She was arrested and charged with the murder. She vehemently denied it saying that she had purchased the rat poison to kill rats in her employer's home. Her mistress, Mrs Maloney, told the police that the house was not infested with vermin and that she had not asked for any rat poison to be purchased.

Mary Ann came to trial at Hertford Assizes in St Albans on 30 June 1899 before Mr Justice Mathew, the proceedings lasting two days. The prosecution made much of Mary Ann's motive for the crime and brought forward various witnesses to bolster their case. A shop assistant from Bloomsbury gave evidence of Mary Ann buying the poison for the purpose of killing rats, which at the time did not seem in any way unusual. Evidence was presented as to the cause of Caroline's death and the origins of the cake.

Mary Ann continued to plead her innocence but had no convincing defence. The jury took two hours to find her guilty and did not make a recommendation to mercy, despite her age.

She was sentenced to death and returned to St Albans Prison. This prison had facilities for female prisoners but had not had an execution since 1880, when Thomas Wheeler was hanged there. It did not have a gallows and had to borrow one from neighbouring Bedford prison.

Even though it seemed like a clear case of premeditated murder there was considerable public agitation for a reprieve, perhaps due to Mary's youth and family background. We have seen this before in other cases of the period. There was resolution passed by the Metropolitan Asylums Board urging for clemency for Mary Ann and some newspapers, such as the *Daily Mail*, also asked for a reprieve on the grounds that she was a mental degenerate. Mary Ann's mother had told the press that she 'had been silly since the time she was at school', and that she sometimes talked to herself. A hundred Members of Parliament had signed a petition on the day before she was due to die, calling for a week's postponement in carrying out the sentence, while her mental state was determined. The Home Secretary, Sir Mathew White Ridley was not moved by all this and determined, as usual in the case of deliberate poisoning, that the law must take its course.

She was therefore hanged by James Billington within the walls of St Albans prison at 8 a.m. on Wednesday, 19 July, 1899. The press were excluded and thus we have no actual details of her death. A crowd estimated at around 2,000 had gathered at the main gate to see the black flag hoisted over the prison and the notice of execution posted. Some knelt silently in prayer at the appointed hour. Mary Ann was interred in an unmarked grave within the prison later in the day. She was the fourth of five women to be executed by James Billington. Edward Lloyd, the Chief Warder, gave an interview to a press reporter in which he stated that Mary Ann 'faltered a little as she walked to the scaffold between two warders. She was sobbing and praying the whole of the time and was heard to say Oh, my God in Heaven and Lord have mercy upon my soul.' He further related that she stood firmly on the drop whilst she was being pinioned, which process lasted a minute and a half.

Mary Ann's body was examined by the prison surgeon, Eustace Henry Lipscombe, who, as was required by law, signed the death certificate. The inquest was held at 10 a.m. before the coroner, Lovell Drage. The Chief Warder told the jury that Mary Ann was given a drop of 7ft, breaking her neck, and that her death had been 'instantaneous'. He produced the death warrant, which read as follows: 'Mary Ann Ansell, convicted of wilful murder, is ordered to be hanged by the neck until she is dead; and her body buried within the precincts of the prison in which she was last confined.' Lloyd confirmed her age as 22.

She was buried in an unmarked grave within the prison later in the day. In 1931, her remains were re-interred in the St Albans City cemetery.

Mary Ann secured her place in history as the youngest woman to be hanged in private and the last woman to be hanged in the nineteenth century. She was the fourth of five women to be executed by James Billington. Of the twenty-three women executed in private between 1868 and 1899, twelve had been convicted of murder by poisoning.

A Home Office file made public in 2000 revealed that Mary Ann had admitted sending Caroline the poisoned cake, mistakenly thinking that the death would not be investigated because her sister was in an asylum.

9

BABY FARMERS

The practice of baby farming grew up in the late Victorian era when there was no effective contraception and great social stigma attached to having a child out of wedlock. Proper adoption agencies and social services didn't exist at this time. Instead, a number of untrained women offered fostering and adoption services to unmarried mothers who would hand over their baby plus, say £10-£15 in cash (quite a large sum of money then), in the hope that the child would be re-homed. Most of the babies were in one way or another. It is probable that some were sold to childless couples and others fostered/ adopted for a few pounds. Unmarried mothers were often desperate so they answered the adverts placed in newspapers by seemingly reputable people. Getting rid of a child in this way had obvious advantages to the mother: it was simple, quick, at the time legal and with few questions asked. The mothers had few real alternatives. Abortion was illegal and the back street abortions that were carried out were a very high risk alternative, sometimes resulting in severe haemorrhaging or even the death of the mother or prosecution and imprisonment if she was found out. Abandonment was similarly illegal and little sympathy was extended by the courts to women who abandoned their children in those days. Murdering of unwanted children by their mothers typically resulted in the death penalty in Victorian Britain. Selina Wadge was hanged by William Marwood on 15 August 1878 at Bodmin for the murder of her illegitimate son, and Louise Massett became the first person to be executed in the twentieth century for murdering her young son.

If having been 're-homed', a baby disappeared, the mother was often too frightened or ashamed to tell the police so it was very easy for the unscrupulous baby farmers to kill off unwanted or hard to foster (or sell?) babies. Sadly, a few of the baby farmers found killing off the babies far easier than re-homing them and these are the cases examined here. Murder yielded a quicker profit without the need for caring for the child for some weeks or months, at their own expense.

In an age of high infant mortality, deaths of babies and small children attracted little attention and were actually quite common. Where a baby's body was found, it was often impossible to trace the mother as the authorities did not have the advantage of DNA tests.

Six baby farmers were hanged in England and one each in Scotland and Wales over the forty-year period from 1870 to 1909.

Annie Tooke

A baby boy named Reginald Hyde was born on 6 October 1878 to a young woman from Cambourne in Cornwall called Mary Hoskins. Mary had moved to Ide near Exeter in Devon to conceal the pregnancy. She was persuaded by her brother to give the child up to a 'nurse' and made contact with forty-year-old Annie Tooke who agreed to take Reginald on for £12, plus 5s a week. Annie moved from

Ide to South Street, Exeter in the spring of 1879 and had difficulty coping with the growing Reginald. The baby was not seen alive after 9 May but a child's torso was discovered on 17 May by a local miller. The head, limbs and genitals were missing but were discovered nearby. This gruesome find made the papers and the story was read by a butcher and a doctor from Ide who knew Annie and the child. They visited her and asked to see Reginald whom she was unable to produce, instead making up a story about an unnamed person having taken him away a fortnight earlier. The police initially suspected that Mary Hoskins had been responsible for the death (presumably to save the 5s a week), and took Annie to Cambourne to identify her. Mary was arrested and charged with the crime, but soon released when Annie gave Captain Bent, the chief constable of Exeter, a statement describing how the child had been taken. Captain Bent became suspicious of her testimony and arrested her. While in Exeter Prison awaiting trial she made a full confession to him, saying how she had suffocated Reginald with a pillow and then cut him up with the fire wood chopper on the coal bunker. She later withdrew this confession. She was tried at the Devon Assizes in Exeter on 21 and 22 July 1879 and the jury convicted her on the basis of the confession, supported by blood stain evidence on items of her clothing and the coal bunker. She was hanged on Monday, 11 August by William Marwood, the gallows being erected in the old prison hospital building. Her execution went without a hitch and the gallows then remained out of use until it was re-erected in the prison van house for the execution of John Lee in 1885. On this occasion the trap doors failed to open on three occasions and Lee was reprieved.

There seems little doubt that she was guilty and that the murder was typical of the 'baby farming' style of crime. However, there is no evidence to show that she was involved with any other children, unlike the other women in this chapter.

Margaret Waters

Margaret Waters, aged thirty-four, was charged with five counts of wilful murder of children in the Brixton area of London, as well as neglect and conspiracy. Sergeant Richard Relf of the Metropolitan Police became the first person to specialise in investigating baby farming murders. He examined the cases of eighteen infant deaths in the Brixton area, leading to the arrest of Margaret Walters. Her case filled the papers in the summer of 1870 with graphic descriptions of how she had poisoned babies, wrapped their bodies in old rags and newspapers and dumped them on deserted streets. When she was arrested, nine babies in very poor health were discovered at her home and taken to the Lambeth Workhouse. Sadly the majority of them died soon afterwards.

Margaret was tried at the Surrey Assizes in September and convicted of the murder of an infant named John Walter Cowen for which she was sentenced to death. Her execution was carried out in private by William Calcraft at Horsemonger Lane Goal, in the county of Surrey, on Wednesday, 11 October 1870. Reporters were not permitted to witness her death, which would have been by short-drop hanging and was unlikely to have led to instant unconsciousness.

Margaret's sister, Sarah Ellis, was convicted in the same case for obtaining money under false pretences and sentenced to eighteen months' hard labour.

Jessie King

Jessie King was a twenty-seven-year-old Glaswegian mill worker who lived with her partner Michael Pearson at lodgings in Canonmills in Edinburgh and ran a small-scale baby farming business. One of the children in her care was an infant boy called Alexander Gunn who initially appeared to be well cared for but suddenly disappeared. Attempts to trace him were defeated by Jessie moving to the Stockbridge area of Edinburgh. Here the couple started looking after a female baby who, like Alexander, suddenly disappeared. Although there was inevitable suspicion, it is probable that Jessie would have got away with it had the body of a male baby not been found by some boys playing in Stockbridge. The baby had been strangled.

Jessie was interviewed and during the questioning broke down and led the police down to the cellar where they discovered the body of the female baby who had been suffocated. Jessie was charged with three murders but the prosecution decided only to proceed with two of them. She was tried before Lord Justice Clerk at the High Court of Justiciary in Edinburgh on 18 February 1889. She told the court that she had strangled Alexander in a state of 'drunken melancholy' and described how she had given the girl whisky to make her sleep, but claimed she had 'overdone it'. She offered no defence and was inevitably found guilty of murder, the jury deliberating for just a few minutes. As she was sentenced to death she gave out a loud shriek and then fainted. She was sent back to Edinburgh's Calton Prison to await execution and whilst in the condemned cell, was examined by a medical commission to see whether she was sane, which they found her to be.

James Berry, the executioner, arrived at Calton Prison on the day before the hanging and, as was customary, went to have a look at the prisoner. She realised who he was and asked him not to hurt her. He assured that he would not and asked her why she had killed the children. According to James Berry's account she burst into tears telling him: 'Oh, Mr. Berry, I must have been mad. The poor little things had to starve like both of us and I thought it was the best thing that could happen to them. I couldn't bear to hear their cries.'

The following morning, Monday, 11 March 1899, she dressed in her own clothes and accepted the sacrament from the Catholic priest who had attended her. She also celebrated mass in the prison chapel before managing some breakfast. Berry went to her cell and allowed her to say goodbye to the wardresses who had looked after her before pinioning her wrists with a leather strap and leading her out. Canon Donlevy read the litany to Jessie as the procession made its way to the gallows and Jessie made the responses to it until Berry tightened the noose around her neck. He did not have an assistant so he also had to pinion her legs. Her last words were: 'Unto thy hands, O Lord, I commend my sprit. Lord Jesus receive my soul. Jesus, son of David have mercy upon me'. With that Berry pulled the lever and she dropped through the trap and became instantly still on the rope. She was left to hang for the regulation hour before being buried in the prison in an unmarked grave that afternoon. Reporters were not allowed to witness the actual execution but were allowed to view her body and talk to the prison staff. She was described as 'calm in the extreme' before her death and Berry was reported as having said that 'in all his life he never saw a woman meet her death so bravely'. She was to be the last woman hanged in Edinburgh.

Amelia Dyer
The Reading Baby Farmer

Amelia Elizabeth Dyer was perhaps the best known and most prolific murderous baby farmer. Mrs Dyer was fifty-six years old when she moved from Bristol to Caversham in Reading in 1895 and began advertising for babies to look after. On 30 March 1896, a bargeman recovered the corpse of fifteen-month-old Helena Fry from the River Thames at Reading. Helena's body was wrapped in a brown paper parcel that had the name of a Mrs Thomas and her address on it – Piggott's Road, Lower Caversham. Mrs Thomas was one of Mrs Dyer's aliases. It took the police some time to trace Mrs Dyer as she had already moved on, changing her address quite frequently and also using various aliases.

In the meantime, a Cheltenham barmaid, twenty-three-year-old Evelina Marmon, had answered a newspaper advert from a 'Mrs Harding' seeking a child for adoption. She met 'Mrs Harding' and paid her a £10 fee to take her four-month-old baby daughter Doris on 31 March 1896. She felt comfortable with the arrangement as 'Mrs Harding' appeared to be a respectable and motherly person. The following day Mrs Dyer 'adopted' another child, Harry Simmons. The police finally located Mrs Dyer, who they kept under surveillance for several days before mounting a 'sting' operation using a young woman to pose as a potential customer. She was arrested on 4 April 1896 when she opened the door to the person she thought would be this customer only to find two policemen standing there. The two tiny bodies of Doris and Harry were found in the Thames on 10 April 1896, both wrapped in a carpet bag and both with white tapes round their necks. In total, the corpses of seven babies, all of whom had been strangled, were recovered from the Thames and each one had the same white tape around their neck. She soon confessed saying: 'You'll know all mine by the tape around their necks.' After arrest she made two attempts to commit suicide in Reading police station.

She came to trial before Mr Justice Hawkins at the Old Bailey on 21 and 22 May 1896 charged with Doris' murder in the first instance, so that if she was acquitted, she could be tried for another. This was standard practice until recently in cases of multiple murders. Miss Marmon identified Mrs Dyer in court as 'Mrs Harding'. The defence tried to prove insanity but failed to convince the jury who took just five minutes to find her guilty. Although there was strong evidence of her dubious sanity, her crimes were also appalling and the jury seemed to give far more weight to that aspect.

During her three weeks in the condemned cell at Newgate, she filled five exercise books with her 'last true and only confession.' The chaplain visited her the night before her execution and asked her if she had anything to confess – she offered him her exercise books saying: 'isn't this enough?' She was hanged the following morning, on Wednesday, 10 June 1896 by James Billington becoming, at fifty-seven, the oldest woman to be executed since 1843. Her ghost was said to haunt Newgate Prison. No one will ever know the exact number of her victims but at the time of her arrest, she had been carrying on her trade for fifteen to twenty years. The Dyer case filled the papers in the second quarter of 1896 and what they didn't know for a fact they speculated upon. One contemporary paper dubbed her case the 'Reading Horror'.

Ada Chard-Williams

Ada Chard-Williams, aged twenty-four, was convicted of battering and strangling to death twenty-one-month-old Selina Ellen Jones at Grove Road, Barnes in London on or around Saturday, 23 September 1899. Florence Jones, a young unmarried mother, had read an advert in the local paper which offered to find adoptive homes for unwanted children. She answered the advert and duly met 'Mrs Hewetson' (Chard-Williams) at Charing Cross railway station on 31 August 1899. She agreed to pay her £5 to take on Selina but could only give her £3 on the day. Being an honest woman, she went back later with the balance and found that 'Mrs Hewetson' and Selina had vanished. Florence reported the matter to the police. The police soon discovered that 'Mrs Hewetson' was really Ada Chard-Williams. However, they had no body with which to prove there had been a murder, at least not until little Selina's corpse was washed up on the bank of the Thames at Battersea on 27 September. They remained unable to trace Ada as she moved frequently but were surprised she took pre-emptive action and wrote them a letter denying the killing (which she had read about) but in effect, admitting she was a baby farmer who bought and sold babies for profit. In the letter, she claimed that she had sold Selina on to a Mrs Smith in Croydon.

Like Amelia Dyer, Chard-Williams had her own 'signature' way of tying up bodies she wished to dispose of using a knot called a Fisherman's Bend, which was a crucial piece of evidence at her trial at the Old Bailey on 16 and 17 February 1900 before Mr Justice Ridley. She was hanged in private by James Billington in the execution shed in the yard of Newgate Prison on Tuesday, 6 March 1900, the last woman to be executed there. She was suspected of killing other children although no further allegations were proceeded with. Her husband, William, who had helped with the business, was acquitted. Like Amelia Dyer, Ada Chard-Williams secured her place in Madame Tussaud's Chamber of Horrors.

Annie Walters and Amelia Sach
The 'Finchley Baby Farmers'

Annie Walters and Amelia Sach became the first women to be hanged in the new women's prison at Holloway, North London, on 3 February 1903. Previously, female executions in London had been carried out at Newgate Prison.

Twenty-nine-year-old Amelia Sach ran a 'nursing home' which offered a haven for unmarried mothers to have their babies in and which, for a fee, claimed it would care for the infant afterwards. Sach told her clients that she could arrange for foster parents for the babies for an additional fee. Once the mother had left the baby with Sach, she would pass it over to fifty-four-year-old Annie Walters who would murder it, either with a dose of Chlorodyne (a morphine based drug that causes asphyxia in babies), or by suffocation if the Chlorodyne didn't work. The baby's body would then be disposed of in the Thames or by burying it on a rubbish dump.

Annie Walters was neither literate nor very bright and in 1902 decided to take one of the babies home. She lived in rented accommodation and her landlord was a police officer. She told him that she was looking after the little girl while her parents were on holiday and his wife helped her change the baby's nappy. The policeman's wife noted that the little girl was actually a boy. A few days later, Annie told the couple that the child had died in its sleep and she seemed genuinely upset about his death.

A few months later she did the same thing again and this time her landlord became suspicious when this second child died. She was duly arrested and charged with the murder of the child, a three-month-old boy by the name of Galley. Further bodies were discovered from the information Annie gave the police which implicated Amelia Sach in the murders. The police had enough evidence to charge them both. Many items of baby's clothing were found by the police when they searched Amelia's home and the pair may have murdered as many as twenty children.

They were tried at the Old Bailey on 15 and 16 January 1903, before Mr Justice Darling. It took the jury just forty minutes to find them both guilty. They were taken back to Holloway Prison and were hanged there by William Billington assisted by John Billington and Henry Pierrepoint on Tuesday, 3 February in the newly constructed execution shed at the end of 'B' Wing. On the day of her execution, Amelia was in a state of virtual collapse in the condemned cell. Pierrepoint recorded in his diary the following:

These two women were baby farmers of the worst kind and they were both repulsive in type. One was two pounds less than the other in weight and there was a difference of two inches in the drop which we allowed. One (Sachs) had a long thin neck and the other (Walters) a short neck, points which I was bound to observe in the arrangement of the rope.

Amelia had to be almost carried to the scaffold while Annie stayed quite calm and is said to have called out 'Goodbye Sach' as she was hooded on the trapdoors. This was to be the last double female hanging in Britain. After hanging the usual hour their bodies were prepared for inquest and later burial. Their remains now lie in Brookwood Cemetery in Surrey.

Holloway prison had been built between 1849 and 1852 to replace the existing Giltspur Street Prison and in 1902 became London's first all-female prison.

Rhoda Willis

Rhoda Willis, also known as Leslie James, was originally from Sunderland but had gone to live in South Wales. She had taken up a position as housekeeper to a Mr David Evans in Pontypool and suggested to him that baby farming would be a way of generating extra income for them. Initially, he was against the idea but she must have persuaded him because an advert duly appeared in *The Evening Press* giving a Box No. to reply to. A reply was received from a Mrs Lydia English, whose sister, Maude Treasure, was pregnant. It was agreed that Leslie James, as she was known to Mrs English, would take the baby when it was born. Rhoda also received other replies to her advertisement, including one from an Emily Stroud who had had a baby on 20 March 1907. Rhoda took this child and kept it until early May when she dumped it outside the Salvation Army House in Cardiff, with a note claiming she was an unmarried mother who could not cope. Sadly, the baby was not discovered quickly enough and subsequently died of exposure. Another child was adopted on 8 May, but this one was able to return to its parents unharmed.

On 4 June 1907, Rhoda picked up Maude Treasure's one-day-old baby girl and took her by train back to her lodgings in Cardiff. Her landlady told the police that Rhoda had gone out later in the day and had returned home drunk. She helped to get Rhoda to bed and noticed a bundle by the bed. When she opened it, she was horrified to find the body of a newborn baby girl. She called the police and they arrested Rhoda on the spot.

She was tried at Swansea before Mr Commissioner Shee on 23 and 24 June 1907. She denied the murder and claimed that the child had been ill and therefore died of natural causes. The prosecution showed that she had died from asphyxia. Handwriting experts claimed that the writing on the note found with the dumped baby outside the Salvation Army House was Rhoda's. She was convicted and sentenced to death and made a full confession to her solicitor in the condemned cell on the morning of her death.

Rhoda was hanged by Henry and Tom Pierrepoint at Cardiff prison on Wednesday, 14 August 1907, her forty-fourth birthday. She was described as an attractive woman. Her blaze of golden hair glinting in the morning sunshine, as she was led across the yard to execution shed had a profound effect on Henry Pierrepoint. She stood 5ft 2in tall and weighed 145lb so a drop of 5ft 9in was given. Rhoda was the last baby farmer to go to the gallows in Britain.

Postscript

As a result of these cases, Parliament passed a number of acts to better protect babies and small children, including the Infant Life Protection Act of 1897 and the Children's Act of 1908. These included requirements that local authorities must be notified within forty-eight hours with full details of any change of custody or the death of a child aged under seven. The Act also empowered local authorities to actively seek out baby farms and lying-in houses, to enter homes suspected of abusing children, and to remove the children to a place of safety. It gave a legal definition of improper care of infants: 'no infant could be kept in a home that was so unfit and so overcrowded as to endanger its health, and no infant could be kept by an unfit nurse who threatened, by neglect or abuse, its proper care and maintenance.' The government also introduced regulations for adoption and fostering which finally brought an end to baby farming in Britain.

10

THE TWENTIETH CENTURY

Just sixteen women were hanged in fifty-five years in England, Scotland and Wales, of whom four were baby farmers as discussed in the previous chapter. No woman was executed between 1908 and 1922 or between 1937 and 1948, although two were to hang in 1936. Louise Masset is included in the total as she was executed in 1900 having been condemned in 1899. (See Chapter 6.)

One hundred and forty-five women were sentenced to death for murder in Britain during the twentieth century, another was condemned for espionage during the First World War and one for treason during the Second World War and both were reprieved. Ten of these women were still teenagers at the time of sentence and all were reprieved. Five women were given death sentences in Scotland of whom one was executed (Susan Newell), and three women were condemned in Southern Ireland prior to 1925, of whom two were reprieved. One death sentence in the Channel Island of Guernsey led to a reprieve. Of these 156, no fewer than 139 were reprieved (89.1 per cent).

There are at least fifty-one instances of women who murdered their infant children being reprieved. Few people felt that these often desperate young women deserved to die and indeed no woman had been hanged for murdering her own infant since 1849. Yet it was not until 1938, with an amendment to the Infanticide Act of 1922, that the law finally caught up with practice and public opinion, and understood post-natal depression and the stigmatisation prevalent at the time caused to a young woman having a baby outside of marriage. A further thirty-three women were sentenced to death and reprieved for murdering older children. In at least two cases, these murders could be described as mercy killings. Many of the remaining cases concerned the murders of husbands and boyfriends. One woman had her conviction for murdering her infant child quashed on appeal and one woman who murdered her boyfriend, his father and one of his employees, was found insane after sentencing and committed to Broadmoor, the secure hospital for the criminally insane.

Emily Swann
The Wombwell Murder

It is amazing what a glass of brandy will do. A few minutes before 8 a.m. on the morning of Tuesday, 29 December 1903, Emily Swann was in a state of virtual collapse, moaning pitifully on the floor of her cell and yet, after a drink of brandy, she was able to regain her composure and walk to the execution shed where she said 'Good morning John', to her hooded and pinioned boyfriend, John Gallagher, as she was brought up beside him on the gallows in Armley Prison in Leeds. He was not aware that she was there and was completely taken aback but managed to reply, 'Good morning love.' As the noose was placed round her neck, she said: 'Good-bye. God bless you.'

Emily was a forty-two-year-old mother of eleven children. She was described as a stumpy little round-faced woman, 4ft 10in tall and 122lb in weight, from a 'respectable' background. She was married to William Swann who was a glass-blower and they had a lodger, a thirty-year-old miner called John Gallagher, who was living with them at Wombwell in Yorkshire.

It is probable that Emily and John were having an affair and it was common knowledge that William beat Emily at times, although whether this was because he felt she was too friendly to John or for other reasons is not known. Attitudes to extra-marital relationships and wife beating were very different a century ago; William probably felt well within his rights to lay into Emily over her liaison with John.

In view of the rows, John had decided to leave the Swann household, although he continued to visit regularly, which always seemed to provoke another fight. Things came to a head on the afternoon of 6 June when Emily went into her neighbour's house with a shawl over her head. She removed the shawl and showed the neighbour her two black eyes and facial bruises, saying: 'See what our Bill's done!'

On seeing Emily's injuries, John, who was also there, became instantly enraged and said: 'I'll go and give him something for himself for that.' Another neighbour saw him dashing into the Swanns' house, followed closely by Emily. John was shouting: 'I'll coffin him before morning.' The neighbours heard the sounds of a struggle from inside the house. The noises of fighting went on for some ten minutes, at the end of which John came out and went back to the neighbour's house.

'I've busted four of his ribs and I'll bust four more', he announced. A few minutes later he told the neighbour: 'I'll finish him out before I go to Bradford.' As he went back into the Swanns' house, he said: 'I'll murder the pig before morning. If he can't kick a man he shan't kick a woman.' Another fight ensued and the neighbour heard Emily say: 'Give it to him, Johnny.'

Ten minutes later Emily and John emerged from William's house holding hands and being described by neighbours as showing 'every sign of affection.' Behind them, in the shambles of the house, William lay dead. John and Emily calmly went over to their friends' house and told them the situation.

The police had been sent for and immediately arrested Emily. John had escaped and went on the run for two months before finally being tracked down to the house of a relative in Middlesbrough, having spent some time living rough.

John and Emily were tried on 9 December 1903 at Leeds before Mr Justice Darling. Their barrister, Mr Mitchell Innes admitted that the relationship between them was 'of a misdirected order', but contended that John had merely gone to the house to remonstrate with William for his brutal treatment of Emily. Their defence insisted that neither John nor Emily wanted William dead.

However, the judge advised the jury that John's remark, 'I'll finish him out before I go to Bradford', showed that there was intent. This remark had been allegedly made between the two fights, after which he had gone back into the house and carried out his threat.

'As for the woman', continued the judge, 'it is my duty to tell you that one does not commit murder only with one's hands. If one person instigates another to commit murder, and that other person does it, the instigator is also guilty of murder.'

Not surprisingly, they were both found guilty on what was very clear evidence, the jury taking only an hour in their deliberations.

Emily remained calm as the foreman of the jury gave the guilty verdict and when asked if she wanted to say anything before sentence of death was passed, told the judge: 'I am innocent. I am not afraid of immediate death, because I am innocent and will go to God.' Both she and John were then formally sentenced to hang. Emily seemed quite unperturbed and smiled and blew a kiss to someone in the gallery as she was led down from the dock.

The judge was aware of some more evidence, which it had been decided would not be put before the jury because it would prejudice Emily's case. After the sentencing and before he discharged the jury, the judge told them that when Gallagher was taken into custody, he had told the police that Emily hit William and beat him with a poker, and that he (Gallagher) did not touch the dead man, although he was present. 'That statement was not direct evidence against the woman but from the proved position of the poker I am convinced that the statement was partly true and that Mrs. Swann did really take part in the actual killing.' Understandably, this caused quite a stir. It was held up as an example of the fairness of the judicial system which declined to take unfair advantage of an accused person. It was also a matter for satisfaction to the prosecution that even without that evidence the jury had still been convinced of the woman's guilt.

They were returned to Armley Prison, Leeds and lodged in separate condemned cells, their executions scheduled for Tuesday, 29 December 1903.

Apparently, John had not expected to be reprieved but Emily had hoped that she would be and had had severe mood swings in the condemned cell. Emily was greatly distressed and in a state of near collapse when the governor informed her that there would be no reprieve. She told her wardresses repeatedly that she was very worried about the disgrace she was bringing on her family. Emily's family made a last, forlorn appeal to the King for clemency but this was, as usual, ignored.

The only time Emily and John saw each other between sentence and execution was at the prison chapel service on Christmas morning where they were kept separate and not allowed to speak. It is reported that they both ate a substantial Christmas dinner.

At this time, mixed sex hangings were still allowed. William Billington was the principal executioner assisted by John Ellis. They went first to John Gallagher who was quite calm and pinioned him, before leading him to the gallows. They then fetched the now much recovered Emily, who was escorted into the execution shed flanked by two male warders.

John was already on the trap, supported by warders, with the white hood over his head when Emily was led in. She would have been able to see her noose dangling from the beam. As she came onto the trap, Billington drew the white hood over her head and then she made her famous remark: 'Good Morning John'. A moment later the lever was pulled and they plummeted down through the trap together. The autopsies found that death had been 'instantaneous' in both cases.

This was very much an 'open and shut' case where the evidence against both defendants was strong and one which involved the doctrine of Common Purpose that was part of English law in 1903 and still is now. The law states that if two or more people commit a crime, they can be held equally responsible where there was common purpose, i.e. they both intended or could have reasonably foreseen the outcome. If Emily's words were accurately reported by her neighbours, it is clear that at that moment, at least, she wanted John to kill William and, therefore, would be equally responsible for the outcome. Her precise role in the actual killing is unclear, although it is probable that she did in fact take part as John had claimed.

It is unlikely that either John or Emily intended to kill William because he was in the way of their affair, but rather

because John lost his temper when he saw Emily's injuries and
between them things went too far in the 'heat of the moment.'
Today Emily might be seen more as the victim than she was
then, but they would almost certainly still both be found guilty
of murder because she played an active role in the killing and
did nothing to restrain John.

Double hangings were ultimately abolished because they
took longer to carry out, and this was felt to prolong the
suffering of the first prisoner especially. Later where two or
more people were to be executed for the same crime, they
would be hanged in separate prisons at the same moment
in time, as happened with Edith Thompson and Frederick
Bywaters (see next). In Emily's case, it was probably far less
cruel to allow her to die beside John rather than make her
suffer on her own.

Edith Thompson
The Ilford Love Triangle

Edith Thompson was a quite attractive twenty-eight-year-old
who was married to thirty-two-year-old shipping clerk Percy
Thompson. They had no children and enjoyed a reasonable
lifestyle, Edith having a good job as the manageress of a mil-
liners in London.

Edith was having an affair with twenty-year-old Frederick
Bywaters who was a ship's steward. Their relationship had
started in June 1921 when he accompanied them on holiday
to the Isle of Wight. He moved in as a lodger while waiting
for his next voyage but had been chucked out by Percy for
getting too friendly with Edith. He witnessed a violent row
between Edith and Percy and later comforted her. His ship
was to sail on 9 September 1921, and he saw Edith secretly
from time to time until ultimately booking into a hotel with
her under false names.

Frederick was a decisive and impulsive young man who according to him, decided on his own to stab Percy Thompson whom he felt was making Edith's life miserable.

On 4 October 1922, Frederick lay in wait until just after midnight for Edith and Percy, who were returning home to Ilford in Essex after a night out at a theatre in London, and then stabbed Percy several times. Edith was said to have shouted: 'Oh don't! Oh don't!' Percy died at the scene and Frederick escaped. Edith was hysterical but was questioned by police when she calmed down alleging that a strange man had stabbed Percy.

The Thompson's current lodger, Fanny Lester, advised the police about Frederick having lodged with them, and they learned that he worked for P&O, the shipping line.

The police discovered the letters that Edith had written to him and soon arrested him and charged him with the murder.

Edith was also arrested and charged with murder or alternatively with being an accessory to murder. She did not know that Frederick had been arrested but saw him in the police station later and said: 'Oh God why did he do it', continuing: 'I didn't want him to do it'.

Bywaters insisted that he had acted alone in the crime and gave his account as follows:

I waited for Mrs. Thompson and her husband. I pushed her to one side, also pushing him into the street. We struggled. I took my knife from my pocket and we fought and he got the worst of it …

The reason I fought with Thompson was because he never acted like a man to his wife. He always seemed several degrees lower than a snake. I loved her and I could not go on seeing her leading that life. I did not intend to kill him. I only meant to injure him. I gave him the opportunity of standing up to me like a man but he wouldn't.

Frederick stuck to this story during the trial which opened at the
Old Bailey on 6 December 1922 before Mr Justice Shearman.

Edith had written no less than sixty-two intimate letters
to Frederick and stupidly they had kept them. In these, she
referred to Frederick as 'Darlingest and Darlint'. Some of them
described how she had tried to murder Percy on several occasions. In one apparently referring to an attempt to poison him,
she wrote: 'You said it was enough for an elephant. Perhaps it
was. But you don't allow for the taste making it possible for
only a small quantity to be taken.' She had also tried broken
glass, and told Frederick that she had made three attempts but
that Percy had discovered some in his food so she had had
to stop.

Edith had sent Frederick press cuttings describing murders
by poisoning and had told him that she had aborted herself
after becoming pregnant by him.

At the trial, Frederick refused to incriminate Edith and
when cross-examined told the prosecution that he did not
believe that Edith had actually attempted to poison Percy
but had rather a vivid imagination and a passion for sensa-
tional novels that extended to her imagining herself as one of
the characters.

Edith had been advised against going into the witness box
by her lawyer but decided to do so and promptly incriminated herself by being asked what she had meant when she
had written to Bywaters asking him to send her 'something
to give her husband.' She said she had 'no idea', which does
not sound very convincing. The judge in his summing up
described Edith's letters as 'full of the outpourings of a silly, but
at the same time, a wicked affection.' Mr Justice Shearman was
obviously a very Victorian gentleman with high moral prin-
ciples. His summing up was fair in law but the judge made
much of the adultery.

He also instructed the jury, however: 'You will not convict
her unless you are satisfied that she and he agreed that this

man should be murdered when he could be, and she knew that he was going to do it, and directed him to do it, and by arrangement between them he was doing it.'

The jury were not convinced by the defence case and took just over two hours to find them both guilty of murder on 11 December. Even after the verdict was read out, Frederick continued to defend Edith loudly. However, the judge had to pass the death sentence on both of them as required by law.

Edith was returned to Holloway and Frederick to Pentonville, prisons half a mile apart in London and placed in the condemned cells. Both lodged appeals; these were heard before the Lord Chief Justice and Justices Darling and Salter on 21 December 1922, and were dismissed.

She was an adulteress, an abortionist and possibly a woman who incited a murder or worse still had tried to poison her husband. At least this is how she was judged against the morals of the time. That is until she was sentenced to death. The public and the media that had been so against her now did a complete U-turn and campaigned for a reprieve. There was a large petition, with nearly a million signatures, which together with Frederick's repeated confession that he and he alone killed Thompson, failed to persuade the Home Secretary, William Bridgeman. Edith was to be the first woman to be hanged for fifteen years.

According to René Weis' book, *The True Story of Edith Thompson*, she had major mood swings even up to the morning of execution, as she expected to be reprieved all along. Dr John Hall Morton, who was both the governor and medical officer of Holloway, decided to give Edith the following medications. At 8.15 a.m., forty-five minutes before her death, she was injected with ½₂ grain (2mg) of strychnine and at 8.40 a.m. she was given ¹⁄₁₀₀ grain (0.65mg) of scopalmine-morphine (Purlight sleep) and ⅙ grain (10.8mg) of morphia. At the stated dose, strychnine is a tonic and the other drugs would have sedated her, with the maximum effect being reached after twenty minutes. It has been variously stated that she fainted and had to be carried to the execution shed and that she was dragged screaming to it. Elizabeth Cronin, who was deputy governor of Holloway and present at the time, refuted these claims. This is supported by a statement in the Commons, reported in Hansard of 27 March 1956, by then Home Secretary Major Lloyd-George, stating that Edith was sedated and thus had to be carried to the gallows and supported on it. Major Lloyd-George told Parliament that he had examined all the available evidence and concluded that nothing untoward happened.

The LPC4 form gives fracture/dislocation as the cause of death and mentions bruising of the neck from the rope. However, it does not mention any blood dripping from between her legs after the hanging.

So, at 9 a.m. on 9 January 1923, both were executed in their respective prisons.

Frederick met his end bravely at the hands of William Willis, still protesting Edith's innocence whilst she was in a state of total collapse.

A few minutes before they entered the condemned cell, the execution party heard a ghastly moaning come from Edith's cell. When John Ellis entered she was semi-conscious as he strapped her wrists. According to his biography, she looked dead already.

She was carried the short distance from the condemned cell to the gallows by two warders and the two assistants (Robert Baxter and Seth Mills), and held on the trap whilst Ellis completed the preparations.

Depending on whose version of events you believe, there was a considerable amount of blood dripping from between her legs after the hanging. Some, including Bernard Spillsbury the famous pathologist who carried out the autopsy on her, claim it was caused by her being pregnant and miscarrying whilst others claim it was due to inversion of the uterus, and the authorities claim that nothing untoward happened at all.

Edith had been in custody for over three months before the execution so would have probably known if she was pregnant. Under English law, the execution would have been staid until after she had given birth. In practice, she would have almost certainly been reprieved. She had everything to gain from claiming to be pregnant so it is surprising that she did not if she had indeed missed two or three periods. However, she had aborted herself earlier and this may have damaged her uterus which, combined with the force of the drop, caused it to invert. The bleeding may equally have been the start of a heavy period. Research done in Germany before and during the Second World War on a large number of condemned women showed that menstruation was often interrupted by the stress of being tried and sentenced to death but could be brought on by the shock of being informed of the actual date of the execution, which in Edith's case was likely to have been only one or two days before she was hanged. Whatever the truth, this hanging seemed to have a profound effect on all those present.

Several of the prison officers involved took early retirement. John Ellis resigned in 1923 and committed suicide in 1931. The chaplain also left the prison service due to suffering a nervous breakdown.

Edith's body was another that was reburied at Brookwood Cemetery in Surrey in 1970, when Holloway Prison was being rebuilt.

Although there is no evidence suggesting that Edith had any physical part in the murder and it is credible that she did not actually intend Frederick to kill Percy, there is the problem of 'common purpose.' In law if two people want a third person dead and conspire together to murder that person, it does not matter which one of them struck the fatal blow, both are equally guilty. The law has always liked written evidence because it is much safer and stronger than hearsay evidence or the confused statements of witnesses. In this case they had a veritable pile of it, mostly incriminating. Letters that talked about poisoning Percy and letters asking Frederick to 'do something' etc. The jury accepted the prosecution case that all this added up to common purpose to murder Percy.

So was Edith evil or just a silly, over-romantic woman who gave no thought to the consequences of her irresponsible letters? My personal view having studied the case is that she was the latter and should have been given the benefit of the doubt. There is no evidence whatsoever that she participated in the killing.

It should be said that divorce was much harder in those days. If Percy refused to divorce her, which he had, her only alternatives were to run away with Frederick or kill Percy.

Susan Newell
A Senseless Murder

Susan Newell was born in 1893 and had lived a hard life in constant poverty. In June 1923, she was living in a rented flat in Newlands Street, Coatbridge, a suburb of Glasgow, with her husband John and eight-year-old daughter Janet McLeod, from her previous marriage. John was apparently a drunkard and a womaniser. After just three weeks their landlady, Mrs Young, had become fed up with their rows and had given them notice to quit.

Susan was noted for having a bad temper and also had some history of violence. On 19 June 1923 she had assaulted John, beating him round the head which he reported to the police. The following day they had another violent argument and he left home going to his sister's house that night.

On the evening of Wednesday, 20 June 1923 around 6.45 p.m., 13-year-old newspaper boy, John Johnson, knocked on Susan's door to see if she wanted the evening newspaper. She told him to come in and took the paper from him. However, John insisted he had to have the money for it. At this, Susan lost control of herself and strangled the poor lad. Her daughter was to see the boy's body when she came in from playing, lying on the settee. Janet had to help her mother wrap it in an old rug. Susan had the problem of what to do with the body. She slept on this problem and by the morning had decided how she would dispose of it.

Susan and Janet carried John's body downstairs and put it in an old pram, which she had found, still covered by the rug. With Janet perched on top of the bundle, they set off together on foot towards Glasgow. Several people noticed them as they walked along the roads towards Glasgow. A passing lorry driver offered them a lift which Susan accepted and dropped them off in Glasgow's Duke Street. As the pram was being got down from the truck, the bundle containing John's small body came undone and a foot was seen sticking out of one end and the top of his head at the other end. Apparently the lorry driver failed to notice this but a lady looking out the window of her house nearby did, before Susan could cover up the body again. She decided to follow Susan and Janet and enlisted the help of her sister. They met a man and asked him to fetch the police while they continued to follow Susan. They were able to keep up with her and saw Susan leave the bundle containing John's body at the entrance to a tenement. Susan attempted to escape over a wall and was immediately arrested by a policeman waiting for her on the other side.

Susan had already worked out her story if she was caught and had primed Janet as well. She told the police that her husband had killed the boy and that she had tried to stop him. He had then forced her and Janet to dispose of the body for him. John was now also arrested and they were both charged with the murder.

Husband and wife came to trial in Glasgow on 18 September 1923 before Lord Alness. The case against John collapsed as he could prove that he was not in the house when the murder took place. He was able to produce several witnesses to prove his whereabouts. The judge freed him immediately saying that he should never have been brought to trial. He left the dock without even a glance at Susan.

The main and most compelling evidence against Susan was given by her daughter Janet. She told the court how she had come back to the flat from playing outside to see the body of John lying on the sofa and how she had helped her mother wrap it up. She also related to the court how she had helped her mother try to dispose of the body and what her mother had told her to say if she was questioned by the police. Susan had given Janet a full story that she was to tell of how her stepfather had killed John.

In her defence, it was argued that Susan was insane, although this was rebutted by the prosecution's expert witness, Professor John Glaister, who had examined her while she was on remand. Her counsel pointed out that the killing was not premeditated and had no obvious motive.

The jury retired and reached their verdict in thirty-seven minutes. Somewhat surprisingly in view of the weight of evidence, Susan was only convicted by a majority verdict. At least one of the jurors believed her defence of insanity. The jury unanimously recommended mercy for her.

Upon receiving the guilty verdict, Lord Alness sentenced her to death and she was taken back to Duke Street (yes, the same Duke Street), where Glasgow's prison stood at the time. Here she was examined by psychiatrists and found to be legally sane.

No woman had been hanged in Scotland for over fifty years and there were considerable efforts made to secure a reprieve for Susan. However, the application of the law in Scotland had to be seen to be in line with that in England where Edith

Thompson had been hanged for what most people regarded as a much less serious crime only ten months earlier.

The Secretary of State for Scotland, therefore, decided that she could not to be reprieved and her execution was set for Wednesday, 10 October 1923. Susan showed emotion for the first time when told by the Lord Provost of Glasgow that there was to be no reprieve. She cried out for her daughter and then fainted.

She was to be hanged by John Ellis, assisted by Robert Baxter. Ellis was noted for the speed at which he conducted executions and it is perhaps for wanting to get the procedure over with quickly and not wanting to hurt Susan he did not pinion her wrists properly. Ellis decided to use the leather body belt that he had had made for Edith Thompson and an additional strap to go round the thighs.

On the gallows, Susan allowed Baxter to strap her legs and thighs without protest but was able to get her hands free from the loose wrist straps on the body belt and defiantly pulled off the white hood saying to Ellis: 'Don't put that thing over me.' Rather than risk another trying scene, Ellis decided to proceed without it, as the noose was already in place and so he simply pulled the lever and Susan went through the trap with her face uncovered. She became the last woman to hang in Scotland and was said to be the calmest person in the execution chamber accepting her fate with both courage and dignity, although she never admitted her crime.

There seem to be few mitigating factors in Susan's case, both she and John Johnson were the victims of her violent temper. The evidence against her was clear and overwhelming.

There is the question of motive. John's father had told the court that his son would not have had more than nine pence on him at the time of the killing. So it seems doubtful that Susan killed him for money and far more likely that she simply could not control her temper.

Perhaps John was somewhat cheeky and said something to Susan when he asked her for the money that made her snap. She was probably already 'wound up' after the rows with her husband and it is quite possible that, unwittingly, young John just pushed her over the edge.

Undoubtedly, there are a significant number of murders committed due to temporary loss of control by people who are sane by any normal definition of that term. The McNaughten rules required that for a person to be found insane it had to be shown that they were, at the time of the crime, suffering from such defect of mind that either they did not know what they were doing or that what they were doing was wrong. Clearly Susan at least knew what she had done was wrong.

Louie Calvert
A Boot Fetishist?

At one minute to nine on the summer morning of Thursday, 24 June 1926, a small group of smartly dressed men silently formed up outside the condemned cell at the end of 'B' wing in the central area of Manchester's Strangeways Prison. Upon a signal from the governor, Thomas Pierrepoint, then Britain's 'No. 1' hangman, entered the cell at precisely 9 a.m. accompanied by two male warders. The two female warders who had been looking after the prisoner told her to stand up and Pierrepoint took her arms and quickly strapped them behind her with a leather strap before leading the way out of the cell through a second door which had been uncovered by sliding away the wardrobe. The prisoner was led forward into the execution chamber by the two male warders and stopped by Pierrepoint on a chalked 'T' precisely over the divide of the trapdoors. The two warders, standing on boards set across the trap, supported her, one on either side, while William Willis, Pierrepoint's assistant, put leather straps round her ankles and thighs. Pierrepoint withdrew what would have appeared to her to be a white pocket handkerchief from his top pocket and deftly placed it over her head following quickly with the leather-covered noose, positioning the brass eyelet just under the angle of her lower left jaw and sliding down the claw cut rubber washer to hold it in place. His eyes darted from side to side to check that all was ready before he lent forward, withdrew the safety pin and pushed the metal lever away from him. The hooded form disappeared through the trap and dangled in the cell below.

The medical officer went down to listen to the weakening heartbeat coming from the small broken body, now hanging motionless, its head drooping to one side.

It had taken no more than twenty seconds to carry out the sentence of the court upon Mrs Louie Calvert. Her body was left on the rope for the customary hour before being taken down and prepared for autopsy. The autopsy found that her death had been 'instantaneous' and confirmed that she was not pregnant. These facts were made public at the subsequent inquest, held later in the day before the Leeds coroner, Mr Stuart Rodgers. She was buried in an unmarked grave within the prison grounds. Louie was calm at the end and was reported to have accepted her fate with considerable courage. It is unclear why her execution took place at 9 a.m. rather than at the customary time of 8 a.m. The hanging drew a crowd outside the prison gates estimated at some 500 people, many of them women, who waited around until the death notice was displayed on the prison gates.

Louie was the first woman to be hanged at Strangeways since Mary Ann Britland in 1886.

It has been said that Louie was somewhat disappointed to find the press were not going to be allowed to witness her death. Apparently, she wanted to be in the limelight for once in her life. In fact, she didn't arouse much media interest at all which was probably another disappointment for her, this being partly due to the General Strike that was going on at the time of her trial.

Louie Calvert was unusual amongst the women executed in the twentieth century in that she was a known criminal who had convictions for petty theft and prostitution although, up to the murder of Mrs Waterhouse, nobody had suspected her of being a killer. She was a small, unattractive thirty-three-year-old who was known to have an unpleasant and violent temper. She had used several aliases, as a prostitute she worked under the name of Louie Gomersal and was known as Louise Jackson to the Salvation Army, whose meetings she attended. She had a six-year-old son, Kenneth, whom she was particularly fond of and asked to have visit her in the condemned cell. He was taken into care after the execution.

Under the name of Louise Jackson, she took a live-in job as housekeeper to one Arthur Calvert who was a night watchman living at 7, Railway Place in the Pottery Fields area of Leeds. Louie's son also went to live with them. She and Arthur had an affair and after a while, Louie claimed that she was pregnant by him and persuaded Arthur to marry her. She was able to deceive Arthur for some time and eventually told him she was leaving him to go to her sister's home in Dewsbury to give birth. She sent Arthur a telegram to let him know she had arrived safely. There was of course no baby and the pregnancy had been feigned purely to force Arthur into marriage.

Louie had in fact returned to Leeds immediately and on 8 March 1926, took up lodgings with a forty-year-old rather eccentric widow called Mrs Lily Waterhouse, in Amberley Road, Leeds. The arrangement between the two women was that Louie would act as maid and housekeeper in return for her board and lodging. While with Lily, Louie had seen an advert on 16 March for a child to be adopted. She agreed to adopt the baby girl from an unmarried teenage mother and she was due to collect the baby on 31 March. Presumably, Louie intended to take the baby home to Arthur and pass it off as her own.

Whether Louie and the girl went through a formal adoption process is doubtful as she would probably have been only too pleased to have been rid of the baby to avoid the stigma of having a baby out of wedlock.

The domestic situation was not at all satisfactory to Mrs Waterhouse because Louie refused to work as agreed and they argued constantly over this and other matters. Also Lily had noticed that her personal items and silverware were going missing and found pawn shop tickets from which she concluded that it was Louie who was stealing them. Lily reported her suspicions to the police on 30 March and was told to return the next day to lodge a formal complaint against Louie.

Sadly for Lily, when she got home, she made the mistake of telling Louie what she had done. The police had arranged for Lily to appear before magistrates on 1 April to apply for a 'process' (an injunction).

On 31 March 1926, Lily was seen by her neighbours entering her house around 6.15 p.m. About 7.30 p.m., her neighbours in the row of terraced houses heard loud banging sounds coming from Lily's house and a few minutes later saw Louie leaving with the baby. One of the neighbours, Mrs Clayton, asked Louie what the noise was all about. Louie told her: 'I put up the baby's bed, and it fell when I was folding it.' Mrs Clayton told Louie that she thought she heard Mrs Waterhouse make some strange sounds. 'Yes', replied Louie, 'I have left her in bed crying because I am leaving her.'

As Lily did not show up in court, two detectives were sent round to Lily's home the following day to find out why she had not appeared. After hearing about the commotion earlier from her neighbours, they opened the window shutters and saw that the main bed had not been slept in. They got a key and went into the house finding Lily lying dead in a small bedroom at the top of the stairs. She had been hit over the head and strangled to death. There were no signs of a struggle as might have occurred in a break in, but one of the officers noticed that Lily was barefoot. There was a mark round her neck consistent with a ligature and marks on her wrists and legs.

Louie was the prime and in fact only obvious suspect, and she was soon tracked down to her marital home in Railway Place. When the police arrived, she opened the door to them. The officers found she was wearing Lily's boots even though they were several sizes too large and some of the missing property was also discovered. She was arrested and taken to the police station to be charged with Lily's murder. As detectives questioned her, a pack of lies unfolded. She insisted that the items of Lily's property had been given to her by Lily to pawn and that Lily was confused and had probably forgotten that she had given them to her.

On Wednesday, 7 April, Louie came before Leeds City magistrates charged with Lily's murder and was remanded in custody to stand trial at Leeds Assizes. Her case was heard at the assizes before Mr Justice Wright on 5 and 6 May and she was, unsurprisingly, found guilty. She accepted her death sentence without apparent shock but claimed that she was pregnant and could not, therefore, be hanged until after she had given birth.

She was taken to Strangeways Prison in Manchester to await execution. This was unusual as it was normal to send the condemned prisoner to the county prison in which the trial had taken place. It was probably because the condemned cell at Armley Prison in Leeds was already in use. Here she was examined and it was thought that it was just possible, although very unlikely, that she might be in the early stages of pregnancy but that it would not cause a problem to hang her. This caused public concern and a petition for a reprieve containing 2,000 to 3,000 signatures, many from her home town of Ossett in Yorkshire, was got up. This was rejected, her execution being scheduled for Thursday, 24 June. There was even a question raised in Parliament relating to her pregnancy. However, on Tuesday, 22 June, the Home Secretary informed her solicitor, Mr E. Ould, that there would be no reprieve and that the story of her pregnancy was not believed to be true. As stated above, the autopsy confirmed that it was just another of Louie's lies.

Whilst in the condemned cell, Louie confessed to the murder of John Frobisher in 1922. At the time, she was again calling herself Mrs Louise Jackson and worked as John Frobisher's housekeeper at Mercy Street, Wellington Lane, Leeds. His body had been found by a policeman floating in a canal on 12 July 1922. He had a wound on the back of his head and a fractured skull. A degree of suspicion had fallen on Louie initially but the Coroner's Court returned a verdict of misadventure and ruled that his death was a simple drowning. Once again, the body was discovered fully dressed but without any boots on. One of the police officers in the Waterhouse case had also been involved in the Frobisher case and remembered that John had been discovered without his boots, and that they were nowhere to be found on the bank, facts which seemed unusual in a case of accidental drowning.

Strangely in two completely unrelated cases of murder, in addition to their 'valuables' she had stolen her victim's boots even though they didn't fit her. Her motive for this is unclear, unless she really did have a boot fetish. It seems the motive certainly for Mrs Waterhouse's murder was gain and it was probably the same in John Frobisher's case. It seems hard to believe that she killed for the boots but rather took them as an afterthought.

Louie was a pathological liar and had a bad temper, but what made her turn to murder? Was it simply the easy way, in her uneducated mind, of covering up her thefts or was it something deeper within her personality? Sadly, we will never know the answer to this, as having been examined and found to be sane for legal purposes nobody was very interested in getting to the bottom of her personality.

Dorothea Nancy Waddingham
The Bogus 'Nurse'

Dorothea was born at Hucknall near Nottingham in 1900 and
after leaving school worked in a factory for a while before
taking up a post at the Burton-on-Trent Workhouse infirmary
in Staffordshire. Here she picked up quite a lot of medical
knowledge whilst working on the wards and afterwards passed
herself off a nurse. She married Thomas Leech in 1925 and
they had three children, Edwin, Alan and Mary over their
eight-year marriage. Thomas sadly developed cancer of the
throat and died in 1933.

Dorothea now reverted to her maiden name and formed
a relationship with their erstwhile lodger, Ronald Sullivan,
who was six years her senior. Together they decided to open a
nursing home at 32 Devon Drive, Nottingham. This was recognised by the county authorities who considered Dorothea
a competent nurse. On 12 January 1935 a Miss Blagg of the
County Nursing Association asked them to take a couple of
new patients for 30s a week. The newcomers were Louisa
Baguley, a widow of eighty-nine, and her daughter Ada who
was fifty. Ada was disabled by a progressive disease that left
her unable to walk and her elderly mother could no longer
look after her. At the time there was one other resident who
died in February leaving Dorothea with a wholly inadequate
income of just the 30s a week. Ronald helped Dorothea run
the nursing home and the couple were to have two children
of their own.

On 4 May Ada summoned her solicitor, Mr Lane, and told
him she wished to change her will. She was to leave all of her
savings, some £1,600, to Dorothea and Ronald on the condition that they would look after both Louisa and herself for
the rest of their lives. It is unclear whether Ada was persuaded
by Dorothea to take this step or whether she had decided on
this course herself. It had been suggested that Dorothea had

threatened to send the two women to the workhouse as she could not afford to keep them. The workhouse would have been a dreadful threat in Ada's mind.

On Sunday, 12 May Louisa died of what was determined to be cardio-vascular problems. In a woman of nearly ninety her death did not arouse any suspicion and a death certificate allowing her burial was issued.

Ada continued to live happily at Devon Drive through the summer of 1935 and was visited by a friend of hers, Mrs Briggs, on Tuesday, 10 September, who found her in good spirits. The following morning Dorothea called Dr Mansfield, Ada's doctor, and told him that Ada had gone into a coma. When he arrived Ada had died and he thought that she had suffered a cerebral haemorrhage. Dorothea showed him a letter that Ada had written on 29 August, expressing her wish to be cremated. Dr Mansfield issued a death certificate and also a certificate permitting cremation. The two certificates together with Ada's letter were sent to the crematorium where they were read by Nottingham's Medical Officer for Health, Dr Cyril Banks. He noted that the words 'my last wish is that my relatives shall not know of my death', appeared to have been inserted after the original letter had been written as they were in a cramped style. Ronald Sullivan had written the letter for Ada but she had signed it. Dr Banks was suspicious and decided to order a post-mortem. This revealed that Ada had actually been poisoned with morphine. Louisa's remains were therefore also exhumed and morphine was found in her too.

Both Dorothea and Ronald were arrested and charged with the murders. Dorothea had recently given birth to her fifth child and nursed it in prison.

The couple appeared before Mr Justice Goddard at Nottinghamshire Assizes on 24 February. Mr Norman Birkett led the prosecution and Mr J.F. Eales the defence. Ronald was discharged by the judge on the second day of the trial due to a lack of any real evidence against him, leaving Dorothea to face trial alone. The court heard the forensic evidence of morphine poisoning and the testimony of Mrs Briggs and Dr Mansfield. Dorothea's defence suggested that Dr Mansfield had given her morphine tablets for Ada for when she was in pain. Dr Mansfield strongly denied having given any tablets to Dorothea, especially morphine. Dorothea described to the court the last two days of Ada's life. According to her, Ada was depressed and in great pain so she had given her up to ten tablets over two days and in the early hours of the Wednesday morning found her in a coma. This information was contained in a statement made to the police on 24 September, after the post-mortem result was known. Previously Dorothea had told the police that Ada had eaten a large lunch on the Tuesday and appeared to be well. Dorothea's evidence was less than convincing as was her general performance in the witness box.

On the third day of the trial the jury took two hours to reach a guilty verdict and for whatever reason added a recommendation to mercy. Mr Justice Goddard sentenced Dorothea to death and obviously did not concur with the jury's recommendation; neither did the Home Secretary, John Simon.

As Nottingham no longer had an execution facility Dorothea was transferred to the Condemned Suite at Birmingham's Winson Green Prison to await her fate. Her appeal was rejected on 30 March and the execution was set for 8 a.m. on Thursday, 16 April 1936. Dorothea was the only woman to be hanged at Winson Green.

Thomas Pierrepoint, assisted by his nephew Albert, carried out the hanging. It was to be Thomas' last female execution and Albert's first.

Dorothea was weighed and measured the day before and was recorded as 4ft 11in tall and 123lbs in weight. She was thus given a drop of 8ft 5in. Large numbers of people had gathered outside the prison on the Wednesday afternoon to protest the execution of a mother of five, even if she had poisoned two vulnerable people for financial gain. The protest was led by the veteran anti-capital punishment campaigner, Mrs Violet Van der Elst. By the Thursday morning the crowd outside the prison had grown to an estimated 5,000 and their hymns could be heard within.

By 8.01 a.m. Dorothea was hanging limply in a room below the gallows and was examined by the prison doctor using a stethoscope to ensure that she was dead. The execution chamber was locked up for an hour. The Pierrepoints returned at 9 a.m. and undressed her and put a rope around her body under her arms, lifting her up with a block and tackle attached to the chain on the gallows beam, for removal of the noose and hood. Her body was then lowered on to a stretcher and made ready for autopsy. A formal inquest was held and Dorothea was later buried in the prison grounds.

Charlotte Bryant
Did She Really Poison Her Husband?

Charlotte Bryant was born in Londonderry, Northern Ireland, in 1904, her maiden name being McHugh. Little is known of her childhood, but by the age of nineteen she was a nice looking girl with raven black hair and attractive eyes who was illiterate, ill educated and notably promiscuous. She fraternised with the British soldiers in the Province and was nicknamed 'Darkie' by them but her activities were strongly disapproved of by the Republicans who threatened her with tarring and feathering, a fate that befell quite a few girls who went out with British soldiers during 'The Troubles.'

In 1922, she met Frederick Bryant who was eight years her senior. Frederick was serving as a military policeman in the Dorset Regiment. He had served in the army during the First World War and was described as a simple country lad. He immediately fell for Charlotte's physical charms. When Frederick's tour of duty ended, he returned to England and Charlotte went with him. They married a little while later at Wells in Somerset. Frederick resumed civilian life as a farm labourer and by 1925, was working as a cowman at a farm near Yeovil, in the village of Over Compton. Like most small rural villages there was little to do and even less excitement. Social life revolved round the local pub. In the thirteen years of their marriage, Charlotte gave birth to five children, although whether Frederick was the father of all of them is open to question.

Charlotte was very highly sexed and soon became bored with village life, compared to the excitement of life around the Londonderry barracks, with plenty of attentive and free spending soldiers and a good sex life. She did not work as such and spent her days drinking and indulging in a little prostitution, as much for the sex as for the money. She was known as Black Bess or Killarney Kate by the villagers and was thought of as a drunken slut. Surprisingly, Frederick seemed indifferent to these goings on. As he told a neighbour: 'I don't care what she does. Four pounds a week is better than thirty shillings', (£1.50 a week, which he earned as a cowman).

In December 1933, Charlotte met Leonard Edward Parsons, a horse trader and gypsy, who took up lodgings in the Bryant's cottage and with whom she had an affair. In 1934, Frederick Bryant was sacked from his job as a farm labourer, as his employer was not happy about what was going on in his tied cottage. They then moved to the village of Coombe, near Sherborne, where again Frederick found employment as a farm labourer. The move did not change the domestic circumstances, Parsons simply moved with them and his and Charlotte's affair continued unabated.

Parsons did not live with the Bryants on a permanent basis but rather stayed there between business trips. He had a common-law wife, Priscilla Loveridge, by whom he had fathered four children. Initially Parsons and Frederick Bryant appeared to get on quite well and drank together in the local pub. Domestic life, however, was somewhat different with Charlotte and Parsons sharing the marital bed while Frederick had to sleep on the sofa on occasion.

Eventually, Frederick could stand the situation no longer and ordered Parsons to leave. Charlotte went too and she and Parsons rented rooms in Dorchester. She soon returned to the family home and a few days later all three had a meeting and Parsons was allowed back into the house. It appeared that Charlotte had become totally besotted with Parsons, and though he enjoyed her sexual favours, her love was not returned and the relationship began to deteriorate. This was something she was to deny at her trial.

In May 1935, Frederick, who was then thirty-nine years old, was taken ill for the first time, with severe stomach pains, immediately after eating the lunch that Charlotte had cooked. Helped by a neighbour who induced vomiting, he began to feel a little easier. The doctor came to see him and diagnosed gastroenteritis. After a few days, Frederick recovered and returned to work. A further attack followed in August and again Frederick made a full recovery.

In November 1935, Parsons dropped a huge bombshell into Charlotte's life by announcing that he was leaving. His stated reason was the lack of work in that part of Dorset, although the deterioration in Charlotte's looks may have had something to do with it too.

On 11 December 1935, Frederick was again taken ill with severe stomach pains from which again he recovered. Charlotte continued to search for Parsons in the local pubs but without success. She did, however, form a new relationship with a woman called Lucy Ostler who was a widow with seven

children. Lucy moved into the Bryants' home and witnessed
Frederick's final attack on the night of 22 December 1935. He
once again suffered extremely severe stomach pains. This time
it was so bad that he was admitted to hospital in Sherborne
where he died in the afternoon of the 23rd. His death was
regarded as suspicious by the doctors and therefore a post-
mortem was carried out. Analysis of his tissues by Home
Office pathologist Dr Roche Lynch found 4.09 grains of
arsenic in the body. These findings were reported to Dorset
Constabulary who visited Charlotte and removed her and the
children to a workhouse in Sturminster Newton while they
conducted a minute search of the Bryant's cottage and garden.
Of the 150 odd samples sent to the Home Office laboratory,
thirty-two contained arsenic. Among the items recovered was
a burnt tin which had contained an arsenic-based weed killer.
Armed with this vital piece of information, the police systematically visited all the local chemists shops to try and establish
where the weed killer had been purchased and by whom.
Their efforts were rewarded when they discovered a Yeovil
chemist who had sold a tin of the weed killer to a woman
who only signed the poisons register with a cross. Charlotte
could not write, a fact known to all who knew her. The chemist, however, was unable to identify either Charlotte or Lucy
Ostler in a subsequent identity parade.

On 10 February 1936, Charlotte, who was still at the workhouse in Sturminster Newton, was arrested and charged with
the murder of her husband. She is reported to have told the
officers that arrested her: 'I haven't got poison from anywhere
and that people know. I don't see how they can say I poisoned
my husband.'

The trial opened on Wednesday, 27 May 1936, at the Dorset
Assizes in Dorchester before Mr Justice MacKinnon. It was to
last just four days, which was by no means unusual in capital
murder trials at this time. As it was a high profile poisoning
case, the prosecution case was led by the Solicitor-General,

Sir Terrence O'Connor. Charlotte was defended by the well-known barrister Mr J.D. Casswell KC.

The prosecution argued that the case was a classic eternal triangle and that Charlotte poisoned her husband to be able to have Parsons. They could not show direct evidence that Charlotte either bought or administered the arsenic although the circumstantial evidence supported this theory. Lucy Ostler testified against Charlotte and told the court that on the night Frederick died, Charlotte had made him an Oxo drink and that he was violently sick after taking it. She also related how she had explained to Charlotte what an inquest was and alleged that Charlotte had told her that she hated Frederick and only stayed with him because of the children. She told the court about the tin of weed killer and how Charlotte had said that she would have to get rid of it.

She mentioned how she had found the remains of burnt clothing in the boiler and then discovered the remains of the tin amongst the ashes which she had thrown into the yard where the police discovered it.

Mr Casswell was unable to shake Lucy Ostler who stuck to her damning allegations against Charlotte. Leonard Parsons' testimony did not help her case either. He told the court how they had intercourse on numerous occasions. Nowadays, this may not seem shocking but in 1936, promiscuity and adultery were considered totally unacceptable and had the effect of painting Charlotte as a 'scarlet' woman, something that probably bore considerable weight with the jury.

Forensic evidence was presented by Dr Roche Lynch who had analysed the various samples taken from the Bryant's home. He demonstrated to the court how arsenic could be dissolved in Oxo and not be spotted by a person drinking it. He also told the court that he had found that the ashes from the boiler in which Charlotte was alleged to have tried to destroy the weed killer tin contained 149 parts per million of arsenic whereas ashes normally contained around forty-five parts per million. Altogether thirty witnesses had testified for the prosecution and painted a dire picture of the woman in the dock.

Mr Casswell called Charlotte as a witness with some trepidation, but in fact she did much better than he expected. She denied knowing about poison or possessing any weed killer. She also demonstrated to the court that an old coat in which traces of arsenic had been found and which it was alleged that she had worn when she bought the weed killer, did not fit her at all.

Interestingly, she told the court that she was pleased when Parsons left their house and that she had lost interest in him, rather than the other way round.

Charlotte's older children gave evidence but their testimony was in fact very damaging to their mother's case. They related how she had asked Ernest, her older son, to dispose of some blue bottles in late December. Her daughter, Lily, told how she had seen Parsons with a blue bottle whose contents had fizzed when poured onto a stone by Parsons in front of Charlotte.

Once all the evidence had been heard and the closing statements made by both sides Mr Justice MacKinnon commenced the summing up. He asked the jury to consider two principle questions, was Frederick Bryant poisoned with arsenic and if so, was that arsenic administered by Charlotte. He noted that Charlotte had been present on each occasion her husband had been ill and that two of the bouts of sickness had occurred before Lucy Ostler, who was a possible suspect, had come into the household.

On 30 Saturday, after deliberating for just an hour the jury returned a verdict of guilty against Charlotte. When asked if she had anything to say before sentence was passed, she replied in a calm voice: 'I am not guilty.' Mr Justice MacKinnon had the black cap placed upon his wig and then passed the death sentence. There was considerable emotion in the court and

Mr Justice MacKinnon seemed to have difficulty saying the dreaded words to her. On hearing her sentence, Charlotte broke down and was led sobbing from the dock.

After the trial, Mr Caswell received a letter from a Professor Bone who had read about the case in his Sunday paper. He told Mr Caswell that the 149 parts per million of arsenic that Dr Roche had found in the ashes was on the low side for ashes and certainly not an unusually high amount as Dr Roche had told the court. Professor Bone later provided the defence with a signed statement to this effect.

Charlotte's appeal was heard on 29 June at the Appeal Court in London. The appeal judges refused to hear the evidence of Professor Bone and concluded that even if the jury had been incorrectly advised by Dr Roche, the outcome of the trial would have been the same. Thus her appeal was denied and her sentence stood. At this time, it would have been unprecedented for the Court of Appeal to admit new evidence, it just concerned itself with the conduct of the trial. It could be argued that Professor Bone's statement was not new evidence but rather a correction of flawed evidence that had already been given at the original trial by the prosecution's 'expert' witness.

Charlotte spent almost six weeks in the condemned cell, where her once raven hair had turned completely white, presumably due to the stress of her situation. She decided, after much agonising, against seeing her children as she felt it would be too much for them to bear. She was visited regularly by Father Barney, a Catholic priest, who prayed with her and had a small altar set up in her cell.

She began to learn to read and write with the help of the shifts of female warders who looked after her round the clock and was able to dictate a telegram to the King asking for clemency. She also wrote a letter in which she said: 'It is all fault I'm here. I listened to the tales I was told. But I have not got long now and I will be out of my troubles. God bless my children.' The Home Office obliterated the name in this note so we will never know whose fault Charlotte thought it was.

A lot had been going on behind the scenes to try and save Charlotte. Sir Stafford Cripps, at that time a Member of Parliament, had applied to the Home Secretary to declare a mistrial and order a new one on the grounds of the flawed evidence. Questions had also been raised in the House of Parliament about the case and the usual petitions got up.

There had always seemed to be an unwritten rule at the Home Office that poisoners should not be reprieved and this practice was followed in Charlotte's case. On the Tuesday, the day before her execution, the Home Secretary, Sir John Simon, declined on the advice of his officials to grant a reprieve or a new trial. The prison governor had the unpleasant job of communicating this to Charlotte and telling her that the execution would take place, as planned, the following morning.

Strangely, Charlotte was not hanged at Dorchester Prison, in the county in which she was convicted and sentenced, although it continued to have an execution chamber which was last used for the hanging of David Jennings in July 1941. Instead she was sent to Exeter, in neighbouring Devon, to await execution.

Charlotte was led to the gallows at 8 a.m. on Wednesday, 15 July 1936 by Tom Pierrepoint assisted by Thomas Phillips. By an odd coincidence, a man called George Bryant (no relation) had been hanged the previous day at Wandsworth.

As was the norm by 1936, Charlotte's execution was an entirely secret affair and there were no reporters present. However, she was attended by a Catholic priest, Father Barney, who was not bound by Home Office rules of secrecy. He later described her last moments as 'truly edifying.' 'She met her end with Christian fortitude.' He reported, however, that she never confessed to the murder. Mrs Van de Elst was present outside the prison to lead a protest against the execution but ended up being fined for obstructing the police.

In accordance with her sentence, after autopsy, her body was buried in the grounds of the prison.

Charlotte left the tiny sum of 5s 8½d to her children, who being now orphaned, were taken into the care of Dorset County Council.

In view of the seriously flawed forensic evidence, should Charlotte have been granted a re-trial? On the balance of probability, she was guilty, but this piece of totally incorrect evidence surely made her conviction unsafe and unsatisfactory to use the modern term. The witness evidence and circumstantial evidence remains strong and it is probable that the right decision was reached. However, flawed evidence leads to a lack of public confidence in the justice system.

One wonders how much Charlotte's lowly status and acknowledged promiscuity played in the decision to neither reprieve her nor grant a new trial. Sadly, Britain was very much a class ridden society in 1936 and Charlotte was virtually at the bottom of the social pile, perceived as an illiterate, immoral slut. Were people like her simply expendable and their well publicised executions considered as a good lesson to other women not to stray from the 'straight and narrow' paths of morality, as perceived by a male dominated society?

Styllou Pantopiou Christofi
A Greek-Cypriot Tragedy?

The penultimate British female hanging was that of Styllou Pantopiou Christofi, a fifty-three-year-old Greek Cypriot, at London's Holloway prison on Wednesday, 15 December, 1954.

Styllou had been convicted of the murder of her daughter-in-law, thirty-six-year-old Hella Christofi whom she had battered and strangled to death at their home at 11, South Hill Park, Hampstead, London on Wednesday, 28 July 1954.

Hella, who was of German origin, had been married to Styllou's son, Stavros, for some fifteen years and the couple had three children. They enjoyed a happy marriage until Styllou went to live with them in July 1953. The two women bickered and rowed about the way that Hella bought up the children which did not accord to Styllou's old-fashioned views. The situation reached the point where Hella had had enough and decided to take the children and herself on holiday to Germany, telling Stavros that she didn't expect to find her mother-in-law still there when she returned.

It was now that Styllou decided to kill Hella. Once her son had gone off to his work as a waiter at the Café de Paris and the grandchildren were safely tucked up in bed, she firstly hit Hella over the head with the ash can from the range. She now dragged the unconscious woman into the kitchen and strangled her with a scarf. In a futile attempt to destroy the evidence of the murder, Styllou pulled the dead body out into the yard where she put paraffin soaked newspaper round it and set fire to it. A neighbour, John Young who was letting his dog out, noticed the fire in the back yard and could see what appeared to him to be a tailor's dummy being burnt. Styllou went into the street and raised the alarm with a passing motorist around 1 a.m. on the Thursday morning, shouting: 'Please come. Fire burning. Children sleeping'. The fire brigade were able to save the house and the children who were asleep upstairs. They discovered the charred body of a woman in the yard and noticed a long red mark around the neck. Styllou had hoped that the body would be too badly burned to reveal anything. The police were now called and a search of the house revealed Hella's wedding ring wrapped in a piece of paper in Styllou's room. She told the officers that she had been asleep and had been awakened by the sound of two male voices downstairs. She went downstairs and had seen one man in the yard, before going to Hella's bedroom where she got no reply when she knocked on the door. She then saw the body on fire in the yard and went for some water to douse the flames with. The police were less than impressed with this tale and arrested Styllou at the scene. She was subsequently charged with murder after Hella's post-mortem and the inquest had established the precise causes of death.

Stavros pleaded with his mother and her lawyers to plead insanity but Styllou declined, saying that 'I am a poor woman of no education, but I am not a mad woman.'

Styllou came to trial at the Old Bailey on 28 October 1954 before Mr Justice Devlin. Evidence was presented by Mr Christmas Humphreys of the injuries to Hella and the subsequent fire and conflicting stories told to the police by Styllou. It took the jury just under two hours to bring in a guilty verdict, to which they added a recommendation to mercy. She appealed against her conviction but this was dismissed.

Under the provisions of the Criminal Lunatics Act of 1884 the Home Secretary had a duty to have a condemned prisoner examined by prison psychiatrists if there was concern over their sanity. Gwilym Lloyd George, the then Home Secretary, ordered this and Styllou was found to be sane against the legal standards of the day. On 12 December it was announced that there would be no reprieve.

Her execution was to be the first at Holloway since Edith Thompson had been hanged there over thirty years previously in January 1923.

In the Condemned Suite she was guarded round the clock by teams of wardresses and asked for a Greek Orthodox Cross to be put up on the wall of the execution chamber where she would be able to see it in her last moments. On the morning of her death Styllou was made to wear the mandatory rubberised canvas underpants. Albert Pierrepoint carried out the execution at 9 a.m. on the Wednesday morning, assisted by Harry Allen. Being of slight build at less than 5ft tall and weighing just 117lb, Albert gave her a drop of 8ft 4in. The notice of execution was posted on the prison gates a few minutes later. Styllou's body was autopsied and a formal inquest held during the morning, prior to burial within the grounds in the afternoon.

Albert Pierrepoint noted in his autobiography how little press interest there was in Styllou's execution. One wonders if it was because she was middle aged, unattractive and foreign.

Styllou's body was exhumed and reburied in Brookwood Cemetery in Surrey when Holloway was redeveloped.

It emerged later that Styllou had been examined by the Principal Medical Officer of Holloway while she was on remand in October 1954. He found her to be suffering from a delusional disorder that made her fear that her grandchildren would not be bought up properly by Hella and that she would in time be excluded from seeing them due to the clash of cultures between the two women. This seems an entirely reasonable conclusion but did it make Styllou insane? Not by Home Office standards.

After the execution it was revealed that Styllou had been tried for murder once before. She had been acquitted of the murder of her mother-in-law in Cyprus in 1925.

Ruth Ellis
The Last Woman
to be Hanged in Britain

On Wednesday, 13 July 1955 at London's Holloway Prison, Ruth Ellis secured her place in history becoming the last woman to be executed in Britain.

Ruth had a passionate and tempestuous relationship with a young man of twenty-five called David Drummond Moffat Blakely with whom she often quarrelled and had recently suffered a miscarriage by, after he punched her in the stomach during a fight. They had been living together on and off for about two years prior to the murder.

David was a motor engineer and racing driver and was also a heavy drinker who used to frequent the Little Club that Ruth managed, which was very popular with the motor racing fraternity. He was building a racing car with his friends, the Findlaters, and over Easter 1955 consistently refused to see Ruth, having promised to do so and despite repeated visits and phone calls by her to the Findlaters' house. They had, unfortunately, taken on a nanny whom Ruth suspected David was having an affair with, although in truth he was not.

So in a pique of jealousy and rejection on Easter Sunday afternoon, 10 April 1955, Ruth persuaded her other boyfriend, Desmond Cussen, to drive her to Hampstead where she lay in wait for Blakely outside the Magdala public house in South Hill Park where David and Anthony Findlater were drinking.

When they came out to the car at around 9.30 p.m., she called to David who ignored her, so armed with a 38 calibre Smith & Wesson revolver she fired a first shot and then pursued him round the car firing a second shot, which caused him to collapse onto the pavement. She then stood over him and emptied the remaining four bullets into him, as he lay wounded on the ground. At least one bullet was fired from point-blank range and left the tell-tale powder burns on his skin. One bullet injured a Mrs Gladys Yule in the hand as she was walking up to the pub.

Other drinkers came out of the pub to see what had happened and Ruth was arrested by an off-duty policeman, Alan Thompson, still holding the smoking gun. She was taken to Hampstead police station where she appeared to be calm and not obviously under the influence of drink or drugs. She made a detailed confession to the police and was charged with murder.

Ruth appeared at a special hearing of Hampstead Magistrates Court on the Easter Monday (11 April), where she was remanded in custody to Holloway Prison to await trial. She was placed in the hospital wing and kept under observation day and night. During her initial interview on the Monday afternoon, she again described the details of David's killing. The Principal Medical Officer, M.R. Penry Williams, examined her twice, finding no evidence of mental illness. Ruth consented to and undertook an electro-encephalograph examination on 3 May. This also failed to find any evidence of brain abnormality. While on remand in Holloway, she was examined on 4 June by Dr D. Whittaker, psychiatrist for the defence and by Dr A. Dalzell on behalf of the Home Office on 9 June. Neither man found any evidence of insanity. Ruth discussed her feelings on the days leading up to and including the murder with Dr Dalzell, and he reported to the Home Office that he found no evidence of delusions, hallucinations or other forms of mental illness.

Ruth's trial opened on Monday, 20 June 1955 in the No. 1 Court at the Old Bailey before Mr Justice Havers. The prosecution was led by Mr Christmas Humphries, assisted by Mervyn Griffith Jones and Miss Jean Southworth; the defence was led by Mr Melford Stevenson, Q.C., assisted by Mr Sebag Shaw and Mr Peter Rawlinson.

Ruth appeared in the dock in a smart black two piece suit and white blouse, her hair re-dyed to her preferred platinum blonde in Holloway with the special permission of Dr Charity Taylor, the governor; hardly the image of the poor downtrodden woman.

She pleaded not guilty, apparently so that her side of the story could be told, rather than in any hope of acquittal. She particularly wanted disclosed the involvement of the Findlaters in what she saw as a conspiracy to keep David away from her.

When the prosecuting counsel, Mr Christmas Humphreys asked her: 'Mrs Ellis, when you fired that revolver at close

range into the body of David Blakely what did you intend
to do?' She replied: 'It was obvious that when I shot him I
intended to kill him.'

There were legal submissions made by Mr Melford
Stevenson regarding provocation. Mr Justice Havers said he
had given careful consideration to these but ruled that there
was 'insufficient material, even upon a view of the evidence
most favourable to the accused, to support a verdict of manslaughter on the grounds of provocation.' Mr Stevenson said
that in view of that ruling it would not be appropriate for
him to say anything more to the jury. The jury of ten men
and two women were then brought back into court and
in their presence Mr Stevenson said: 'In view of the ruling
which your Lordship has just pronounced I cannot now with
propriety address the jury at all, because it would be impossible for me to do so without inviting them to disregard your
Lordship's ruling.'

Mr Christmas Humphreys indicated that in the circumstances, he would not make a final speech to the jury either.

The judge then summed up. After reviewing the evidence
for the prosecution, his Lordship said:

> You will remember that when Mr. Stevenson made his
> opening address to you he told you that he was going to
> invite you to reduce this charge of killing from murder to
> manslaughter on the grounds of provocation.
>
> …The House of Lords has decided that where the ques-
> tion arises whether what would otherwise be murder may
> be reduced to manslaughter on the grounds of provocation,
> if there is not sufficient material, even upon a view of the
> evidence most favourable to the accused, that a reasonable
> person could be driven by transport of passion and loss of
> control to use violence and a continuance of violence, it is
> the duty of a judge, as a matter of law, to direct the jury that
> the evidence does not support a verdict of manslaughter.

I have been constrained to rule in this case that there is not sufficient material to reduce this killing from murder to manslaughter on the grounds of provocation.

… It is therefore not open to you to bring in a verdict of manslaughter on the grounds of provocation.

Mr Justice Havers continued: 'But I am bound to tell you this, that even if you accept every word of Mrs Ellis' evidence there does not seem to be anything in it which establishes any sort of defence to the charge of murder.' The jury then retired and not surprisingly found Ruth guilty after deliberating for only twenty-three minutes.

To convict a person of murder two things have to be proved: that the person actually killed the victim (known as the '*actus rea*' or the 'guilty act'), and that they intended to kill the victim (known as the '*mens rea*' or the 'guilty mind'). Clearly there was no question as to whether Ruth had actually killed David Blakely and by her famous answer to the question as to her intention when she fired the shots, there could be no question as to her intent. If it had been possible to show that she had not intended to kill him, the correct verdict would have been guilty of manslaughter.

Mr Justice Havers had no alternative but to sentence her to death. The black cap was placed on his head and she was asked if she wished to say anything. She remained silent and stood impassive as he then sentenced her to be taken to the place where she had last been confined and from there to a place of execution and there suffer death by hanging. To which she replied, 'Thank you'. Ruth now turned on her heel, smiled to her friends in the public gallery and walked calmly down the stairs at the back of the dock.

She was taken back to Holloway in a prison van and placed in the Condemned Suite, where she was guarded round the clock by shifts of female warders.

It has been disclosed from Home Office files in the National Archives that as Ruth awaited her execution she only once broke down and cried. Wardress Griffin was present when Labour MP, George Rogers, tried to persuade Ruth to appeal for clemency and the warder claimed he had browbeaten her into agreeing. Dr Charity Taylor, the governor of Holloway, reported:

> I have never seen Ruth Ellis so distressed, and the officers reported that for the first time she had cried. She told me she supposed it was too late to change her mind as he was going to the Home Secretary in the morning. ... I did not ask her, but I formed the strong impression she did not wish Mr. Rogers to pursue the subject of a reprieve.

Mr Rogers had taken up the case at the request of one of his constituents in North Kensington, Ruth's friend, Jacqueline Dyer.

The High Sheriff of London provisionally set Wednesday, 13 July for Ruth's execution, pending an appeal. However she decided against this and indeed there were absolutely no legal grounds for one. The final decision on Ruth's fate rested with the Home Secretary, Major Gwilym Lloyd George, later Lord Tenby. Despite considerable public and press pressure, he ruled against her. His decision was announced on the afternoon of Monday, 11 July and communicated to Ruth by Dr Taylor. She was visited by her mother and her friend, Jacqueline Dyer, within an hour of hearing there would be no reprieve. Petitions containing several thousand signatures were sent to the Home Office.

There was to be one final attempt to save Ruth. She had requested a meeting with Leon Simmons, who had represented her at her earlier divorce, to discuss her will, and he and Victor Mishcon went to see her at 11.15 a.m. on the Tuesday morning. Unbeknown to Ruth, they had been asked by her trial solicitor, John Bickford, to make one final attempt to find out from her where she got the gun. Victor Mishcon was surprised at the woman he saw in Holloway who had by now less than twenty-one hours to live. He recalled that she greeted him saying: 'how kind of you to come. I wanted Mr Simmons to know certain facts which I think may have some bearing on my will.' She told Victor Mishcon: 'I am now completely composed. I know that I am going to die, and I'm ready to do so. You won't hear anything from me that says I didn't kill David. I did kill him. And whatever the circumstances you as a lawyer will appreciate that it's a life for a life. Isn't that just?' Victor Mishcon was so struck by these words and her calm demeanour that he never forgot them. However, she did reveal some more details of the case, against a promise from Mr Mishcon that he would not try and use them to save her. She told him that she had been drinking with an unnamed man over the weekend and had told him that if she had a gun she would shoot David. He told her that he did indeed have a gun and took her to practise shooting with it. He later drove her to Hampstead. Ruth did not name Desmond Cussen as this man, although it was assumed that it was he. All this was taken down in writing and Ruth finally and grudgingly allowed it to be taken to the Home Office. But warder Griffin, who was present during the interview, told the Home Office that Mr Mishcon omitted a statement by Ruth that she had asked Desmond for the gun.

The Permanent Secretary, Sir Frank Newsam, was out at the races that afternoon and her statement was left with another senior official. They had the police check this new story but it really didn't make matters any better. All it actually did was to show even clearer evidence of premeditation.

Ruth had her last meeting with her parents and brother on the Tuesday afternoon and they left Holloway around 5.15 p.m. Her brother, Granville Neilson, told reporters that 'she seemed absolutely calm and unafraid of what was going to happen to her.' The news of her new statement had made the evening papers and there was now even greater agitation for a reprieve.

Ruth began a final letter to Leon Simmons that evening in which she said, 'I did not defend myself. I say a life for a life.' She wrote a postscript to it the following morning telling him that she had not changed her mind at the last moment (about being hanged). She also wrote a letter of apology to David's mother, Mrs Cook.

Prisoner 9656 Ellis spent just three weeks and two days in the Condemned Suite at Holloway. On the Tuesday evening, the eve of the hanging, the governor at Holloway was forced to call for police reinforcements because of a crowd of more than 500 who had gathered outside the prison's gates singing and chanting for Ruth for several hours. Some of them broke through the police cordon to bang on the prison gates, calling for Ruth to pray with them. Inside the usual preparations had been made.

Ruth had been weighed at 103lbs clothed, so Albert Pierrepoint calculated a drop of 8ft 4in. The gallows had been tested on the Tuesday afternoon using a sand bag of the same weight, which was left overnight on the rope to remove any stretch. Around 7 a.m. on the morning of execution, the trap was reset and the rope coiled up so as to leave the leather covered noose dangling at chest height above the trap. A cross had been placed on the far wall of the execution room at Ruth's request.

She was made to wear the compulsory rubberised canvas pants and was given a large brandy by the prison doctor to steady her nerves.

At about 8.55 a.m., a telephone call was received at Holloway from a Miss or Mrs Holmes purporting to be the private secretary to the Home Secretary, saying that a stay of execution was on its way. Dr Taylor (the governor) immediately telephoned the Home Office and discovered that the call was a hoax. Dr Taylor consulted Mr Gedge, the under sheriff of London, and they decided to proceed. This led to a delay to the execution of one minute. Thus a few seconds before 9.01 a.m., Albert

Pierrepoint entered her cell, pinioned her hands behind her back with his special soft calf leather strap and led her the 15 feet to the gallows.

Pierrepoint recalled that Ruth said nothing at all during her execution. When she reached the trap, the white cotton hood was drawn over her head and the noose adjusted round her neck. Pierrepoint's assistant, Royston Rickard, pinioned her legs with a leather strap and when all was ready, stepped back allowing Pierrepoint to remove the safety pin from the base of the lever and push it away from him opening the trap through which she now plummeted.

The whole process would have occupied no more than fifteen seconds and her now still body was examined by the prison doctor before the execution room was locked up and she was left hanging for an hour.

Around 1,000 people, including women with prams, stood silently outside the prison that morning, some praying for her. At eighteen minutes past nine, the execution notice was posted outside the gates and after that the crowd dispersed.

Ruth's body was taken down at 10 a.m. and an autopsy was performed by pathologist Dr Keith Simpson, which showed that she had died virtually instantaneously. Unusually, the autopsy report was later published and Simpson noted the presence of brandy in her stomach.

An inquest was held by Mr J. Milner Helme, the then coroner for the City of London, later on the Wednesday morning and Ruth's brother made a formal identification of her body. A scarf had been put round her neck to hide the rope marks. The inquest report gave the cause of death as 'Injuries to the central nervous system consequent upon judicial hanging.'

Ruth's body was buried within Holloway Prison around lunchtime, in accordance with her sentence, but later disinterred and reburied in a churchyard in Buckinghamshire when Holloway was rebuilt.

One feels that for whatever personal reasons Ruth did everything she could to obtain her death from the justice system. The media were largely in favour of a reprieve and a lot of the public were too at the time.

On 8 February 2002, at the behest of Muriel Jakubait, Ruth's sister, and Ruth's daughter Georgie, who died in 2001, the Criminal Cases Review Commission (CCRC) referred Ruth's case to the Court of Appeal to have the conviction reduced from murder to manslaughter.

The appeal finally came before the Appeal Court in London on Tuesday, 16 and Wednesday, 17 September 2003. The judges were Lord Justice Kay, Mr Justice Silber and Mr Justice Leveson. The court was asked to overturn the murder conviction and substitute a verdict of manslaughter on the grounds of provocation and/or diminished responsibility. Michael Mansfield QC appeared for the appellant and introduced evidence to show that Ruth was suffering from battered-woman syndrome when she shot David. It should be noted that 'battered-woman syndrome' was only accepted as defence to homicide in 2000 and therefore could not apply retrospectively. Michael Mansfield claimed that she had been 'disgracefully treated' and that this could have left her in an intensely emotional state.

He also claimed that Justice Havers and the prosecution and defence barristers involved in the case were 'labouring under a misconception of the law'. They believed that, to establish provocation, the defence had to prove the killing was not motivated by malice, but that what happened was in the 'passion of the moment', without any intent to kill or cause grievous bodily harm.

Mansfield argued that this was an incorrect view and that the correct construction of the law on provocation as it then stood was that there was an intent to kill, but that it arose out of a passionate loss of control and provocative conduct. He suggested that 'cumulative provocation' incited her to shoot David and that this was not considered in the original trial.

Evidence was adduced to show that, despite Ruth giving up her job, and the flat that went with it, and providing David with money, he regularly beat her up, at one point so badly that she went to hospital. Afterwards, he apologised with flowers and a card, and she accepted him back again as she always did.

In January 1955, Ruth discovered that she was pregnant with David's child. In her original testimony, read to the Appeal Court, Ruth described a fight in which 'David got very, very violent. I don't know whether that caused the miscarriage or not, but he did thump me in the stomach.'

David returned to Ruth on the Wednesday before she murdered him to profess his 'undying love' for her and promised to marry her. On the Saturday night, it is claimed that Ruth sat in an empty house opposite and watched a party where David was cavorting with a nurse. A doctor at the original trial said, 'The situation was now absolutely intolerable for her. She considered he was being unfaithful at that moment but she was convinced he would return and she wouldn't be able to resist him.' This behaviour was the trigger, Mansfield said, for manslaughter, not murder.

Further evidence came from a retired midwife now living in Australia, who gave a written statement to the Criminal Cases Review Commission in 1999. Moreen Gleeson, then in her twenties, saw Ruth in the street, allegedly on the night she shot David. She was 'stressed and weeping'. Apparently, she told Moreen: 'It's my boyfriend. He's in there with another woman. He won't let me in!' Ruth was 'quite distraught'. To calm her, Moreen suggested taking her home for a coffee. She said, 'Ruth was crying again and said, as if surprised, "Oh! I've got a gun!"' She also said a bulky man with a 'proprietary air' loomed up and stood 'possessively' over Ruth. This was understood to be Desmond Cussen. (It is difficult to see how Moreen's statement helped the appellant's case, as all it does is provide further evidence of pre-meditation and intent to kill.)

David Perry appeared for the Crown at the appeal. He told the court that, at the time of her trial, there was no such defence as diminished responsibility, and the defence of provocation required evidence of a sudden loss of self-control in immediate response to a provocative act.

In Ruth's case, although it is accepted that she had been violently ill-treated by her lover in the past, the only provocation on the day of the killing was his breaking off their affair by failing to contact her, even though he had promised to do so. Even if that amounted to provocation, her response to it was wholly disproportionate, he said.

On Monday, 8 December 2003, Lord Justice Kay delivered the Appeal Court's ruling, dismissing the appeal as 'without merit' and finding that Ruth had been properly convicted of murder at her original trial. The Homicide Act of 1957 changed the law to allow a defence of diminished responsibility but the Appeal Court ruled that this defence was not available at the time of Ruth's trial. If the defence of provocation was to succeed, it had to be proved that Ruth had been subjected to violence immediately before the murder rather than in the recent past.

Lord Justice Kay said:

> Under the law at the date of the trial, the judge was right to withdraw the defence of provocation from the jury and the appeal must fail ... If her crime were committed today, we think it likely that there would have been an issue of diminished responsibility for the jury to decide. But we are in no position to judge what the jury's response to such an issue might be.

The court was critical that the case had been referred to it at all, by the Criminal Cases Review Commission (the body which examines possible miscarriages of justice), and stated that it could have dealt with eight to twelve cases had it not had to consider this one.

Lord Justice Kay said:

We have to question whether this exercise of considering
an appeal so long after the event, when Mrs. Ellis herself
had consciously and deliberately chosen not to appeal at
the time, is a sensible use of the limited resources of the
court of appeal ... On any view, Mrs. Ellis had committed a serious criminal offence. This case is, therefore, quite
different from a case like that of James Hanratty, where
the issue was whether a wholly innocent person had been
convicted of murder.

EPILOGUE

Although Ruth Ellis was the last woman to actually suffer the death penalty, three more women were sentenced to hang for murder before the Homicide Act of 1957 came into law, but were all reprieved. They were Annie Drinkall in November 1955 for the murder of her daughter; Freda Rumbold in November 1956 for the murder of her husband, who was the last woman to occupy the Condemned Suite at Holloway; and twenty-one-year-old Maureen Hanrahan who, with twenty-three-year-old Patrick Doran, was convicted of a robbery/murder on 20 March of 1957. She was sent to Manchester's Strangeways Prison to await execution.

The Homicide Act of 1957 came into law at the end of March 1957 and re-classified some forms of murder as non capital which did reduce both the number of death sentences and reprieves. It also introduced the notion of diminished responsibility into English law. These changes came about as a result of the report of the 1949-1953 Royal Commission on Capital Punishment. From March 1948 to October 1948, twenty-six people were reprieved while this Royal

Commission was being set up. Between August 1955 and July 1957, everyone sentenced to death was reprieved, amounting to forty-nine cases, while the government tried to frame the new Act.

Under the Homicide Act of 1957 the five categories of murder for which the death sentence was still to be mandatory were:

Murder committed in the course or furtherance of theft.
Murder by shooting or explosion.
Murder whilst resisting arrest or during an escape.
Murder of a police or prison officer.
Two murders committed on different occasions.

Only one woman was sentenced to death after the Act came into force. She was Mary Wilson who was dubbed by the press the 'Widow of Windy Nook.' She was reprieved in 1958, probably because of her age (she was sixty-six), even though she had poisoned two husbands. Under the provisions of the Act, she could have been executed, as the two murders were committed on different occasions.

INDEX